The First Immigrants from Asia

A Population History of the North American Indians

The First Immigrants from Asia

A Population History of the North American Indians

A. J. JAFFE

Senior Research Scholar, Retired
Columbia University
New York, New York
and Research Associate
National Museum of the American Indian
New York, New York

With the assistance of

CAROLYN SPERBER

Late of Columbia University
New York, New York

PLENUM PRESS • NEW YORK AND LONDON

Library of Congress Cataloging-in-Publication Data

Jaffe, A. J.
   The first immigrants from Asia : a population history of the North
American Indian / A.J. Jaffe with assistance of Carolyn Sperber.
      p.   cm.
   Includes bibliographical references and index.
   ISBN 0-306-43952-2
   1. Indians of North America--Asian influences. 2. Indians of
North America--Migrations. 3. Indians of North America--History.
I. Title.
E98.A84J34   1992
970.004'9705--dc20   92-13590
                                                              CIP

ISBN 0-306-43952-2

© 1992 Plenum Press, New York
A Division of Plenum Publishing Corporation
233 Spring Street, New York, N.Y. 10013

Printed in the United States of America

To my good friend,
the late Dr. James G. E. Smith,
Curator of North American Indians
at the National Museum of the
American Indian

Foreword

This study by a distinguished social-science analyst must have been a labor of love. No lesser motivation can explain its panoramic sweep over prehistory and history, across sea-change sociodemographic transformations—and all this in the face of intimidating evidentiary challenges that persist to this day.

Tracing the evolution of the "Amerindians," the "first immigrants" to the North American continent and their American and Canadian descendants, would be a daunting task even for recent intercensal periods, given the informational obstacles at play. In the present case, the temporal span being reviewed has been expanded by extraordinary orders of magnitude. On the origins side of his evolutionary examination, Jaffe goes back in time to Asiatic internal migration streams some 10 to 15 (or perhaps over 50) thousand years ago, continues with what could have been land or sea crossings in today's Bering Strait vicinity, and presents plausible inferences concerning what must have been multimillennial processes of dispersal over the Western Hemisphere before, during, and after its glacial age. Eventually, when his analysis reaches its most recent temporal aspects ages later, Jaffe's coverage extends to the 1980 U.S. and 1981 Canadian censuses, with interpretative findings as timely as current press reports on censuses just appearing for the 1990s.

The result is a descriptive, analytic, and surely prime reference work of many parts: combinations of demographic, anthropological, and sociological insights; reviews of major Paleolithic-era population redistributions and their presumptive temporal phases; crisp evaluations of available prehistoric and early historical source materials; distinctions in abundance between what is known, remains speculative, or may well be inherently unknowable about preagricultural livelihoods; inferences about life-cycle transformations when hunting or gathering gave way to agricultural sources of food supply; references in depth

vii

and new contributions to the paleodemographic literature on ancient mortality and fertility; accounts of millennial, multicentury, and finally intercensal vital-trend phases since antiquity; identifications of informational minefields and the challenges these will continue to pose to new researchers; and sociodemographic deductions linked to case studies of the Amerindians' extraordinary—yet little noted—demographic transitions within this century in both the United States and Canada.

Students of historical linkages between population change and resource availabilities will encounter illustrations galore of circular and cumulative possibilities under both primitive and contemporary societal circumstances, whether natural or manmade. Instances when demographic pressures on food supply have led to high mortality and this to high-fertility norms that then generated renewed food-supply pressures have been recurrent circular causal patterns. Migration—induced by tribal, ethnic, or class struggles over scarce arable lands in older settled areas—has generated repeated competitive and emigration outcomes, leading over time to settlement of major regional aggregates—a cumulative pattern not unlike North America's history of repeated expulsions visited on the continent's Amerindians. With modifications to allow for contemporary nation-state influences, analogous cause–effect sequences are still to be found today, as in major parts of Africa and Brazil's Amazon region. Or with direct reference to the present volume's geographic compass, consider that "a court ruling denying a claim by Canadian Indians to a vast region of British Columbia has further embittered relations between this country's aboriginal peoples and its nonnative majority, at a time when tensions have been running as high as at any time in decades" (see "Ruling Limiting Land Embitters Canadian Indians," *New York Times,* March 13, 1991, p. A4).

A long active researcher on uses and abuses of social statistics in diverse subject areas, Jaffe has a field day identifying definitional and enumerative shortcomings or inconsistencies in both the U.S. and Canadian census reports on the Amerindians. His exposures on these scores could well serve as prime textbook examples of an important—yet much too often overlooked—branch of social analysis. Applied to the 1990 Amerindian census findings being issued in the United States, Jaffe's evaluations of their validity could serve as required background reading on a question of headline interest today (see, for example, "Census Finds Many Claiming New Identity: Indian," *New York Times,* March 5, 1991, p. A1).

Fortunately, the data at hand for both the United States and Canada appear adequate to demonstrate that recent Amerindian demographic trends in the two countries have been instances of phenomenally accelerated population change. Essentially unnoted by trend students, including this one, U.S.

Amerindian fertility according to Jaffe's estimates came to over 5 children per woman as of 1960—a level not much above what it had been a half-century earlier, far above the industrialized world's contemporary average, and only moderately below the Third World average. Only 20 years later, by 1980, the corresponding ratio had dropped by no less than a 13-child amount to an order of magnitude that approximated bare replacement behavior, was only somewhat above the industrialized world's average, and came to not much more than half the Third World's average ratio. United Nations fertility surveys reveal practically no comparable rates of decline, at least with respect to national populations. Similarly for the Canadian Amerindians: Although their fertility transition record has apparently been a bit less dramatic than that in United States, the 2.5 child–woman ratio decline registered between 1960 and 1980 again ranks with the most rapid national transition experiences encountered anywhere.

With respect to the second major aspect of modern-era demographic transitions—mortality declines—substantial Amerindian downtrends began much earlier than 1960 but have since then also been succeeded by dramatically rapid convergence to low-mortality national levels. As of the pre-World War I years, estimated Amerindian life expectancy in the United States was about 15 years below the contemporary average for both that country and developed areas generally; hence it lagged behind the latter by at least three-quarters of a century. By 1980, the corresponding difference with both developed areas and U.S. averages had plummeted to some 2 to 3 years, mainly because of accelerated survival rate upsurges since about 1960. In Canada, where mortality documentation for its Indian population has been less extensive, it is again possible to infer that considerable convergence with the country's overall longevity levels has taken place, although the gap here is larger than in the United States.

Studies of very long-run demographic evolutions have been rare for any population, whether national or nonnational, and rarer still—if indeed any exist—for ethnically identified subnational groupings. It is to be hoped that this contribution will stimulate and help guide at least partially analogous undertakings in one or more of several ways: by encouraging intensified demographic research on prehistoric eras, ancient historic periods, and the many subsequent premodern centuries that also unfold before one reaches the beginning years standard for research in historical demography; by illustrating how the technical tools of modern demographic analysis can be fruitfully blended with those of other disciplines, both physical and behavioral, when seeking to advance demographic knowledge for premodern subject areas; also and not least, by illustrating how valuable conclusions concerning extended demographic transitions can be deduced for ethnic or other groupings subject

to large-scale intergroup exchanges when one has to cope with seemingly un-
revealing source materials.

A subjective aspect of this volume worth noting, one pervasively inter-
twined with its social-scientific aspects, is that the reader will not long be kept
in doubt about the harsh injustices and severe human costs implicit in the
cold statistical findings being presented. Although the evidence is consistently
weighed objectively for what it can and cannot tell us—given its innumerable
estimating warts, interpretive uncertainties, and all—Jaffe's outrage at the centu-
ries-long brutalizations visited upon North America's "Native Americans" by
European settlers and their descendants is neither kept concealed nor manifested
infrequently. His protest against the significant discriminations and inequalities
that are still found to exist—and will surely persist despite increasing attempts
at reform—is no less evident. None of this will be a surprise to those who know
the author personally or are aware of his prolific contributions to other subject
areas. Candor and indignation in exposing social inequities have been hallmarks
of his long career as an analyst of American and global human resource development issues and comparative patterns, subjects that all too often translate into
instances of subdevelopment, superior–subordinate hierarchies, outright subju-
gations, or (in the Amerindian history) all too easily verified accounts of un-
disguised or at best crudely disguised cruelties.

Happily in the Amerindian case, reasons exist for hopes for the future. A
series of objective indications point, at least directionally, toward more humanitarian outcomes. As late as 1900, when the present century began, the U.S.
census showed an Amerindian population count no less than three-fourths
below its estimated size when the Pilgrims landed—abundant testimony to the
demographic eradications that must have prevailed during the better part of 300
years, whether from directly physical or lethal socioeconomic causes. Three-
fourths of a century later, a very different message can be read into the fact that
the Amerindian population sizes—according to the U.S. 1970 and 1980 censuses—indicated a far greater increase than could be expected from natural
increase causes (births minus deaths) alone. The excess, by some 400,000 or
fully one-fourth of the intercensal increase, Jaffe interprets to have stemmed
largely from the newly expanded willingness of Amerindians to identify openly
with their Indian ancestry—in marked contrast with previous tendencies during
twentieth-century enumerations to overlook or conceal such affiliations. The
generally similar trend patterns found in Canada through 1981 point to analogous factual and interpretive conclusions.

Since 1980, the last census date Jaffe could cover at the time of his writing,
the 1990 U.S. census has reported a further unexpectedly large intercensal
increase in Amerindian numbers for the 1980s, thereby adding fresh support to

Jaffe's hypothesis that there has been a dramatic turnabout in this country of how Amerindians respond when identifying their ethnic origins. Canada is similarly testable in these respects in the light of its 1991 census undertaking.

Should the actual trends and Jaffe's interpretations both prove to be sustained, they would add another chapter—all too rare—to those historic occasions when a group's survival instincts, supported by renascent pride in its ancestral roots, were found to triumph over seemingly overwhelming odds.

GEORGE J. STOLNITZ

Director Emeritus, Population Institute for Research and Training
Indiana University
Bloomington, Indiana

Preface

People, societies, and cultures are always in a state of change. Sometimes change occurs very slowly, or so it seems; at other times the pace appears to be very rapid and hectic. We like to think that the pace, or rate of change, is most rapid in our world of the twentieth century, at least in the more economically developed areas. Whether or not the speed of change is truly most rapid today or whether it pleases our collective ego to think so, I leave to philosophers to decide. I know of no way of ascertaining and comparing the speed of change today with that of the past.

William Fielding Ogburn was intrigued by the idea and the reality of social change. How do you measure it? What influences bring it about? His writings on this subject are documented in his book *Social Change* (1922), in the report to President Hoover entitled *Recent Social Trends in the United States* (1933), and in innumerable other writings.

Ogburn visualized social trends, or changes, as the end products of many forces all operating on each other—an interrelated matrix of factors. Each newly generated change, in turn, reacts upon the other forces and so induces additional social changes. Or, depending on events, it may reinforce other existing social trends. This is the analytical framework within which we undertook a comprehensive demographic history of the American Indians.

Ogburn also put great emphasis on the question: How do you know it? He examined all research "findings" that came to his attention to ascertain the quality of the data used and the validity of the analytical procedures employed. Thus, he could satisfy himself as to the probable correctness of the "findings." We have tried to follow Ogburn's principle by informing our readers of "how we know it."

But why study the Amerindians? This is a purely personal matter. Recollections from my early years of memorizing *Hiawatha* for school, the story of the

Indians and the first Thanksgiving feast, Pocahontas and Captain John Smith, reading *The Last of the Mohicans* and who knows how many other stories and myths, stoked my imagination. In later years I learned of the brobdingnagian human-rights violations inflicted upon the Indians by the European settlers and their descendants. Then the Museum of the American Indian, now the National Museum, came to my attention. After spending many hours examining the collection of smoking pipes at the museum and reading everything I could find of Catlin's, and listening to Ralph Solecki's lectures, it seemed to me that the Amerindian was a suitable subject for a study of social change. Obviously, the Indians of my recollection as a youngster had changed considerably by the latter part of the twentieth century. How? Why?

The experiences of carrying on statistical research in population and the social sciences for over a half-century told me that I could not encompass every aspect of Indian life and society. In the absence of a budget and a staff, and being dependent upon my own efforts and the assistance of good friends—all named in the Acknowledgments—I trimmed the contemplated research down to what I thought was a manageable study. This "manageable" study is limited to the original inhabitants of Canada and the United States, and consists of their population characteristics: origin of the Amerindians, their migrations as settlers and/or refugees, their birth and death rates, where they lived, who they married, and so on. I leave to others the task of investigating other aspects of social change among the Amerindians.

The interrelated matrix of factors that resulted in the observed social change became larger and larger and more and more complicated. But because all must come to an end, I am stopping. Sufficient interrelated influences, which can result in social change, are presented forthwith, based on the Amerindians as my case study. I begin with *Homo erectus,* Beijing (Peking) man or woman of a half-million years ago or longer, and follow him/her and descendants almost to the end of the twentieth century.

He/she today is *Homo sapiens sapiens,* the same as you and me. He/she has changed physiologically as well as socially.

Acknowledgments

Many friends—probably close to 50—helped us, gave us information and/or statistics, reviewed early drafts that led to improvements in the final version, and otherwise assisted us in one way or another. We are grateful to them and sincerely thank them. But we alone are responsible for the contents of this volume.

We apologize to any of those whose names may have been inadvertently omitted from the following alphabetical listing. As we often mention, "counting is difficult." We have tried to provide the affiliation of each person, but because of retirement, job changes, and other events, we are not certain of the present affiliation of everyone.

We are also most grateful to the Columbia University Seminar on Population and Social Change for several opportunities to test some of our ideas. Talking to the members and exchanging ideas with them greatly sharpened our own thinking and analyses.

And we are most appreciative of the efforts of Eliot Werner, Herman Makler, Robert Freire, and staff in converting our original manuscript into a publishable book.

May other would-be authors have as many helpful friends as we have. Without them we could not have prepared this volume.

Robert Austerlitz, *Columbia University*
Carol Berger, *Canadian Consulate*
Robert Carleton
Paul Carter, *Columbia University*
John A. Cavallo, *L. Berger & Associates*
Ralph S. Clem, *Florida International University*
Jerome A. Cybulski, *Canadian Museum of Civilization*

Tony d'Angelo, *U.S. Indian Health Service*
Martha de Montano, *National Museum of the American Indian*
Frank Findlow, *Lockheed Aircraft*
Rosalind S. Fink, *Columbia University*
David J. Finkel
J. R. D. Fowell, *Canadian Consulate*
Nathalie Friedman, *Columbia University*
Alan S. Gilbert

Michael Greenberg, *Rutgers University*

Sheila Grimm, *U.S. Census Office in New York City*

Aaron Handler, *U.S. Indian Health Service*

Larry Heligman, *United Nations*

Bill Hill, *U.S. Census Office in New York City*

Ralph L. Holloway, *Columbia University*

Robert Johansen, *Fellow, Society of Actuaries; Consulting Actuary*

Sheila Klein, *Indian and Northern Affairs, Canada*

Robert Lewis, *Columbia University*

Irving Lukoff, *Columbia University*

Evelyn Mann, *New York City Planning Office*

Carlos Medina

Maria Morales-Harper, *U.S. Census Office in New York City*

Mary E. Mygatt, *Columbia University*

Margaret Padin-Bialo, *U.S. Census Office in New York City*

Edward T. Pryor, *Statistics Canada*

Theresa Rogers, *Columbia University*

Anna C. Roosevelt, *National Museum of the American Indian*

Nan A. Rothschild, *Columbia University*

Julia Roybal, *San Ildefonso, New Mexico*

Leo Roybal, *San Ildefonso, New Mexico*

William Ryan, *Columbia University*

Joseph Salvo, *New York City Planning Office*

James Smith, *National Museum of the American Indian*

Ralph Solecki, *Texas A & M University*

Herbert F. Spirer, *University of Connecticut*

Eugene Sterud, *National Endowment for the Humanities*

Douglas H. Ubelaker, *Smithsonian Institution*

Larry F. Van Horn, *U.S. National Park Service*

R. W. Venables, *National Museum of the American Indian*

P. Willey, *California State University, Chico*

Howard Winters, *New York University*

*   *   *   *

Carolyn Sperber, associate director for research and analysis in the office of equal opportunity and affirmative action of Columbia University, died April 25, 1992 following a heart attack. She was a good friend, co-worker, and expert statistician. Carolyn was instrumental in helping to design the analysis and in obtaining the information on the ancestry of the U.S. Amerindians. Without these data, our analysis of the population in the twentieth century would have been meager and unsatisfactory.

Contents

PART II • WHAT COLUMBUS HAD WROUGHT: THE PERIOD FROM 1492 TO THE 1980s

PROLEGOMENON

It was intended to present here some facts bearing on the *causes* of increase or decrease of Indian populations as affecting them in a state of savagery or barbarism, and as they yield to civilizing influences, but the limits of these notes do not allow. They will appear hereafter.

It is to be understood that the statements and facts presented are not brought forward to attack or defend any theory whatever; nor are they submitted as by any means conclusive evidence on the subject to which they relate. But it is hoped that, by bringing them to the notice of competent observers, enough other facts may be obtained to warrant a general conclusion respecting the influence of civilization upon the Indian population.

It may not be impertinent for the writer to observe that the above and a multitude of other facts that have come to his knowledge during several years of study of the question of Indian civilization have convinced him that the usual theory that the Indian population is destined to decline and finally disappear, as a result of contact with white civilization, must be greatly modified, probably abandoned altogether.

S. N. CLARK

BUREAU OF EDUCATION
November 24, 1877

Chapter *1*

Some Observations

INTRODUCTION

We present as comprehensive a picture as possible of the population changes, the ever-changing demography, of the original inhabitants of that part of the earth's surface known today as Canada and the United States. We follow them from the time of first arrival in the Western Hemisphere to the end of the twentieth century.

These people have many names: Native American is the most general term and includes the Inuit, or Eskimo, and Aleut; we omit the latter two groups. We concentrate on the *Indians* or *Amerindians,* who constitute the great majority of all Native Americans. North American Indians are those who live, or lived, in the United States and Canada. *Ancestors* and *Ancients* are those Amerindians who lived long before the arrival of the Europeans. The names *Indian* and *Eskimo* were assigned by the Europeans. Indians thought of themselves only as members of specific tribes or bands, to use the Canadian term. Debates are possible over what name to apply to the groups in which these people lived: bands, tribes, ethnic groups, entities, nations, or whatever. We hold no brief for any name. We use the *tribe* only because most writers and most currently available information about the Indians use *tribe* in the United States and *band* in Canada.

We prepared this comprehensive demographic history for the interested nonprofessional as well as for demographers, archaeologists, and anthropologists. Most demographers know very little about pre-World War II Amerindian population history and even less about archaeology. Too many archaeologists and physical and cultural anthropologists know too little about demographic and actuarial studies and population dynamics. Yet the demography of the people in whom they are interested is of the greatest importance for understanding the Native Americans.

1

Three major topics underlie our discussions of both the prehistoric and historic periods (the dividing line is Columbus's first trip to the Western Hemisphere), and these we discuss in summary form. One is "Changes in the Natural Environment" and its influence upon population. The second is the question "Who Is an Indian?" The third is the ever-recurrent problem of "Inferring History from Fragments of Information" and drawing conclusions about the remote past as well as the present. We revert to these three topics time and time again in the following chapters. In hope of preventing undue repetition in the body of the book, we include the summaries in this introductory chapter.

OUR INTERESTS

Our aim is threefold:

1. To document the changing population characteristics of the North American Indians from the earliest times possible to the latter part of the twentieth century, a period of 15,000 to perhaps 30,000 years or more
2. To ascertain the extent to which their population characteristics may be converging, or resembling, those of the general populations of Canada and the United States in the twentieth century
3. To relate these changing demographic characteristics to changes in the natural and social environments.

Coverage

Population characteristics include where they came from and when, age and sex, how many years they lived (length of life), causes of death, how many children the women have, intermarriage with non-Indians, and other traits that describe the people and how they live. Here we place our main emphasis.

We place much less emphasis on the absolute numbers of Amerindians. Prior to the late nineteenth century, all numbers are uncertain, and a uniquely correct number of natives never will be had. We see no point in arguing how many there were in 1492 or any other early date. As for the present, the end of the twentieth century, until an agreed-upon definition of "who is an Indian" is arrived at—we suspect that this will never happen—there can be no uniquely correct number. The best that can be done, and all we attempt, is to note the probable direction of change over time, increased or decreased numbers.

There is a large literature about the Amerindians, but very little of it is concerned with their changing population characteristics. Before the Europeans landed, the Indians were masters in their own lands. Within the following four centuries, they were relegated to the status of pariahs and subject to the whim of the white man. How did this social change impact on their demographic characteristics?

Or, consider the introduction of agriculture long before the Europeans arrived. How did the gradual transition from a hunting and gathering economy to an agriculture-based life affect Indian demographics? Did relegating the natives to reserves (in Canada) and reservations (in the United States) affect their demographic behavior? What impact might World Wars I and II have had upon Amerindian life and demographics?

We emphasize the pre-European period, for in order to understand twentieth-century demographic and social conditions, we must have a baseline. What were the conditions in the millennia prior to the arrival of the Europeans at the end of the fifteenth century? We know when and what changes occurred in the political, economic, and social conditions since the advent of the Europeans. Determination of when and what demographic changes occurred, then, throws light on the relationships between the changing social scene and changing demographics.

We divided the pre-European millennia into two major categories: the time of the hunters and gatherers and the time of the agriculturalists. The first category includes practically all of present United States and Canadian Amerindian population prior to about 1,500 to 2,000 years ago. (All dates and time periods are approximations; these people did not have calendars and did not keep written records.) Some did survive as hunters and gatherers into the twentieth century, but we doubt that there are many in the 1980s.

The second group, the agriculturalists, first appeared perhaps 2,000 years ago (see Chapter 6). Slowly and gradually agriculture spread across much of North America. By the time the Europeans arrived, perhaps half of the Amerindians had some cultivation. Hunting and fishing could not be given up entirely because there were no domestic animals to provide meat, except for the dog.

In light of this economic transformation, we seek changes in the population characteristics that may have occurred between the hunters and gatherers and the agriculturalists. We can then study changes between the agriculturalists and twentieth century Amerindians.

We omit study of the Eskimo (called Inuit in Canada) and the Aleut partly for technical reasons and partly because they live under geographic and climatic conditions that may make their demographics different from those of their southern neighbors. For example, in constructing life tables for the prehistorics (Chapter 4), we set the end of the fifteenth century as the end of the prehistoric period. For these far northern dwellers, however, little information can be found for the prehistoric period. Further, we have no way of knowing to what extent their length of life may differ from that of the more southern natives—the Indians—due to climate.

We also excluded those who live south of the Rio Grande if for no other reason than it is impractical to study them. We do not have the resources, personnel, budget, and time to cover the entire Western hemisphere.

Further, we omit study of individual tribes for the following reasons:

1. Tribes are constantly in transition. A tribe in existence in the twentieth century cannot be traced back to its original immigration from Asia. Over time, tribes or bands increase, decrease, join other tribes or absorb others, or simply disappear.
2. The information needed for a long-time (several centuries) demographic–historical study of individual tribes is nonexistent.
3. Very little that would have applicability to the demographic history of all Amerindians would be learned by the study of single tribes.
4. As far as we can determine, the bands and tribes in existence in the latter twentieth century are most interested in their current social and economic conditions. Their long-time demographic histories are of less concern to them.

SOURCES OF INFORMATION

There are large amounts of population information sequestered away in government basements, very little of which has been analyzed adequately. With the help of good friends, we have found and processed many of these miscellaneous statistics in an effort to make them as comparable as possible over time and between Canada and the United States, and taking into account the quality of the data. The resulting statistical analysis is then interpreted in light of the nonstatistical historical literature. The reader who is interested in following further the "Trail of the Missing Information" should see Meyer and Thornton (1988).

From the very beginning, the European invaders kept written records of their exploits, together with descriptions of the native people whom they met. The Vikings who landed in Vinland (now Newfoundland) in the eleventh century, and Columbus upon his first trip in 1492, commented about the natives. Much of this record is only partially correct. Some of it appears to be accurate as far as it goes but is incomplete. The explorers and fur traders, the people in the Hudson Bay and other trading posts, for example, had good information about the natives with whom they were in contact and got to know (as far as we can determine). But they did not necessarily know much about those natives with whom they had little or no contact. To illustrate, Dr. James Smith, late curator in the Museum of the American Indian, believed that it was as late as the twentieth century before all the tribes or bands of the Cree (who live west of Hudson Bay) became known to anthropologists, the public, and the Canadian government.

We have drawn upon information from several disciplines—physical anthropology, archaeology, demography, economics, geography, history, sociology, and statistics—and attempted to weave them together. For the demographer we explain some of the archaeology of the prehistorics as described by archaeologists and geologists, in relation to population. For the archaeologist we explain something about population dynamics. In this process we have learned considerably about the relationships of these diverse subjects.

CHANGES IN THE NATURAL ENVIRONMENT— MOTHER NATURE AT THE CONTROLS

If we were to choose the single most influential event or series of events, for the North American Indians, we select the glaciers and interglacial periods that in the past millennia, covered most of Canada from time to time. Humans, *Homo sapiens sapiens,* reached the Western Hemisphere from the Eastern with the help of the glaciers. And ever after, the glaciers and their melting left long-lasting influences—influences that affect life in North America even in the twentieth century.

Mother Nature constantly makes changes in the natural environment, in addition to the changes in glacial activity. Many of these environmental and climatic variations and changes affect small areas, for example, the Southern High Plains of western Texas and eastern New Mexico, as described by Bamforth (1988). The Great Plains (ranging from the southern Canadian Prairie Provinces to the Rio Grande), which he studied, at first sight seem to have a rather uniform geography. Nevertheless, there is sufficient variation and changes therein, over time, so as to have affected human adaptation via the differential availability of buffalo, a primary food source for the Indians.[1]

Such changes impact on humans, and *Homo,* in turn, impacts on the natural environment. Both *Homo* and the environment change.

The published literature is far too vast for us to attempt to summarize in our Amerindian study. We can only call to our readers' attention the excellent information in Bamforth (1988) and the volume edited by Nicholas (1988) and their references to additional readings.

The amount of water on the earth is always more or less the same. If much of it freezes over into glaciers on land, then the sea level falls. As the glaciers

---

[1] Under favorable climatic conditions, there was more grass for the buffalo, and the herds were larger and less mobile. The food supply for the Indians was more assured, and the human aggregations somewhat more complex and larger. The climatic conditions varied from one segment of the Great Plains to another at any moment of time and from one time to another in any given segment. The Plains Indians adapted as best they could to such variability on the part of Mother Nature.

melt, the water runs back into the seas, and their levels rise.[2] This sequence of events has occurred a number of times during the course of the world's history, lowering and raising the sea level between the Eastern and Western Hemispheres, where Siberia and Alaska almost meet. Further, the present waters—the Bering Strait and parts of the Bering Sea and Arctic Ocean—are very shallow, well under 500 feet, or about 150 meters. If enough water freezes into glaciers on land, the sea level in the vicinity of the Bering Strait may drop 100 meters (330 feet) or more, thus exposing vast surfaces of land, as much as 1,000 miles if not more, from north to south.

According to Hopkins,[3] a land bridge was open intermittently between about 25,000 and perhaps 15,000 years ago (during the Wisconsin glaciation). About 15,000 years ago, the rising sea level was drowning Beringia, as the land bridge is named; the "final" complete separation of Siberia from Alaska occurred some 14,000 years ago. The sea level continued to rise to its present level.

Between about 25,000 and 60,000 to 70,000 years ago, the sea level also had its ups and downs, according to Hopkins (1982). There were times when the Bridge was fully open, and other times when stretches of water intervened. The sea level had fallen about 85 meters 60,000 or 70,000 years ago (according to the oxygen-isotope record). According to the coral reef record, there was a decline from −20 meters about 60,000 years ago to −45 meters about 28,000 years ago, an overall decline of almost 100 feet.

Clearly Beringia had its ups and downs. There were times when the land bridge was fully open, and *Homo* and animals were able to walk across; at other times a kayak was needed.

As for the ever-changing climate of Beringia, Hopkins (1982, p. 430) states, "Beringian climates were most severe during the Duvanny Yar interval (about 30,000 to 15,000 years ago)." Presumably, the solar front was pushed southward and probably lay south of the Beringian shoreline during much of the year. It is thought that during the Duvanny Yar interval, annual precipitation was about one-half of what it is today. "This reduction (in precipitation) in the face of widespread evidence of very low snowfall must mean that average annual temperatures also were substantially lowered" (Hopkins 1982, p. 430).

We summarize:

1. Presumably the Ancestors crossed over from northeast Asia with the help of a lowered sea level (see Chapter 2).
2. If the Ancestors had been in northeast Asia 50,000 years ago or earlier, they could have taken an early bridge to reach the promised land, or come anytime by water.

---

[2] For an interesting and readable discussion of glaciers, see John and Katherine Imbrie (1979).
[3] Hopkins 1982; see p. 12, Figure 3, and pp. 430 ff. Also 1967, Chapter 24, especially pp. 461–465.

3. If they arrived over the last land bridge during the Duvanny Yar interval, they chose a period with adverse climate. If they had arrived before or after the Duvanny Yar period—more than 30,000 years ago, or less than 15,000 years ago—they would have had a somewhat more benign climate, with better food potentials.

The glaciers also benefited farmers in the United States in the twentieth century. The movement of the glaciers over the millennia and the great volume of melt water rushing across the landscape pushed much of whatever fertile soil there had been in eastern and central Canada, into what is now southern Canada just north of the U.S. boundary and east of Lake Superior. The bulk of the soil was moved further south into what, today, is the northern part of the United States. The farmers in the Midwest and to the east received free excellent farmland.

Most of Canada today has very little farmland. The Laurentian Plateau or Canadian Shield left behind by the melting glaciers (Figure 1.1) is the predominant land feature—hard granite, gneiss, and schist rock. The glaciers scooped

Figure 1.1. The Laurentian Plateau (Canadian Shield). See *Handbook of North American Indians,* Vol. 6, p. 87. Smithsonian Institution, 1981.

out numerous lake basins and created an untold number of rivers and streams. Transportation, except by air, is difficult because of the broken terrain.

In the twentieth century, the Laurentian Plateau is a source of minerals, timber, fur-bearing animals, and hydroelectric power. To the prehistoric Amerindians and the early European arrivals, however, the only resource of value was the fur-bearing animal. These people did not know about the minerals nor about hydroelectric power, and the market for Canadian timber was limited.

For these early Europeans, the gold rush was for beaver fur (Innes 1956). Beaver-fur hats were all the rage in Europe, and the demand for skins was very great. Fads change, however, and by the nineteenth century silk had replaced beaver fur to a large extent, in the manufacture of hats, and other fancy furs began to replace beaver for coats and other garments. Changing fashions and fads and the natural environment affect markets. This "fur-mining," as we shall see, together with lack of much farmland, had a long-time effect upon the Amerindians in Canada. One effect was the creation of a new ethnic group, the Métis,[4] or those of mixed Indian–European ancestry.

Let us return to the topic of available farmland and agricultural possibilities in Canada versus the United States.

The climate of North America going from south to north gradually becomes colder and the land less suitable for agriculture. People must eat, and agriculture is capable of supporting a higher population density than can hunting and fishing. (There are limited areas, e.g., the West Coast of the United States and Canada, where fish and other sea creatures are sufficiently abundant so that they provided a steady and dependable food supply in pre-Columbian times.)

There are about 3.5 million square miles of land in each country. If Alaska and the Arctic and sub-Arctic areas of Canada are omitted there are about 3 million square miles in each. The countries are close to equal in size, but the geography and climate are vastly different. The area suitable for cultivation stops just above the Canadian–United States boundary close to the southern limit of the Laurentian Plateau.

In Canada a little under 10% of these 3 million square miles, about a quarter-million, is classified as being in farms.[5] About half of the one-quarter million, or one-eighth of a million square miles, however, is woodland or not under cultivation for whatever reason; only about 4% of the total surface is actually under cultivation (1981). Today's wheatland in the Prairie Provinces was largely uncultivatable by the prehistoric Indians or by the early European settlers (see Chapter 7).

In the United States,[6] about half of the land surface is classified as "land

[4] Slobodin, 1981, pp. 361 ff.
[5] *Statistics Canada, 1984,* Catalogue 96901, Table 1.
[6] *Statistical Abstract of the United States, 1989,* Tables 1078 and 1112.

in farms," and between 15 and 20% of the total surface is used for growing crops (1980).

Maize (Niethammer 1978, Chapter VI) was the main but not the only crop cultivated by the Amerindians and was grown in much of the eastern half of the United States and in portions of the Southwest where water was available. In southeastern Canada, in particular that section lying between about Quebec City and Lake Superior (in the United States between New York State on the east and Michigan on the west), maize was an important crop also. Minor crops included beans, chilis, pumpkin, squash, and others that require more or less the same growing conditions as maize. In addition, various wild grasses including what we now call "wild rice" were eaten when available. Wild acorns and nuts and other food items were used, but little of these foods grew in Canada north of the cultivable land.

In summary the amount of land suitable for agriculture in the United States is four or five times as great as in Canada. The number of Native Americans in the United States at the time of the first European arrival was four or five or more times as great as in Canada. Coincidence?

Growth of the Amerindian population after the European invasion also was influenced by these geographic considerations. The Europeans who settled south of the St. Lawrence River and Great Lakes wanted land for farming. They felt that they had to rid the land of the Indians and killed very many of them, thus reducing the native population in what is now the United States. In Canada the settlers had less interest in farmland once they had appropriated the small amount available, and there was less felt need to decimate the native population. Indeed, the Indians were needed for the fur trade. Hence the population was not reduced as much as in the United States. Again we see the interplay of natural and manmade forces.

The discussion following in Part II of our story will explore in more detail the relationship of geography to the changing size of the Indian population from 1492 to the end of the nineteenth century. During the twentieth century, however, the geographic differences between the two countries have not been as important (as far as we can determine) in influencing population size and rate of growth of Amerindians. Other social and economic factors are far more important in the latter twentieth century, in influencing their population size and characteristics.

WHO IS AN AMERICAN INDIAN?

When the first Europeans arrived, it was clear to them who was an Indian—anyone who lived away from "civilization" and did not look like a European nor an African. As fighting broke out between the natives and the settlers, the "enemy" was the Indian, if he was not another European (see Appendix 1). This "definition" was formalized in the United States Constitution when Indians *not taxed* were specifically excluded from the population counts for each state on the basis of which the number of state's Congressmen was determined. After all, what census enumerator (they were at first called U.S. marshals) wanted to travel through the "wilderness" looking for Indians to count for the 1790 census? So the Indians were defined as the "enemy," unless they paid taxes.

This difficulty and unwillingness to locate and count the Indians in the decennial censuses continued from the first census, that of 1790, to that of 1870. The ninth U.S. census was the first to recognize Indians as a separate "race" and attempt to count them.[7] The census office argued that if vagabonds and horses and cattle were counted, the natives also should be counted. By 1870 almost all Indians were on reservations or otherwise known to government Indian agencies. It was now more nearly feasible to count them. Actually, only about one-quarter were enumerated, and three-quarters estimated, according to the published census table.

An Indian was defined, apparently, as any inmate of a reservation or client of an agency, someone whom the enumerator thought "looked like an Indian." If this definition sounds like a tautology, so be it. The 1910 census tried to tighten this definition as follows: "All persons of mixed white and Indian blood who have any appreciable amount of Indian blood are counted as Indians, even though the proportion of white blood may exceed that of Indian blood."[8] In 1910 all people living on reservations and considered by the enumerators to be Indians were reported as Indians. The working definition seems not to have changed over the decades.

Until about World War I and the Great Depression most of the Amerindians continued to live on reservations, or reserves. Hence, the traditional definition continued to be applied by the censuses; nonwhites who lived on reservations were considered to be and were recorded as Indians.

By 1980 in the United States and 1981 in Canada, people were asked to classify themselves as to race. This enumeration innovation shifted the burden of definition to the respondents as far as the census is concerned. "You are an Indian (or whatever race you prefer) if you say you are."

In Canada the definition of an Indian over the decades was much the same as that south of the border, insofar as we can determine. The Canadian Department of Indian Affairs published information on numbers of Indians during much of the nineteenth century, but we suspect that these figures were largely estimates. The Canadian census conducted its first count of Indians in 1871. The 1981 census reported the Métis separately, those of mixed Indian and non-

---

[7] *Ninth Census of the United States*, 1870, pp. xvi and xvii.
[8] *Indian Population in the United States and Alaska 1910*, p. 10.

Indian ancestry (see also Chapter 10). Prior to the 1981 census, we do not know
how nor where the Métis may be in the census statistics. The U.S. census
contains no such classification, and we do not know how any Métis who may
have migrated to the United States may have identified themselves to the United
States census.

The Indians are classified as "status" or "non-status" in the 1981 Canadian census. These two groups are legally defined, and it is assumed that
everyone who self-identifies as an Amerindian knows what his or her classification is. The first group generally, but not always, lives on the reserves and
is entitled to government benefits. The latter group lives off the reserves and
only some are eligible for government benefits.[9] These two groups combined
presumably are reasonably comparable to the United States Census classification
of American Indian.

In both countries there are legal definitions of who is an Indian. This is the
result of the various treaties and contracts signed over the centuries, which
together with subsequent legislation set the framework for the present government agencies that are supposed to help the Indians. To receive benefits, officially one must be an Indian. Question: Who should be so classified? The
agencies that supposedly service the Indians, their varying definitions of who is
an Indian, and their modes of operation are too numerous and complex for us
to describe here. Also, in both countries, a reserve or reservation is such only if
the appropriate government agency so recognizes it. This has led to many court
battles between groups that desire to be officially recognized as Indian bands or
tribes and granted official reserves, and government agencies.

The most complicating factor in defining the Amerindians and analyzing
the information about them is that so many are of mixed Indian–non-Indian
ancestry (see Chapter 10). Should a person of dual heritage be counted as an
Indian or non-Indian? We have no "correct" answer. We are only certain that
such mixtures affect the reported numbers. The United States census of 1910
(p. 10) noted:

> Since there is an increasing amount of white blood . . . in what is classed as the
> Indian population, it follows that the number of persons included in that class
> [Indian] would tend to increase from census to census without necessarily any increase
> in the total amount of Indian blood in the country. . . . If there were no marriages of
> Indians except between full-bloods, a decline in the total Indian population might
> appear, the number classed as Indian might increase very materially as the result of
> marriages between persons of other races and Indians or between full-blood and
> mixed-blood Indians.

As the population of mixed ancestry becomes larger, a point is reached
where many can report themselves to the census as either Indian or non-Indian

---

[9] *Canada's Native People* (1984).

depending on how they feel. If once having decided, they retained their self-classification we should have no statistical problems. But we suspect that there has been considerable changing of self-identification since World War II—Indian one time and non-Indian another.

Consider a simple case: An Indian woman of mixed ancestry is married to a non-Indian man and they live, let us say, in Philadelphia—definitely not on a reservation. They have two children. Upon reaching the age of self-identification, one declares himself as Indian and one as non-Indian. Sometime later the Indian offspring decides to reclassify himself as non-Indian; the original non-Indian retains his non-Indian self-identification. Was there a decrease in the Indian population and an increase in the non-Indian population? If these two offspring, in turn, marry non-Indians, the eventual result is almost certain absorption of the Indian into the general population. That is why so many self-declared non-Indians report having Indian ancestors (see Chapter 10).

This ambiguity in definition and classification has led to a proliferation of numbers. In the United States, the maximum number of Indians, based on self-identification in the 1980 census, is about 1,478,000. The minimum number is 295,000 self-identified Indians who live on reservations and report being enrolled in a tribe.

In Canada also there is considerable variation. The maximum including the Métis and based on self-classification is 466,000 as reported in the 1981 census. Excluding the Métis reduces the count to 368,000. The minimum number is 225,000 status Indians who live on reserves or Crown lands.

How many Indians are there in Canada and the United States?

THE PROBLEM OF UNCERTAINTY—OR INFERRING HISTORY FROM FRAGMENTS OF INFORMATION

People, including historians, make decisions continuously despite the fact that they do not have full and complete and accurate information. The decision may be as simple as choosing the entrée in a restaurant without knowing precisely how each of the dishes on the menu tastes. Or it may be as complicated as that of the business executive trying to decide whether to build a new factory, or the Congressman trying to decide how to vote on a proposed new tax bill. Juries often must decide guilty or innocent without knowing all the facts. Indeed, if complete information was available, perhaps there would be neither litigation nor murder trials. Did Y murder Z or did Z die as a consequence of "rough sex"? Z is not available to provide information.

Medical doctors must make decisions regarding the nature of the patient's ailment and what medicines may be effective. Often the ailment is not diagnosed instantly and correctly. Once the doctor has received test results, he/she must

(a) decide whether the test results look plausible or the test should be rerun; (b) assuming the tests look satisfactory, determine the diagnosis; and (c) decide what medicines to prescribe.

In every case, the decision maker wishes for more information in order to decide which course of action will produce the maximum "best results." The historian wishes for certain that he or she knew what really happened.

This problem of trying to arrive at a decision without having all the information is known as the "surmise," *decision making under uncertainty.* Everyone continuously faces this surmise; we provide examples throughout the book. Examples range from "when was the growing of maize (corn) first conceived in Mexico?" to "how many Indians are there in the United States and Canada in the 1980s?" to "what were the birth and death rates of the North American Indians in the past and what are they today?"

We have here the statistical problem of *probability,*[10] no different from that taught in statistical courses throughout the length and breadth of North America and elsewhere, and we cannot devote the remainder of our volume to a fuller explanation of this subject. Everyone goes through life making decisions, non-statisticians as well as statisticians, and especially social scientists. Basically the statistical procedures for *decision making under uncertainty* are the guidelines that all of us follow in thinking through a problem. Unfortunately, in our opinion, too many researchers and decision makers fail to make proper use of probability.

The *first* requirement is knowledge of the subject matter. (For further discussion of "know the subject matter," see Jaffe and Spirer [1987, Chapter 3].) They write: "A number is a number—no more and no less. It can make sense and be understood only in light of specific subject matter. The writer or analyst must know the subject matter before the numbers can be explained" (p. 32). To illustrate, consider the question—were goats or sheep domesticated first? The only information consists of skeletal remains from many millennia ago. *The Babylon Times* did not print an article on domestication of goats (*Capra*) versus sheep (*Ovis*). A knowledgeable zooarchaeologist knows that (a) sheep and goat skeletal structures differ slightly, and an inexperienced investigator may confuse the two; and (b) the domesticated form of each differs from the wild form (this is how we know whether or not an ancient people had domesticated animals).

Skeletal remains are found in digs, and the earliest domesticated forms of goats and sheep must be identified. Next, these remains must be dated. Now, perhaps, our question as to which was domesticated first can be answered. For the sake of the concerned reader, we note that the Brothwells are of the opinion that sheep may have been domesticated some 11,000 years ago and goats 8,000 to 9,000 years ago.

---

[10] Readers wishing to pursue this topic will find useful Vazsonyi and Spirer (1984); also Robert Schlaifer (1961).

The *second* requirement is that we have all the information available and possible to obtain. Are there other skeletal remains, as yet unfound, which would provide evidence that goats were domesticated before sheep? Did the zooarchaeologists who reported on these animals properly classify the skeletal remains? When only parts of a skeleton are found, and which parts, how accurate is the diagnosis of sheep or goat? Was the dating of the earliest domesticated form of each correct? Each of these questions has the potential of introducing uncertainty.

On the basis of our knowledge of the subject matter and the available fragments of information, and assisted by conventional statistical procedures, we arrive at conclusions. Sometimes no conclusion is possible. Such is life. For example, we shall never know exactly when the first immigrants arrived in the Western Hemisphere from northeastern Asia. Does this lack of a specific conclusion make any difference to anyone? If not, why argue about it?

Because arriving at a decision in many fields such as population and business generally involves numbers and always information, correct numbers and definitions are necessities. As Jaffe and Spirer emphasize (Chapters 4 and 5), very often people do not define precisely what their subject of interest is. To compound their difficulties, they fail to count correctly or otherwise fail to obtain proper information. Indeed, often the proper and correct information is not available, for example, the exact number of Amerindians in the United States and Canada in 1491.

We emphasize decision making and *probability* because very much of the demographic history of the Amerindians that we describe in the following chapters stems from the use of probability. Neither demographers nor archaeologists nor anthropologists know the complete history. Each has but fragments of knowledge. Probability can help in welding these fragments into a history.

There is no guaranteed certainty in this world. Only probable levels of certainty may be had. And only after William F. Ogburn's famous question "How do you know it?" has been answered.

Now, let us continue with our account, from the time of Beijing Man, a half million years ago, to the 1980s.

Part I

The First Arrivals

Chapter 2

Origins and Entry into the New World

INTRODUCTION

Human beings had to have come from the Eastern Hemisphere to the Western, since *Homo sapiens sapiens* originated in the Eastern Hemisphere. We ask: from where in the Eastern Hemisphere did the Amerindians come? How did they reach the New World? When did this happen? We summarize the available literature insofar as possible.

There is no complete agreement among the archaeologists, anthropologists, geologists, and sundry other professionals who have expressed themselves on these questions. A general consensus in the late twentieth century is that the first inhabitants came from northeastern Asia, probably Siberia (Fladmark 1983). Japan has also been suggested as a possible source. Reynolds (1986) wrote: "The early dating of human presence in Japan is important for the peopling of the New World question . . . . They provide a population close to the land bridge routes to the Americas, at a time when human presence elsewhere in northeast Asia is very poorly, if at all, documented" (p. 331).

There is less agreement on how people reached the New World and when, and just how many waves of immigrants there may have been. Presumably the first immigrants reached the Western Hemisphere by walking to what is now Alaska, across a land bridge, Beringia, which existed in the past. Alternatively, some may have come by a combination of walking and watercraft. The land bridge did extend far south of what is now Bering Strait, perhaps as much as 1,000 miles from south to north (Figure 2.1). They had their choice of routes from the Eastern to the Western Hemisphere. They could have crossed over from

17

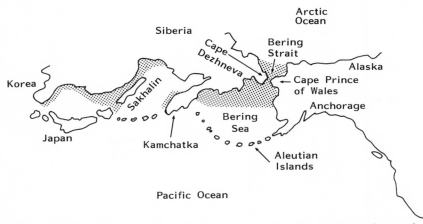

Figure 2.1. Beringia—the Land Bridge—and adjacent areas. Shaded areas indicate where sea level was probably more than 200 feet below its present level at some time during glaciation, thus exposing Beringia.

Cape Dezhneva to Cape Prince of Wales where the two hemispheres are about 50 or 55 miles apart. Or they could have started from Kamchatka or elsewhere in Asia and proceeded along the southern coast of the bridge, ending at approximately where Anchorage is now. Or they could have followed some route in between.[1] Bryan (1978a) suggests that the southern shore of Beringia was probably not much colder than the Aleutian Islands are at present because the Arctic Ocean waters could be cut off and the Japanese Current would keep the southern shores relatively mild.

Those who came along the southern coastline of Beringia may have had to use watercraft from time to time, as well as shank's mare. Bordes (1978, p. 4) argues that they could have come by water to the Western Hemisphere and all points south. "If man could cross many miles of open sea to get into Australia, he could probably cross the Bering Strait . . . even at high sea level."[2]

When these people came is much less certain than from where because there are problems with all the dating techniques, as we discuss subsequently. We should like to know, also, how these Ancients reached Tierra del Fuego, how

---

[1] There are many routes for traveling from one place to another. The old Santa Fe Trail is a good example. Wagon trains took many different routes, but they all ended in Santa Fe, New Mexico, supposedly at the La Fonda Hotel. Ancient people probably were no different. We cannot visualize the Ancestors lining up in Asia, one behind the other, and all following an identical route to the Western Hemisphere.

[2] Because *Homo sapiens* has been in Australia for many millennia and because there does not appear to have been a land connection to the Asian mainland, it is thought that he/she must have come by water sometime in the remote past.

long the journey from Alaska to the southern tip of Chile took, and when this journey occurred. The possible answers to all these questions are the subjects of controversies and arguments today. We shall try to summarize these discussions briefly and in so doing expect to intensify rather than ameliorate the disputes.

THEIR ORIGINS

European Thinking in the Sixteenth to Eighteenth Centuries

Several decades after Columbus reached the Western Hemisphere, burning questions arose among European writers and philosophers. Who are these creatures who met Columbus and other explorers? What is their origin? (Huddleston 1967). At first these questions were not raised because Columbus and the other explorers thought that they had reached islands off the coast of Asia. Everyone knew that people lived in Asia so there were no questions to be answered. Columbus did not know that he had stumbled upon the Western Hemisphere, which was a long way from and separate from Asia.

Magellan's expedition of 1519 to 1522 rounded South America through the Straits of Magellan and sailed across the Pacific. Magellan was killed in the Philippines in a battle between two native groups, but his expedition continued, saw Asia, continued westward and returned to Spain, thus sailing around the globe. This revelation, that there was an Eastern and a Western Hemisphere separated by mighty oceans, convinced the European philosophers that they had serious problems. If these natives were not Asians, who were they and how did they reach the Western Hemisphere?

The Europeans at this time—sixteenth to eighteenth centuries—had great difficulties in handling these questions because any possible answer had to fit into the theological framework of the times. All humans had to have been created by God, and following the Flood, had to be descendants of Noah. But nowhere in the Bible is there even a hint of humans living in a New World. Was there an unrecorded second creation of humans? The problem was complicated further by the presence of wild animals in the Western Hemisphere. How did they get there? And all this creation and movement into the Western Hemisphere had to have been completed within the last 5,000 to 6,000 years. This was the age of the world as computed from the Bible.

Sir William Petty wrote to his cousin, Sir Robert Southwell, in 1681, "I find that the world being 5630 years old" (Marquis of Lansdowne, 1928, p. 92). About the same time, Scalinger's Chronology "placed the Creation in the year 3948 B.C." or exactly 5,440 years before Columbus "discovered" the Western Hemisphere in 1492. Remarkable!

To complicate matters, if these inhabitants were not human beings, what were they? Many theories were advanced. The Indians were descended from the survivors of the "lost continent of Atlantis," of the "ten lost tribes of Israel," of "migrants from Troy, Phoenicia, Carthage," and so on. Huddleston (1967, p. 11) wrote that all origins postulated were "limited by the necessity to conform to Christian theology. . . . At no time before 1729 did anyone offer an origin theory which could not be made consistent with the Bible."

Joseph de Acosta (*Historia natural y moral de las Indias,* published in 1590) was the first to set forth the thesis that the people in the Western Hemisphere must have come from Europe, Africa, or Asia (see Huddleston 1967). He pointed out the flaws in other theories (e.g., there was no second creation). He then concluded that there must be a land connection because the Bible makes no mention of a second Ark, or at worst a narrow strait that could be navigated, in the undiscovered north or south.

Next Enrico Martin, an engineer in New Spain (present-day Mexico), in 1606 suggested that the most likely route for the earliest migrants from Asia to the New World would be in the region of Anian that he located in the extreme northeastern part of Siberia and northwestern America. Both man and animals could have crossed at this point to the Western Hemisphere.

Beringia, or the Land Bridge as it came to be known, was finally recognized as a route of men's and women's entry into the New World from northeastern Asia.

How Do We Know That They Came from Asia?

The Bering Land Bridge—Beringia—that we describe later is a route that the ancient Siberians or other northeastern Asians could have taken to reach the New World. Since there are no witnesses alive today who could give testimony, we must rely on circumstantial evidence, on the probabilities. Let us begin by asking from where they might have come. It appears obvious from their physical appearance that the Amerindians could not have arrived from Africa.

Europe as an origin also is very unlikely because of the intervening Atlantic and Arctic oceans. Substantial oceangoing craft were needed before the Europeans could cross the North Atlantic, the narrowest part of that ocean. The Amerindians did not have such craft 10,000 years ago or even earlier. Europeans first managed to sail across the Atlantic only 1,000 to 1,500 years ago.[3]

Only Asia is left as a possible source, and it must be the far northeast (what is now Siberia and adjacent lands); the middle and southern Pacific is far too wide for these ancient ones to have crossed by water. The Polynesian voyagers

---

[3] Morison (1971). By about 800 A.D. the Scandinavians were roaming the North Atlantic Ocean. There are stories about Irish religious earlier sailing over the North Atlantic to North America, but these earlier voyages, if there were such, have not been verified (see also Sauer 1968).

(Sharp 1964, Chapter 9), who settled the various South Pacific islands, embarked on their journeys recently, so to speak, perhaps only within the last 2,500 years, and long after the Amerindians arrived in the Western Hemisphere.

Turning to less speculative information, we note that Steward (1973, pp. 24–25) wrote of the "resemblance between Asiatics and American Indians." He refers to Hrdlička (an expert on human skeletal material) as stating that the "Neolithics of eastern Siberia show a close relation to the oblong-headed lower vaulted tribes of America."

Turner (1983 and 1987) provides dental evidence that the Native Americans, the Amerindians, Eskimo or Inuit, and Aleut are related to and descendants of the people of northeastern Asia—the northern Chinese, Japanese, Mongolians, and Siberians. The teeth of the Native Americans are similar in many respects to those of the Asians of 30,000 years ago or earlier. The cluster of tooth characteristics that he finds to be similar in these two groups of people he calls *sinodonty*. "Sinodonty appears in these skulls from the 18,000-year-old upper cave site of Chou-K'ou-Tien [see following section on China] in northern China, so it must have evolved some time earlier, perhaps 30,000 years ago."

Most archaeologists agree that the ancestors of the present native American population immigrated from northeastern Asia. They figure that the probability of this being the case is very high. We know of no further evidence.[4]

We discuss the part that probability or decision making under uncertainty plays in determining "irrefutable facts" in archaeology and anthropology, indeed, in all life. At present we simply point out that the only irrefutable evidence would consist of seeing, interviewing, and photographing the first Ancestors from their point of departure in northeastern Asia to their port of entry into the New World. Such a test is analogous to that applied by some archaeologists to determine the date of the first arrivals. Because we have no such evidence, we simply state that the probability of a northeast Asian origin is very high.

THE PEOPLING OF NORTHEASTERN ASIA

Since the Amerindians are believed to have come from northeastern Asia, their ancestors must have arrived in that part of the world before the migration to the Western Hemisphere began. Hence, we are faced with more questions: From where did they come? Why? When did people first reach northeastern Asia?

---

[4] Language and blood tests have been studied in an effort to determine relationships between the Siberians and the Amerindians. But the results are too inconclusive to be more than suggestive. For additional information about Indian languages, see Austerlitz (1980). See also Ruhlen (1987) on languages and Zegura (1987) on blood.

Because northern China is within walking distance of the far north, let us begin with China as a possible source of Amerindians.

China

Homo has lived in China since at least the lower Pleistocene, a million years ago or longer (Chang 1977; Jia 1980).[5] Although *Homo erectus* presumably originated in a warm climate, by the mid-Pleistocene, between 400,000 and 600,000 years ago (Chang 1977, pp. 43 ff.; Jia 1980, pp. 21 ff.), he/she was found to have lived in north China near Beijing at a site named Zhoukoudian (formerly Chou-K'ou-Tien).

Homo erectus beijing was an important player in the Siberian ancestry tree, so a few more words about him/her are in order. The original discovery of skeletal remains was made by J. Gunnar Andersson. But it was David Black who identified them as relics of a new type of early man and the oldest ever found in China. The original identification was made on the basis of two teeth and subsequently confirmed in 1928, when cranial and mandible fragments were found, and in 1929, when a well-preserved skull was found.

Lantian man (*Homo erectus*) was found at a site a little south of Zhoukoudian and was assigned an age of 600,000 years on the basis of paleomagnetism (Cybulski 1981, pp. 237 ff.).

Jia (pp. 13 ff.) dates Lantian Man between 650,000 and 800,000 years ago, depending upon which specimen is analyzed. Further, he states: "On the whole the Lantian specimen is very closely related to *Sinanthropus pekinensis* of Zhoukoudian. Nevertheless it cannot be identified exactly with *S. pekinensis*." The problems of dating and classification are too complex to discuss here. Cybulski doubts that "agreement will ever be reached" (p. 227) as to the uniquely correct classification of fossil *Homo* remains.

Stewart (1973, p. 23) noted: "This primitive form of man had reached a point close to the Pacific coast of Asia at 40° north latitude where it is cold in winter. There is evidence that he had achieved control of fire, and that is one of the reasons he was able to survive this far north. Also, there is evidence that he was making stone tools."

The January weather in this part of northern China in the twentieth century is more or less similar to that in the United States in the area between about Philadelphia and Boston, an average of about 32° Fahrenheit. A half-million years ago, at the time of Beijing Man, the weather may have been colder at times than now (Chang, p. 46). As the glaciers advanced and retreated, the weather

---

[5] The problem of dating these ancient findings is discussed in some detail in conjunction with each early man finding. Apparently dating to within 100,000 years or so, during the Pleistocene may be the best that can be done with present technologies.

either cooled or warmed. *Homo erectus* may have needed more firewood than Stewart conjectured and may have invented warm clothing and shelter.

If Beijing Man had made a successful adaptation to a cold climate (at least in wintertime) a half million years ago or longer, we may hypothesize that he could have reached the colds of Siberia 100,000 years ago, or perhaps even earlier. Definitive evidence on this point is unavailable, but we cannot rule out that possibility.

That the northeastern Siberian ancestors of the Native Americans are most likely to have come from northern China or Mongolia is implied by Turner's analysis of dental traits (1987, p. 6). He adds that the northeastern Siberians are unlikely to have come from western Siberia: "Thanks to help from USSR Academy of Science anthropologists, I have established that there are no known skeletal remains west of Lake Baikal and the Lena River that could serve as ancestral stock for any group of sinodonts." Therefore, the Ancestors could have arrived only from the south—that is China or Japan presumably from Zhoukoudian to Siberia to Beringia to Alaska to Tierra de Fuego. Are the Amerindians relatives of the Han?

Japan

Forty thousand years ago, more or less, the Japanese archipelago was part of mainland Asia. Hence, at that time *Homo sapiens* could have walked from China to the present Japanese islands. Certainly, by 30,000 years ago people were all over the archipelago, as documented by a number of sites. Indications that people were there before 30,000 years ago is less certain, according to Ikawa-Smith (1978, pp. 42 ff.).

Northern Japan is cold in winter. For people to have lived there 20,000 to 30,000 years ago they must already have had, or very quickly developed, a culture that could cope with cold weather. How long did it take for them to develop such a culture? Were they descendants of Beijing Man who brought with them to Japan the ability to cope with cold weather? From Japan did they go by water and/or land to the Western Hemisphere, a possibility suggested by Reynolds?

Siberia

People were living here far north of the Japanese islands at least 33,000 to 35,000 years ago. Such sites were discovered on the Alden River. Obviously the people must have reached Siberia earlier than the sites uncovered by archaeologists; how much earlier is not known insofar as can be determined. Mochanov (1978) writes:

> Beginning with the Konoshel'skoe [Southwold] cooling [33,000 to 30,000 years ago] individual Diuktai (Siberian dwellers) populations, following the "mammoth" fauna,

were able to settle Beringia, including the unglaciated part of Alaska. . . . Later Diuktai migrations, presumably between 18,000 and 11,000 years ago are clearly fixed. (p. 67)

If, 33,000 to 30,000 years ago, some Siberians had settled in Beringia and some had reached Alaska, clearly then their forefathers must have entered Siberia many millennia prior to 33,000 years ago. Might they have entered 100,000 years ago?

Derevianko (1978) seems to agree with Mochanov "that man settled the southern regions of North Asia in the middle and upper Pleistocene"; this suggests at least 100,000 years ago. (Compare this date with the estimate of about one-half million years for the middle Pleistocene as given for Beijing Man in the section on China.)

He then refers to reports of discoveries of North American sites presumably older than 30,000 years. "Although not well documented and very controversial, [these sites] cannot be unconditionally rejected and left unstudied. The discovery of early complexes in Siberia and the Far East in recent years does not exclude, but rather proposes, that the first discoverer of the New World was not even *Homo sapiens sapiens,* modern man, but a more ancient creature . . . which passed through Beringia earlier than 35,000 years ago." Might this more ancient creature have been *Homo sapiens neanderthalis*? Or may it be that *Homo sapiens sapiens* had already appeared 100,000 years ago or earlier as we mention in the following pages?

Ancient man was ready to migrate to the New World from the Old 30,000 or more years ago. Why did he migrate, how did he get there, and when?

THEIR TRIP TO THE WESTERN HEMISPHERE

Why Did the Ancients Migrate?

Probably for much the same reasons as present-day *Homo* migrates. Food and warfare may be the two most prominent forces that move people about. (In the twentieth century, people who are seeking food are said to be seeking "economic opportunity"; migrants resulting from warfare or natural catastrophe are referred to as refugees or displaced persons.)

Eugene Michael Kulischer (see Jaffe 1964) formulated a model that describes the interrelationships of population, technology, the economic structure, natural resources, the political structure, political developments (including war), and man's psychology and personality. He postulated that in ancient times, when a tribe or group found its available natural resources—that is, food—inadequate, it moved on, or attempted to do so. If another tribe blocked its way, fighting ensued, and the defeated group was forced to move elsewhere. In so doing it probably impinged on yet another group that, in turn, impinged on a third group, and so on and on—the domino effect.

Let us return to the ancient Siberians-to-be-Amerindians. When Beringia, the land bridge, existed, there was also the Mammoth Steppe, a vast northern grassland as described by the Guthries (1980). This steppe extended from interior Alaska to the west and south of the Urals; it may have extended as far as present-day Ireland. Glaciers covered northwestern Europe, and in North America, the area east of interior Alaska. People could and probably did wander back and forth across the Mammoth Steppe insofar as they desired and were able to do so. There were no boundaries manned by immigration police to halt these wanderers, or migrants. Since *Homo* did not originate in Siberia, only by wanderings in very ancient times could he have reached northeastern Siberia from his place of origin.

This steppe supported large numbers of grazing animals, camels, horses, the wooly mammoth, the steppe bison, antelopes, ibex, and others. And, of course, the predators, especially lions. There was plenty of meat available for the Siberian Ancestors.

Hence, if and when a tribe living in eastern Siberia found its food supply to be insufficient or was driven away by some other tribe that wanted the territory, it could move, or flee, sometimes toward Beringia. The geography and food resources were similar on both sides of the nonexistent boundaries separating Siberia from Beringia, or Beringia from Alaska. This process of forced movement, we suggest, was repeated time and time again. Until finally, perhaps after untold centuries, Alaska was reached. An imaginative archaeologist may compare these wanderings with those of the ancient Israelites, from Egypt to the Promised Land.

Those people in Siberia, if any, who had developed a maritime culture could have migrated partly by land to take advantage of all this meat on the hoof. And partly by water to enjoy the fruits of the seas.

No one knows or will ever know the precise scenario of why and how they migrated eastward. The one scenario that we cannot accept is that one sunny morning, for no apparent reason, entire tribes started walking to Alaska and stopped only when they reached the Promised Land.

When Did They First Arrive?

The answers given to this question range from about 15,000 to 50,000 years ago, and earlier. In the absence of official immigration statistics, only indirect evidence is available. To begin, it is thought that people arrived in the Western Hemisphere irregularly, or in waves. Some Ancestors may have arrived thousands of years before others. Some trickled in, a few this century, a few the following century, and so on. Even today there may be an occasional immigrant who arrives by kayak. This type of irregular immigration adds to the difficulties of attempting to date the time of arrival by means of the customary dating techniques, as we shall discuss subsequently.

But first let us return to the question of man's first arrival in northeastern Asia. Obviously, if northeastern Asia was the staging area for entry into the New World, immigrants to the Western Hemisphere could not predate the peopling of this part of Asia. Hence we may reason as follows. If migrants came from Japan, we have as a time limit perhaps 30,000 years ago or somewhat longer, since this is how long ago people have lived in northern Japan (as previously discussed).

Those who arrived from Siberia may have done so several millennia earlier, since Soviet archaeologists believe that *Homo* was in Siberia long before 30,000 years ago.

One of the arguments advanced for a recent date of first arrival, under 15,000 years ago, stems from the observation that all Indian skeletal remains found to date are of modern man, *Homo sapiens*. Furthermore, the argument goes, *Homo* (ourselves) supposedly first appeared someplace on earth only about 40,000 years ago (Fagan 1987, p. 11). Presumably it would require many millennia for modern man to reach northeastern Asia and then the Western Hemisphere. So, it is argued, he/she could not have arrived in Alaska longer ago than 15,000 years, or at the most, perhaps 20,000.

This logical scenario was upset in 1988, or so it appears, when the discovery of the skeletal remains of early modern *H. sapiens* dated to about 100,000 years ago was announced.[6] This date implies that *H. sapiens* must have begun to emerge many millennia earlier; a new variety of humankind does not spring up overnight fully developed. If so, had some of these *H. sapiens* reached northeastern Asia more than 50,000 years ago? Perhaps even over 100,000 years ago? Or still earlier? Failure to find archaeological evidence does not prove that *H. sapiens* was or was not there.

If any were in Siberia 100,000 years ago, could they have crossed over to northwestern North America 100,000 years ago? Beringia has had its ups and downs for as long as can be ascertained. No one can specify the precise millennia in the remote past when it might have been possible to cross over. All that we can say is that if modern *H. sapiens* had been in northeastern Asia more than 50,000 years ago, he/she could have managed to reach Alaska far earlier than the conventionally accepted date of around 15,000 years ago. Did he/she do so?

In summary, the earliest date at which migrants may have arrived is either about 30,000 years ago, or perhaps as much as 100,000 years ago. The Western Hemisphere was available at all times, and there were no immigration officers to stop the flow of immigrants.

---

[6] Stringer (1988). His article is based on a more technical article by Valladas *et al.* (1988).

HOW TIME OF ARRIVAL IS ESTIMATED

Introduction

The earliest site-dating method is that used for estimating how long people have been in the Western Hemisphere. If a site that contains the remains of a cooking fire, human bones, bones of animals killed or butchered by humans, stone tools, or whatever, can be dated, then that date is at least the minimum number of years since the Ancestors arrived. Let us suppose that a site is dated to 12,000 years before the present. To this, the archaeologist adds whatever length of time he/she thinks may have been required for the Ancestors to reach that spot from Beringia. The sum denotes when the investigator thinks that the immigration occurred. To illustrate: Suppose that the earliest agreed-upon site that has been located in the Western Hemisphere is dated at 15,000 years. Add to this whatever the investigator deems appropriate, one or more millennia, for travel from Alaska.

Martin represents the "recent arrival" school with his statement: "The possibility of a human society inhabiting America much before 12,000 years ago ranks as highly improbable" (1987, p. 13). Note that if Hopkins's (1967) estimate of when Beringia was last open, that is, above water, is accepted, about 15,000 years ago, the migrants must have arrived just before the bridge disappeared. If they arrived by water, of course, they could have come any time.

At the other end of the time scale are the sites reported to be well over 12,000 years old. The sites so mentioned are too numerous to list and describe here.[7] Statements about them range from "the first immigrants into South America sometime before 12,000 years ago" (Bryan, p. 137) to Meadowcroft, which is said to be from the twentieth millennium B.P. "Put succinctly, the data from Meadowcroft appear to confirm at least a 'middle entry' date range for the peopling of the New World and place the initial human crossing of Bering Strait no later than 20,000–25,000 years ago" (Adovasio et al. 1983, p. 188).

Wormington (1983, p. 191) summarized the feelings of the optimists—the believers in early arrival—by saying: "We still lack universally acceptable proof of occupation before Clovis times (10,000 to 12,000 years ago). This does not mean . . . that I feel that fully acceptable proof will not be found for the presence of people on earlier time levels" (i.e., before 12,000 B.P.).

Obviously no conclusion as to date of first arrival that is acceptable to all parties can be reached. Perhaps all we can say is that it is improbable that *Homo* was in the Western Hemisphere 100,000 years ago.

---

[7] Many of these sites are described by Shutler (1983), and in many journal articles by Childers and Marshall (e.g., Bordon 1979 and others).

Therefore, let us try to determine why there is a lack of agreement among the archaeologists. We suggest the following obstacles to agreement:

1. The various procedures for determining the age of a site or a tool or other evidence of *Homo* lack sufficient precision.
2. Archaeologists rely considerably on lithics (stone tools) to indicate the presence of human beings and the age of a site, because stone survives whereas organic products deteriorate.
3. Even if an early site can be identified and agreed upon as to its age, it is obvious that *Homo* must have arrived before the site was established. How much earlier is unknown.
4. A number of generations—how many?—were required before the Ancestors could adapt to conditions in the New World.

The various measures of time elapsed are not as precise as we desire.[8] We shall not discuss these measures in detail but shall simply illustrate that different methods produce different ages for a site. Scientists argue long and loudly about dating—how old is the object or how many years ago did this event occur. Sometimes the people and the methods agree; other times not.

Some Measures

Different materials require different measuring procedures. A widely used measure for determining the age of bone or other organic material is carbon-14. Other measures are available (either for organic or nonorganic matter) including thermoluminescence, amino acid racemization, tree-ring-calibrated dating, fission track dating, paleomagnetism, and uranium series. Still other techniques are available, and new ones (e.g., thorium-uranium method) are being introduced constantly.

Each of these, in turn, has numerous variations. Laboratories that use different variations of the carbon-14 test, for example, obtain different results. An extreme example of such difference is seen in the "Case of the Caribou Fleshing Tool." This tool (made from the bone of a caribou and used for cleaning the flesh off the animal skin) was found in the Old Crow locality in the northern Yukon (Nelson *et al.* 1986, pp. 749–751). The original carbon-14 date published for this bone was 27,000 B.P. This reading resulted from analysis of the carbon in one part of the bone. A reanalysis in which another part of the bone was tested resulted in a reading of 1,300 to 1,400 years ago. The authors wrote that

[8] Following are some of the many reports that describe these measures of time past. A general review is that of Berger (1983). Some technical articles on carbon-14 or radiocarbon dating are Hogg (1982), Stuiver and Polach (1977), and Olson (1963). Marshall (1990) reviews some recent developments.

"the four Old Crow artifacts . . . are all of late Holocene age [within the last 10,000 years] and not of the earlier Pleistocene period." Apparently the original dating was done on that part of the bone more easily contaminated by ground water. The second dating was done on the collagen that, reportedly, is more reliable.

An example of how different methods differ in their results is that of the presumed Paleo-Indian skeleton found in southern California (R.E. Taylor *et al.* 1983, pp. 1271 ff.). This was dated by the process of aspartic acid racemization to an age of approximately 70,000 years ago, the upper Pleistocene. Back to the laboratory the "age measurers" went. Uranium series isotopic ratios produced dates of 8,300 to 9,000 years ago. They then employed several carbon-14 measures and found an age of 3500 to 5000 B.P. Perhaps all the skeletal material was under 10,000 years of age. Probably most archaeologists accept the more recent dates. This variation in dating simply illustrates the fact that knowledge of the technical aspects of the measurement of time is needed in order to interpret properly the sacrosanct laboratory report.

Cybulski (1981, pp. 252–253) presents an insightful example of dating fossil skulls. Although from Africa rather than North America, it is nevertheless a relevant illustration of the problems and disagreements in timing. Four specimens of *Homo sapiens rhodesiensis* were attributed a range "from possibly 130,000 B.P. . . . to 34,000 B.P. . . . Other dating techniques, however . . . suggest that the four fossils might also be contemporaneous at *ca.* 40,000 B.P. and, therefore, more than very late with respect to accepted *Homo erectus* forms." Different dating, different interpretations.

One of the ways of trying to obtain a fairly accurate reading of the age of a site is to obtain several dates from a variety of objects in the site, and from two or more laboratories, if possible. If all the dates are close to each other, the age of the site can be accepted. This is attempted where and when feasible.

An excellent example of different-measuring-procedures-plus-different-labs-equal-different-ages-of-the-same-site is reported by James B. Benedict (1989, p. 5). In north-central Colorado at the Caribou Lake site excavation, charcoal attributable to humans and fragments of pottery (sherds) were excavated. One laboratory dated two samples of the charcoal by conventional radiocarbon dating using beta counting. The calibrated dates in calendar years B.P. were 1175 and 1310. (Radiocarbon dates were converted to calendar-year dates using tree-ring calibration.) The difference is not significant because the error of measurement is about the same as the size of the difference. A sample of soot was then dated by accelerator mass spectrometry by a different laboratory, to 665 years B.P. Finally, two samples of sherds were dated by thermoluminescence to 450 and 210 years B.P.

How old is the site? Benedict evaluated the results in light of his knowledge of the site and concluded that the age produced by accelerator mass spectrometry most likely was the most nearly accurate. He warned that "second opinions" are essential.

All this advice is well and good. But in too many instances only one sample from a dig is subjected to one method of dating by one laboratory. The archaeologist could obtain only one sample to test or did not have the funds for several tests. So how do we interpret the results of such "one-shot" dates? Benedict insists that depending on a single technique, or even two techniques, can result in wrong numbers and misinterpretation of the findings.

The Limitations of Lithics

The presence of tools made by *Homo* is sufficient proof that *Homo* was there. Date the tool and you have a date for *Homo*. Unfortunately, stone tools are the most likely to survive over the millennia and are difficult to date. If no stone tools are found, it is tempting to say that *Homo* was not there. We know that the Amerindians did not have metal tools (with some minor exceptions). But it is very likely that they made tools out of bones, antlers, wood, and other perishable materials, as Bryan describes (1978a, pp. 72–73). So how do you date something that is not there?

A second limitation of lithics for detecting the presence of Ancient man/woman lies in the fact that sometimes natural processes (flowing water, freezing, etc.) shape stones very similar to those shaped by the Ancestors. When such a stone "tool" of debatable origin is found, the conventional archaeologist's reaction is to reject it as evidence of *Homo*. If natural processes could have shaped it, one cannot say that Ancient Man was there.

To the nonarchaeologist, for example, the statistician, in the absence of other information, it would appear to be equally valid to say that if *Homo* could have shaped it we cannot say that this "lithic tool" resulted from natural processes. We are in the field of probability.

Let us consider the following; although the information needed is not now available, permit us to outline it. Of all, or a proper sample, of the objects that may have this ambiguous origin, how many were the result of *Homo's* efforts and how many of natural processes? Let us assume, for example, that out of 100 such lithic objects, 10 can be shown to have been fashioned by man. Then when we find such a debatable character we can say that there is 1 chance in 10 that it was manmade. We do not summarily reject it as evidence that man/woman was not there.

If we found a large number of such ambiguous origin stones, for example, 1,000, we could say: Given the probability of 1 in 10, perhaps 100 of them were fashioned by humans. (The precise number of manmade objects is unknown because there is always some variation around the probable, or expected, number.) We shall never know which are *Homo*-made objects. We only know that he was there.

All this is hypothetical at this moment. But perhaps some day carefully prepared tests will provide probabilities.

Homo Must Have Preceded the Date of the Site

Regardless of the date ·of the "oldest-known-agreed-upon-site," it is obvious that people must have preceded it in the New World. The Ancestors did not fly over from Siberia instantly and construct the site in one moment. How long did it take from the time he/she passed through immigration in Alaska to the time that he/she reached a place where he/she could leave a sign of his/her presence for future archaeologists to attempt to date? This time must be added to the age of the site. No one knows how long this journey required, and so the debate.

How Long Did It Take the Ancestors to Adapt to Conditions in the New World?

Given the physical and cultural variation among the Amerindians when first seen by the Europeans, we can only conclude that many—an unknown number—generations must have been required for this to happen. 10 generations? 100 generations? More? Who knows? We assume that the original immigrants had in common an adaptation to cold Arctic or sub-Arctic weather. Those who ended as high-mountain dwellers, or as Amazon or tropical dwellers, had to adjust their physiologies. If it were possible, for example, to determine how many generations were required for the high Andean dwellers to develop their enormous lungs and chest, we should have a better idea of how long the Amerindians have been in the Western Hemisphere. Stewart discusses the possible effects of environment upon physical appearance but does not attempt to estimate how long or how many generations were required for such adaptation.

THE FIRST SIGNS OF AGRICULTURE— ANOTHER CLUE TO TIME OF FIRST ARRIVAL

We have not seen this possible indicator of time of first arrival—or how long has *Homo* been in the New World?—in the literature but believe that it is statistically logical. Given an estimate of the earliest date known for domesticated plants, or the beginning of cultivation, that is, incipient agriculture, we can estimate the possible minimum number of millennia since the first Asian immigrants arrived.

Let us illustrate with maize, or corn. It is believed that maize first appeared (in Mexico) in recognizable form between 8000 and 9000 years B.P. In the earliest stages of domestication, it is not possible to distinguish between the wild and cultivated forms. Hence cultivation, or first attempts at domestication, must have been started, perhaps one or more millennia prior to the earliest recognizable domestic form.

This uncertainty regarding the exact moment when the idea of agriculture was conceived is obvious in the way in which writers have presented the "first date." For example, Woodbury and Zubrow (1979, p. 47) wrote that "by about 3500 B.C. [5500 B.P.] the Tehuacan maize was certainly being cultivated along with a number of other plants."

The Brothwells (1969, p. 104) say that "early use and sowing of wild maize [began] in the El Riego phase (ca. 7200–5200 B.C. [or 9200–7200 B.P.]), the true cultivation of maize during the Coxcatlan phase (5200–3400 B.C. [or 7200–5400 B.P.]). . . . Maize has developed as a crop within the last 7000 years."

Weaver (1972, p. 26) says that "the earliest samples date from about 5000 B.C. [7000 B.P.]. . . . This was either a wild maize, or maize in its first stages of domestication. . . . There is definite evidence that maize was domesticated by 3000 B.C." [5000 B.P.].

How many millennia passed between the time of arriving at the concept of people growing crops, the first steps at cultivation, and the appearance of recognizable domesticated plants? In the process of domestication, the plant acquires characteristics that the wild plant does not have. Maize, for example, began as a small cob, perhaps an inch in length; modern domesticated corn may be 6 to 8 inches in length. The original was capable of seeding itself; modern corn is unable to do so. Generally it is not possible to distinguish the wild form from that planted by *Homo* in the earliest stages of incipient cultivation. So how do we know when people first got the idea of growing crops?

As far as we can determine, most (if not all) study of the length of this wild-to-recognizable-domestication period has been carried on in the ancient Levant. It is thought that 1,000 to 3,000 years or more may have elapsed between the initial idea and the achievement of recognizable domestication. A. M. T. Moore[9] reports a study carried out by Gordon Hillman in Eastern Turkey. Hillman tried to determine whether selection pressures such as various methods of harvesting and patterns of crop rotation might affect domestication of wild einkorn wheat. He concluded that as long as the cultivation methods of simple husbandry were followed, wild einkorn would remain unchanged even over long periods. Only after unusual cultivation techniques

[9] See Moore, A. M. T.

have been applied for many hundreds of years do mutations characteristic of domestication appear.

Hillman (see Moore 1979) also studied the plant foods found in Abu Hureyra (in Syria) during the Mesolithic, that is, over 10,000 years ago, and concluded that many centuries must have passed before domestication was clearly visible.

A. H. Simmons *et al.* (1988, p. 35), in reporting on 'Ain Ghazel in central Jordan, state that the earliest attempts at domestication occurred 10,000 to 12,000 years ago and that a number of plants had been domesticated by about 9,000 years ago.

Furthermore, we have every reason to believe that the early arrivals from northeastern Asia did not bring knowledge of agriculture with them: (a) the environment there does not permit agriculture, and (b) any who may have come from parts of Asia where the climate was favorable to agriculture most likely arrived well before agriculture was invented in the Eastern Hemisphere (Eckholm 1964). Therefore, these immigrants must have been hunters and gatherers. They must have continued as such for untold millennia prior to becoming agriculturalists.

This period of being hunters and gatherers can be subdivided into at least two components: (a) walking from Alaska to Mexico if that country is the womb of maize, and (b) familiarizing themselves with the local flora and fauna of Mexico.

How many millennia did all these steps require? Our best estimate is that to have produced recognizable maize some 9,000 years ago, they must have reached the New World at least 15,000 to 20,000 years ago. They could have come much earlier, of course, but we are only seeking the minimum time that they must have been in the Western Hemisphere. We arrive at this estimate as follows:

Step	Years before the present (B.P.)		
	Minimum	Intermediate	Maximum
Cultivation begins	7,000	8,000	9,000
Precultivation period—idea of planting takes root	3,000	4,000	5,000
Hunting and gathering including walking from Alaska to Mexico	5,000	7,000	10,000
Total years since first immigration	15,000	19,000	24,000

This line of reasoning, we suggest, is a logical approach to the question: What is the latest date for the first arrivals to the Western Hemisphere? We do not claim that our calculations are correct and definitive. Rather we hope that future research will result in some agreement regarding the length of each step in the chain. As new information is obtained our preliminary time estimates will be revised. By adding the millennia for each step, we arrive at the minimum time since first arrival. We feel that such component or step analysis holds more promise than simply attempting to obtain a migration date in one fell swoop.

PROBABILITY—ALSO A CLUE TO TIME OF FIRST ARRIVAL

The controversy and disagreement among archaeologists on how long *Homo sapiens sapiens* has been in the Western Hemisphere stems from the insistence on 100% absolute proof of age. Many archaeologists insist more vehemently on 100% proof than do government officials who ask people for age information. The Census Bureau (in every country), for example, does not insist that one produce a notarized birth certificate to validate the age he or she reports. Yet many archaeologists insist on the equivalent of a notarized birth certificate for the age of a site or whatever indication of human presence may be found.

We can guarantee that the probability of such proof of human presence in the remote past is highly unlikely. There are problems with all of the measures of time past, as we saw. Further, nature confuses today's archaeologists by destroying ancient sites via earthquakes, glacial erosion, and so forth. If any Ancients had occupied sites in Canada that were subsequently covered by glaciers, for example, these sites were obliterated as the glaciers receded. Evidence of any early immigrants who may have come down the Pacific Coast during the height of the glaciation was obliterated by the rising sea level, if they walked too close to the water line. Given all these frustrations, the best that can be done today is to estimate the probability that people had been in North America prior to some specified cutoff date.

As we read today's archaeological literature (that of the latter part of the twentieth century), there is substantial agreement that people have been in North America for at least 10,000 years. Proposals that they have been here longer often have not been received gracefully. A number of sites have been proposed as of "very ancient" origin (as we mentioned earlier in this chapter). Let us call the cutoff age X millennia B.P. Decide for yourself what it should be, 10,000 years, 15,000 years, or whatever. Now let us use probability—decision making under uncertainty—in an attempt to decide whether there is evidence for a more ancient date. This is analogous to a judge and court trying to render a verdict in the absence of 100% guaranteed proof. Or analogous to the businessman trying to plan for the future.

In theory, the following calculations can be carried out. How practical it may be today we do not know, judging from the present disputations that appear in the literature. Perhaps some future seventh-generation archaeologists via a

CIAA (Commission to Investigate Archaeological Aging) will attempt to do these calculations. Given several sites that have been proposed as being over X millennia of age, the probability of its age being over X millennia is assigned to each site. For example:

Site	Probability of being over X millennia	Probability of being under X millennia	Total
1	.5	.5	1.0
2	.7	.3	1.0
3	.3	.7	1.0
4	.6	.4	1.0
5	.7	.3	1.0

Multiply the probabilities of being younger (.5 × .3 × .7 × .4 × .3), and we obtain .012, or 12 chances in 1,000. We can now say that the probability of *all* these sites *being under X millennia* is extremely slight, only 12 in 1,000. Conversely, the probability of *all* these sites *being over X millennia* is but slightly larger, 44 in 1,000. It is very unlikely that all are older. Therefore, we conclude that some of these sites are over X millennia and that some are younger.

We can not know which site, or sites, may be older than X millennia but can feel confident that at least one site is of this older age. Archaeologists can now dispute over which one it is.

Is it possible to obtain agreement among the archaeologists on the probability to be assigned to each site? Today no; perhaps tomorrow. Or are archaeologists, as their kin, destined to argue interminably over that which can never be determined, the ultimate "truth?" Or, how many angels can dance on the head of a pin?

URANIUM–THORIUM MEASURE AND REDATING OF SITES

Very many of the sites analyzed by archaeologists, and including those from which date of emigration from Asia is inferred, were dated by carbon-14 (^{14}C). How solid are these dates?

Bard and associates compared the dates obtained by using mass spectrometric uranium–thorium (U–Th) with accelerator mass spectrometry ^{14}C dates. Corals off the Island of Barbados were measured by both procedures. Below a ^{14}C date of about 7000 to 8000 B.P., both procedures seem to be equally valid insofar as they accord with the dendrochronological calibration. Hence the comparative measurements of the corals were reported by Bard only for older ages. When U–Th is about 8,000 years B.P., ^{14}C is about 7,000 years. When U–Th, according to the investigators, provides a measure of about 21,000 years B.P., ^{14}C provides an estimate of 17,000 or 18,000 years B.P.

At every age, U–Th produces a greater age then does ^{14}C. But the ratio of the two processes is not a constant; the ratio seems to vary randomly by age. U–Th is greater than ^{14}C by between 10% and 20%; there is no indication that it might be increasing with increasing age. The average ratio is between 15% and 17%. Thus a ^{14}C reading of 10,000 years B.P. may mean 11,000 to 12,000 years by U–Th.

Ought 'all sites that were ^{14}C dated and used to estimate possible time of arrival of the Asian migrants be inflated to U–Th dates? Discussions and arguments can continue for untold generations or at least until such time as a newer time measure is devised. Note that the two measures have differing applicability in the real world, and both must be processed in laboratories. Clearly, both are subject to error.

Previously, we noted Wormington's feelings that there is a consensus of sorts among the archaeologists that the first Ancestors arrived 10,000 to 12,000 years ago. Nevertheless, she thought that in the future there would be evidence that they had arrived even earlier. May we suggest that her optimism seems justified; by shifting from ^{14}C to U–Th dating techniques, the Ancestors arrived perhaps 2,000 years or more earlier, around 14,000 B.P., give or take 1,000 years or more (the confidence limits).

In Chapter 2, we noted the impossibility of precise measurement of past times. Each new method of measurement complicates dating problems.

SUMMARY

Archaeologists agree that the ancestors of the Native Americans came from northeastern Asia.

It is agreed that many must have crossed over on the Bering Land Bridge (Beringia) when it was open, that is, when glaciers on land had lowered the sea level enough to expose a land passage, at times perhaps as much as 1,000 miles wide. Beringia was intermittent; sometimes it was there and other times not. Some archaeologists say it is possible that some of these Ancient peoples came over by watercraft. We presume that they came both by land and water.

The unanswered question is: When did they first arrive? Geologists think that it would have been possible to cross from Siberia to Alaska almost anytime during the last 100,000 years, perhaps, if anyone wanted to do so. Some Soviet archaeologists think that *Homo* may have been in Siberia, the staging area for the emigration, 75,000 to 100,000 years ago. Did some cross the Bering Strait that long ago?

Present efforts to answer the question *when* are made by seeking the most ancient sites that have definitive proof that human beings were there. A big problem is that the techniques for measuring elapsed time and or being certain that *Homo* was there are too inexact. What is acceptable evidence and timing to one archaeologist is unacceptable to another. The estimates of *first entry* into the New World range from about 12,000 years ago to, perhaps, 50,000 years. The majority of archaeologists lean toward the lower date. But the final verdict is not yet in.

Chapter 3

Growth and Dispersion in the New World

INTRODUCTION

How many immigrants arrived from Siberia and adjacent areas will never be known. By the time that the Europeans appeared at the end of the fifteenth century, there were well over 1 million north of the Rio Grande and perhaps between 10 and 100 million throughout the Western Hemisphere (see Chapter 7). The great majority were American Indians. The number of Inuits (Eskimos) and Aleuts probably amounted to no more than 100,000.

These people entered the New World via the northwest corner of North America. By 1500 their descendants were living all over the Western Hemisphere. Hence we ask:

1. How far did they have to go by shank's mare or watercraft to reach their promised lands?
2. How did they "escape" from Alaska?
3. How long did it take them to reach all parts of the Western Hemisphere?

Finally, we note where they lived at the beginning of the sixteenth century and how their geographic distribution was influenced by geography and climate.

HOW FAR AWAY IS MY NEW HOME?

From the western coast of present Alaska to the tip of South America, Tierra del Fuego, is between 10,000 and 11,000 miles as the proverbial crow flies. Exactly how many miles must be walked or paddled is indefinite. It depends on whether the journey is a straight line or has innumerable twists and turns and ups and downs. The Chinese (at one time) measured distances in terms of the effort required to cover them. What we call 1 mile, if traversed uphill is a longer distance than downhill. And many are the rivers to be crossed and the hills and mountains to be climbed between Alaska and Tierra del Fuego.

Presumably the first southward movement by land was in the western part of North America. From Alaska to about the center of California and eastward to New York is on the order of 5,500 miles. Any wandering to and fro instead of following a straight line to the East Coast increases the mileage considerably.

Any Ancestors who reached South America presumably did so via Central America and Panama. This leads directly into Columbia and the western side of the continent. To reach the east coast of South America around Recife, Brazil, is about 10,000 miles.

Others may have preferred warmer climates and opted for the now-fashionable Caribbean Islands. From Alaska to Colombia, South America, and across water to the closest of these islands amounts to around 7,500 miles. Presumably the first visitors to these islands (and possibly to Florida) came north from Venezuela via island hopping.

Covering such vast distances by shank's mare or paddling a boat was difficult physical work. Further, these early people did not know where they were going. They must have followed the "food trail," whether it be animals to hunt, fish to catch, or wild plants to gather.

Let us next examine how they "escaped" from Alaska if they had walked over Beringia and how long it may have taken them to spread throughout the Western Hemisphere.

"ESCAPE" FROM ALASKA

How?

The situation faced by the original immigrants was complicated indeed. If they traveled by water they could have crossed over any time that there were people in northeastern Asia capable and desirous of emigrating. If they came walking overland, there were times more favorable and others less favorable.

By Water

Those who may have come from Asia by watercraft (Fladmark 1983, pp. 119 ff.) had to have possessed a maritime culture—knowledge about fish and sea mammals and how to catch them, how to build watercraft, and so forth. These people probably hugged the Pacific Coast as they proceeded east from Asia and then southward. They had no need that we can visualize, to stop in Alaska.

Indeed, they could have continued to Tierra del Fuego if they saw any reason to do so. We suppose that any such sea nomads would have settled on land sooner or later, as all Native Americans seen by the first Europeans were land dwellers. (A possible exception may have been some Tierra del Fuego natives.) Such landings could have occurred in Alaska, Vancouver, San Diego, or anyplace else on the Pacific coast. In short, they pose no problems for the "escape-from-Alaska" story.

Ackerman *et al.* (1984, p. 7) report that people possessing a well-developed maritime culture lived on Heceta Island (off the coast of British Columbia) 8,000 to 9,000 years ago.[1] The authors wrote: "The early inhabitants were well adapted to a marine type of resource exploitation." They caught offshore sea mammals, fished, hunted birds, and gathered molluscs and crustaceans.

> Data suggest that the northwest coast was initially settled by peoples with a maritime tradition who were experienced in the exploitation of off-shore resources and who made extensive use of water transportation. The Kroeber hypothesis of an early settlement of the north Pacific coast by interior people who approached tidewaters by interior rivers can now be seriously questioned. (Ackerman 1984)

The authors do not state whether these Heceta Island inhabitants were recent or very early arrivals from Asia. However, we understand their findings to imply that these people probably came from Asia many millennia ago, with a developed maritime culture, and perhaps were slowly on their way south along the Pacific coast.

By Land

Those who arrived via the Bering land bridge were faced by "escape" problems. Beringia had its ups and downs; sometimes it was all there, and sometimes part of it was under water, between about 70,000 and 15,000 years ago (Hopkins *et al.* 1982, pp. 12 and 426). Those who walked into Alaska found an area that was relatively free of glaciers and held sufficient game and other foods to support these newcomers.

To leave Alaska for points south, however, meant that these people confronted glaciers sooner or later, depending on the stage of the glaciation. The glaciers were intermittent. During the Mid-Wisconsinan Interglacial, about 40,000 years ago, the glaciers were much smaller; it was relatively easy for people to move south (Figure 3.1). During the Late Wisconsinan Glaciation, about 18,000 years ago, however, they were at their maximum and covered most of Canada and much of northern United States (Figure 3.2).

Furthermore, there was intermittent glaciation in the Cordilleran region (the range of mountains nearest the Pacific coast) (Fladmark 1983, pp. 13 ff.;

---

[1] Photocopy received from author.

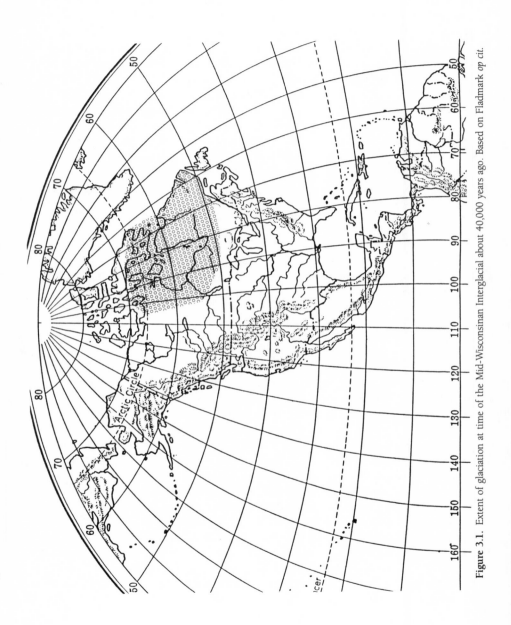

Figure 3.1. Extent of glaciation at time of the Mid-Wisconsinan Interglacial about 40,000 years ago. Based on Fladmark *op cit.*

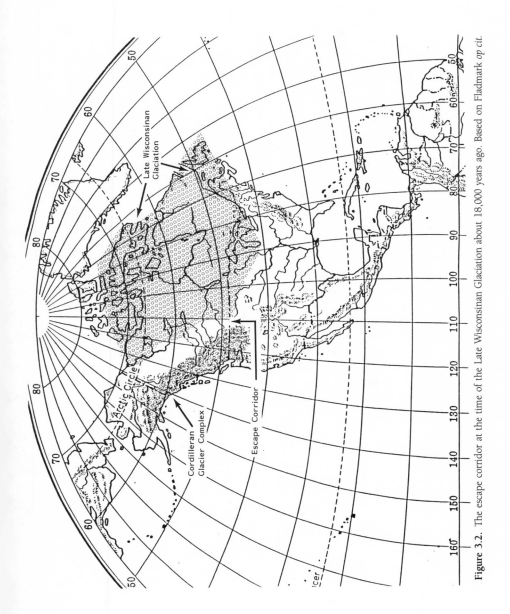

Figure 3.2. The escape corridor at the time of the Late Wisconsinan Glaciation about 18,000 years ago. Based on Fladmark *op cit.*

November 1986, pp. 8 ff.). Between these two glaciations was an intermittent ice-free corridor that could be used by escapees from Alaska. Both glaciations expanded and contracted from time to time but not necessarily simultaneously nor in step. Hence, it is impossible to specify exactly when the best-time-to-go-south was. If this best time could be determined precisely, it would help in determining when the first settlers may have reached southern Canada and the United States.

During the Late Wisconsinan there were only three maybe passable routes out of Alaska, according to Fladmark (1983, p. 40). One was along this ice-free corridor where there were pockets of habitable space. This was not impossible, at least for short distances, if the people were sufficiently motivated to move. But life at this time and in this place would have been very difficult.

A second route that Fladmark thinks was theoretically possible was across the Arctic and down the Atlantic coast. Fladmark considers this to be the least likely due to probable environmental harshness. A third possible route may have been a midcontinental ice-free corridor adjacent to the maximum Laurentide Ice Sheet. This, too, Fladmark considers to have been a marginal area for human survival.

What may have been the savior of these early people is the fact that the regions in which glaciers developed at one time or another were not all uninhabitable at the same time. Under the worst of glacial conditions, there were pockets where human and animal life could survive.

Subsequently the Wisconsinan (or most of it) receded and melted as most glaciers do. By about 15,000 years ago, most of Beringia was underwater, and perhaps about 12,000 years ago, southward passage out of Alaska was easing.

Fladmark summarizes "when" by stating that human occupation in North America cannot be shown to have been impossible at any time during the last 60,000 years but was probably most feasible during the last 15,000, when the retreating glaciers and a warming climate presented the best conditions for people south of Beringia (p. 41).

When Was the Exodus from Alaska?

The first immigrants to the Western Hemisphere may have arrived sometime between 50,000 or more and perhaps 15,000 years ago. Nature's vagaries operating through the process of glaciation set changing limits and times when people could have left northeastern Asia and wandered all over the Western Hemisphere. The problem of when the Ancestors first reached one part or another of the New World is compounded by our inability to time these geological events and changes precisely. If there was a time when it was most feasible to walk over via Beringia *and* continue southward out of Alaska with least difficulty, such a time cannot be specified exactly.

If substantial numbers of immigrants arrived by sea, their passage into the heart of North America would have been greatly eased. But then, due to the subsequent rise in sea level, they would have left few if any clues for twentieth-century archaeologists to find and speculate about. These clues would all be under the sea today. Fladmark suggests that coastal people, those who could have lived off the bounty of the Pacific Ocean, would have been at a great advantage over those who lived inland. Did the coastal dwellers originally arrive by sea? It is possible. Is it possible that most of the original Asian immigrants were people with a culture, or cultures, adapted to the sea and who arrived by watercraft?

DISPERSAL AND GROWTH OF POPULATION

In order to know how long it took the Ancestors to spread throughout the Western Hemisphere we ought to know (1) exactly when the first contingent reached Alaska or some other point on the Pacific coast; (2) exactly how long they stayed there before moving on; and (3) how rapidly they wanted to move. Such information is unavailable. Consequently we must rely on the circumstantial evidence that appears to be most probable. And therein lies another subject for disputation. How long did it take to occupy the entire Western Hemisphere?

The "Schools of Speed"

The Jack Rabbit School

This school insists that only a short time was required. We have not seen any precise number of years specified. Nevertheless, the impression left by these advocates such as Martin (1987, p. 13) is that the hemisphere was completely occupied within 1 or 2 thousand years. Martin states that with easy hunting and no disease, the population could grow 2% or 3% per year and double in numbers every 20 to 30 years.[2]

The Take-It-Slow School

This school does not claim to know how long it took to reach Tierra del Fuego but believes that it took far longer than the jack-rabbit school proposes.

The reasons for our favoring the take-it-slow school are:

1. All the information available about the death rates of these prehistorics indicates that life was short. They probably lived no more than 20 years on the

---

[2] We assume that he means growth per year. The author does not specify.

average (length of life at birth), if that long. (We discuss this in Chapter 4 and Appendix 3.) A length of life of 20 years means that about 50 years are needed for doubling. To arrive at this doubling number of 50 years let us assume that the live birth rate was about as high as is physiologically possible, about 65 per 1,000 population (see Chapter 9). Life expectancy of 20 years implies a death rate of about 50 per 1,000. The difference, 15 per 1,000 population, or 1½% per year, amounts to a doubling in about 50 years.

If length of life was only 17 years on the average, doubling requires about 120 years. If length of life was as low as 15 years, it would require about 175 to 200 years for the population to double. Clearly, Martin's statement that "a doubling in numbers every 20 to 30 years" is a gross exaggeration unless he can prove that infants born at that time and under those conditions of life survived (on the average) 30 or 40 years.

2. We begin with the figure of 100 million people in the Western Hemisphere around the time of first European contact; this is the maximum estimate anyone has proposed.[3] Next we assume that 1,000 immigrants arrived 10,000 years ago and ask—at what rate of average annual growth would 1,000 people become 100 million?

First we note that if the population doubled every 20 years (as suggested by Martin), starting with 1,000 people, in 350 years there would be 100 million. If the population doubled in 50 years, about 850 years are needed to reach 100 million. If the doubling time was 200 years, in close to 3,500 years the population would reach 100 million.

Even with a slow doubling time of 200 years, we must account for the remaining 6,500 years, 10,000 years minus 3,500. The people would have had to reduce their birthrate greatly in order to achieve a no-growth population after 3,500 years had passed. One need not be a population expert to know that this did not happen. People do not suddenly greatly reduce the number of children that they have. Nor do they suddenly start committing suicide in great numbers in order to maintain a constant size population.

We may test our calculations on time required for doubling by asking: What is the average annual rate of growth required for 1,000 people to become 100 million over a time period of 10,000 years (the minimum time estimated since migration from Asia)? The growth rate per year turns out to be about 11.5 per 10,000 population (Table 3.1). To realize how slow this growth rate is, consider Mexico; between 1960 and 1980 the population of Mexico grew at a rate of 360 per 10,000 population, or 3.6% per year.[4]

We can make other assumptions. Suppose that there were only 10 million

---

[3] Borah, in 1964, estimated that there were 100 million at the time of European "discovery"; see Dobyns (1976, p. 12).

[4] Cowgill (1975) has an excellent discussion of this topic of population growth.

Table 3.1. Rates of Population Growth per 10,000 Native Americans under Varying Conditions, and Mexico 1960–1980

Estimated number in 1492	Years since first entry	Number entered	Average annual increase per 10,000 population
North America			
1,000,000	10,000	1,000	6.9
2,000,000	10,000	1,000	7.6
2,000,000	20,000	1,000	3.8
Western Hemisphere			
100,000,000	10,000	1,000	11.5
50,000,000	10,000	1,000	11.0
10,000,000	10,000	1,000	9.2
100,000,000	20,000	1,000	5.5
Mexico	1960	1980	
1960–1980	34.9 million	70.1 million	360.00

people in the total Western Hemisphere when Columbus landed. Then the average annual rate of growth is only 9.2 per 10,000.

Turning to North America (Canada and the United States), if 1,000 migrants arrived, remained there for 10,000 years, and numbered 1 million in 1492, the rate of growth need be only 6.9 per 10,000 population per year. If 2 million people greeted Columbus, an average annual growth rate of 7.6 per 10,000 would suffice.

If many more than 1,000 immigrants arrived, or if the original Ancestors had arrived well over 10,000 years ago, the smaller need be the average annual rate of growth to achieve any desired total population in 1492. The reader can set whatever assumptions desired and calculate the rate of growth. But under no conditions could these Ancients have equaled the Mexican experience of 1960 to 1980.

3. Finally, many generations were required for the physiological and cultural adaptations to the diverse conditions in the Western Hemisphere (as noted in Chapter 2). For example, how long did it take the Amazon dwellers to learn how to eat poisonous (bitter) manioc or handle the poison curare and survive? We suspect that this knowledge was not achieved overnight.

In short, many millennia must have passed before the Amerindians had spread to all parts of the Western Hemisphere. Five thousand years? Ten thousand? Who knows?

Probable Pattern of Population Growth

Over a long period of time, every population experiences cyclical rates of growth, similar to the ups and downs of the business cycle or stock market.

Sometimes the population may be increasing rapidly, at other times slowly. Sometimes there may be actual losses of population—decreases. These cycles can be of any duration; a people may increase rapidly for one decade, let us say, then neither increase nor decrease for three decades, and then slowly lose people for five decades. If the loss continues long enough, that population will disappear. On the other hand, after a while it may start increasing rapidly again. And so on and on, millennium after millennium. Figure 3.3 illustrates this pattern.[5]

Previously we examined population growth in terms of the number of years required for doubling. This implies a continuous rate of growth. For example, if it doubles every 20 years, then this goes on continuously. Every 20 years it doubles throughout the millennia. But in the real (nonacademic) world, this does not happen. Martin (1987, p. 13) was misusing statistics when he wrote: "Growth rates of two to more than three percent *with a doubling of numbers* every 20 to 30 years were feasible." The implication of his remarks is that this doubling is a continuous process, millennium after millennium.

GEOGRAPHIC DISTRIBUTION AND REDISTRIBUTION

Distribution in Past Millennia

No one has estimated the possible geographic distribution of the American Indians at various times in the past, say 10,000 years ago, 5,000 years, 1,000 years. In the absence of such a study, we can only speculate that the people moved about as climate changed and the food supply increased or decreased. Changing climate always is a fact of life.

The glaciers that hindered the Ancestors in "escaping" from Alaska were the immediate machines that ultimately led to the redistribution of population. When the glaciers, centered in Canada and the Arctic, advanced southward, any people living in their path retreated further south. Conversely, as the glaciers receded, the people advanced north. Hopkins *et al.* (1982, p. 442) comment on the "changing of the glaciers." The Beringian ecosystem experienced abrupt and radical changes between 12 and 13 millennia ago. A rising sea level, submerging shelf, and melting glaciers were all part of worldwide climatic and paleogeographic changes.

Men and women were not the only ones to be affected by the comings and goings of the glaciers and the changing climate. The flora and fauna that provided the food supply for the Ancestors also were affected. In order to eat,

---

[5] The rates of average annual increase shown in Figure 3.3 are averages of the cycles calculated on an annual basis. There is no implication that the population increases continuously at the specified rate, year after year, *ad infinitum.*

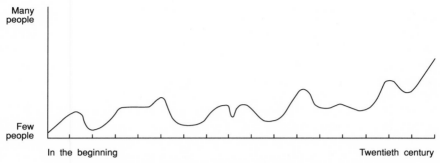

Figure 3.3. Generalized pattern of population growth over many millennia.

the early Amerindians—the Paleo-Indians—had to follow the game and vegetation. Hopkins *et al.* state that the rapid changes in climate at the end of the cold cycle, between 12 and 13 millennia ago, considerably reduced the total area of suitable grazing land, hence reduced the numbers of grazing animals available to the Paleo-Indian hunters.

The Wisconsinan glaciation at its height covered virtually all of Canada and northern United States with the exception of the Pacific coast. For millennia perhaps the only Amerindians in Canada were those who lived along the Pacific coast and in the United States those who lived south of the Mason–Dixon line or on the Pacific coast.

As the glaciers retreated northward, eventually flora and fauna and people followed. Funk (1978, p. 16) describes this sequence as follows: The Northeast was populated between about 10,000 and 6,000 years ago as the Wisconsinan ice sheet gradually withdrew northward. The Paleo-Indians had hunted on the tundra at the edge of the glaciers. As the ice withdrew, the tundra followed northward and was replaced by spruce woodland and then the broad-leaf forest following from the south. The fluted-point hunters probably entered the Northeast from the south and west as they followed the retreating ice.

Some parts of North America became more arid as the ice retreated, in addition to becoming warmer. The Great Basin,[6] for example, now a rather arid area, had many rivers and large lakes that were fed (in part at least) by melting ice prior to about 10,000 years ago. Herds of camels, horses, and mammoths grazed the steppes and fertile marshes. Mehringer (1986, p. 49) notes that a trend toward aridity continued for the next few thousand years, and large game disappeared. It was no longer a hospitable environment for people.

In summary, we suggest that just as the climate "yesterday" differed from

[6] The states, whole or part, included in the Great Basin are Arizona, California, Colorado, Idaho, Nebraska, Oregon, Utah, and Wyoming in the United States, and parts of the southern Prairie Provinces in Canada (Manitoba, Saskatchewan, and Alberta).

that of "today," so did the geographic distribution of the people. Changing climate leads to changing food resources that lead to changing population distribution.

Where They Were in the Sixteenth Century

The Amerindian population at the beginning of the sixteenth century was distributed approximately as was the land suitable for agriculture. The distribution of suitable land, in turn, resulted from the activities of the glaciers over the past many millennia. The glaciers in their repeated process of advance and retreat shoved much of whatever fertile soil there had been in Canada, into the United States and parts of southeastern Canada just north of the border (see Chapter 1). They left behind the Laurentian Plateau that covers the greater part of Canada east of the Pacific coast mountains. It is a scenic area of rocks with little soil suitable for agriculture (Figure 1.1). If the fertile soil that is now in the United States had remained north of the border, Canada would have had far more farming land. Despite the colder climate in comparison with the United States, a considerable amount of agriculture could have been carried on, if the soil was there. And if the glaciers had not distorted the surface.

Much of Canada just a few miles north of Ottawa and Montreal is now covered by forests and innumerable lakes and rivers, making surface transportation difficult. These lakes and rivers were gouged out by the moving glaciers and the waters flowing from the melting ice. The Great Lakes and the St. Lawrence River system, for example, are glacier-made.

In the United States, farming was carried on in most of the area east of the Mississippi River, in the irrigated parts of the Southwest, and in small pockets elsewhere. These are the areas that had sufficient water and in which the Indians could work the soil. In Canada, farming was carried on only in the east, close to the U.S.–Canadian border. Amerindians tended to live where raising crops was possible (Figures 3.4 and 3.5). Because these people had no livestock, hunting of game was also necessary for obtaining meat.

Those who lived on the Pacific coast were an exception. The sea was so bountiful that it could support a very large population. Fishing supplemented by gathering wild plants and hunting of animals supported a human population as dense, or denser, than agriculture and wild game could.

In the United States (Figure 3.4), denser population and agriculture were synonymous; given agriculture, the average was about three or four persons per 10 square miles. The Pacific coast with its plentiful produce of the waters supplemented by acorns and other wild foods had a density of five or more per 10 square miles. The center of the country from about the western boundaries of the states of North Dakota south to Texas, to about western Idaho and Nevada, had a density of one or two persons per 10 square miles. There was too

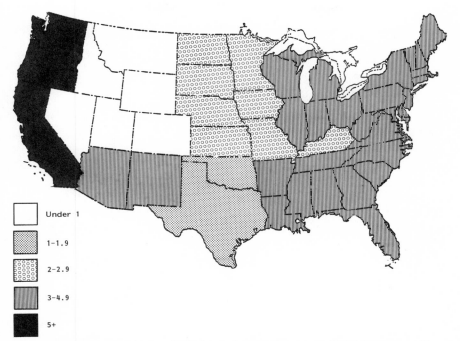

Figure 3.4. Estimated density of U.S. Amerindian population around 1500 (persons per 10 square miles). Based on Mooney's (1928) estimates.

little rainfall and too many mountains throughout this central area. And absent the horse, hunting buffalo was difficult.

In Canada (Figure 3.5), density was greatest in British Columbia, over five people per 10 square miles. Next were the eastern provinces with a density of between one and two people. The Prairie Provinces had a density of less than one person—they had no farmland that they could cultivate, no seas, and no horses.

For Canada, we measured density by dividing the population by half the number of square miles of land surface, because we do not know precisely where the Indians had lived within each province. We only know that they concentrated in the southern portions. In the forested northern lands, few lived and they survived by hunting game and foraging for wild plants. This forested area was a major source of the fur trade with the Europeans (as described in Chapter 7).

The lower part of the Prairie Provinces was the home of the buffalo, almost extinct in the twentieth century. Without the horse, however, they were not easy to hunt. The northern parts were, and still are, the home of the caribou,

Figure 3.5. Estimated density of Canadian Amerindian population around 1500 (persons per 10 square miles). Based on Mooney's (1928) estimates.

moose, and the musk-ox, animals more or less comparable to the ancient megafauna of North America. These animals, in addition to furnishing meat to eat, also furnished skins for clothing, bones that could be fashioned into tools, and so forth.

SUMMARY

Population growth over the many millennia was slow. The Indians moved about North America as the food supply shifted from one area to another. This geographic redistribution resulted in large part from the comings and goings of the glaciers. When the glaciers expanded, flora, fauna, and people were forced southward. As the glaciers retreated and melted, they watered large areas that are now arid; these lands supported much vegetation, many animals, and presumably people. Aridity set in when the glaciers had run their course and no longer were furnishing meltwater. As the food trail dried, people probably left these areas.

By the time the Europeans reached the New World, the climate had long since adjusted itself to about that of the twentieth century. The Amerindian geographic distribution also had adjusted itself to the climate changes.

To aid in the process of human geographic distribution, agriculture arrived in the United States from Mexico and possibly also the Caribbean between 1,000 and 2,000 years ago. Areas suitable for agriculture were suitable for humans.

Chapter 4

Length of Life: Short and Not So Merry

INTRODUCTION

A Brief Description of a Life Table and Length of Life

How long *might* a newly born human infant live? No one knows how long it *will* live because some infants die almost at birth and others live to be over a century of age and see their pictures published in the local newspapers. So we average (so to speak) the number of years lived by a group of people—a cohort—for example, all those born in 1910 or 1970 or any other specified time period, and that is length of life. That is how long the new infant *might* live.

Actuaries have devised complicated procedures for measuring length of life based on the age and sex of deaths that occur in any specified time period—the current life table. But we shall not attempt to describe these procedures here. Instead, we shall simply explain how the nonactuary can use the information in a life table. Suffice it to say that the average person wants to know: How long an infant might expect to live between birth and death, and how long one may expect to live from some specified age, for example, 15 or 30 or whatever, to death. In addition, some readers may wish to know the death rate at various ages. These values can be read in Appendix Tables 3.4 and 3.5. For example, among men agriculturalists at age 40, about 29% (column q_x) can expect to die before their 45th birthday. Such a 40-year-old individual can expect to live 10.6 years more (column e_x), for a total life span of about 50 or 51 years (for further information, see Appendix 3).

Reasons for Constructing New Life Tables

How long people live may be the best single measure of their physical well-being and of the kind of society in which they live. Even today, differences among social classes, ethnic groups, or other segments of society reflect, and are thought of as indicating differences in economic position, in degree of healthfulness of their living conditions, adequacy of diet, adequacy of health care available, and so forth.

We know that people in the economically more developed countries live longer than do those in the underdeveloped countries. We also know that length of life has increased considerably in many parts of the world, especially during the last century or two (United Nations 1973, Chapter 5). We know that the pre-European Amerindians lived much shorter lives than do the Amerindian people in the latter part of the twentieth century.

However, we do not have comprehensive life tables for the prehistorics of North America. Only fragments of life tables for single sites are found in the literature, fragments that indicate that life was short. But these fragments cannot be combined into a larger story that tells us significantly more than we already know about the prehistoric Indians of Canada and the United States.

We need a figure for the totality just as we have today for the total population of Canada or the United States or any other country. It does us little good to infer length of life in the United States and Canada based on information for a few places such as Chicago, El Paso, New York City, Vancouver, and Trenton, for example.

There are several topics of particular interest that can be investigated by means of overall life tables. One subject is the relationship of population growth to the development of agriculture. Some anthropologists[1] hold to the view that increasing population among the hunters and gatherers led to the "invention" of agriculture as a means of feeding more people. A second school holds the view that agriculture arose as a result of a variety of "causes" or changes (see Chapter 6). Agriculture does furnish a larger and more dependable food supply (with minor exceptions) than does hunting and gathering, and food can be stored to carry over lean periods. As a result, population growth followed. Hence, our first objective is to calculate length of life for hunters and gatherers—the nonagriculturalists—separately from the agricultural population. We reason that if the agriculturalists lived longer than did the nonagriculturalists we may infer that the introduction of agriculture was conducive to somewhat more rapid population growth. We infer that population growth, sometimes called "population pressure," among the hunters and gatherers was not the main reason for the introduction and development of agriculture. We shall explore this topic in the present chapter.

---

[1] For a brief summary of the anthropologists' interest in prehistoric demography, see Armelagos and Medina (1977).

Another topic that can be studied by means of life tables consists of some of the social and family conditions under which these Ancestors lived. What may have been their birth rate? How important was the nuclear family versus the extended family, clan, tribe? How frequent was widowhood and orphanhood? In short, what can be inferred about their way of life from life tables for men and women, and for the agricultural and nonagricultural populations? (This topic will be explored in Chapter 5.)

Another reason for new life tables is to obtain separate information for women and men. Too many of the published life tables combine the two sexes. We have reason to suspect that there was a sex difference in length of life. Every life table throughout the world that has ever been calculated for the two sexes separately has shown a significant difference. Why should the prehistoric North American Indians have been any different? Hence, all our calculations are for men and women separately.

Finally, we want an overall pre-European life table as a basis for estimating demographic characteristics prior to 1500. Such characteristics then can be compared with those of the latter twentieth century, as we describe them in Part II. How has the demography of the Amerindians changed in response to the European conquest and influences? This question is central to our thinking.

Following that, we shall present our life tables, discuss some of the diseases and other bodily mishaps that may help to account for prehistoric length of life, and compare the prehistoric Amerindians with other premodern populations. Were the Amerindians unusual?

LENGTH OF LIFE

Some Previous Studies

That Ancient people[2] lived shorter lives in comparison with the average 70 or more years that the people today who live in the economically developed parts of the world take for granted is long known. For example, in 1902 Pearson published length of life for ancient Egyptians as ascertained from mummies. Valoras published in 1936 an estimate of 30 years for Greece around 400 B.C. Willcox in 1938 published an estimate for the early Roman Empire. In 1913, McDonnel published material on ancient Rome. Franz and Winkler, in 1936, published an analysis of Bronze Age people in Austria for the period 1500 B.C. to 700 B.C.

---

[2] For sources of information on life expectancy of early people, see, for example, United Nations (1973); Acsadi and Nemeskeri (1970); and Vallois (1981). One can devote a lifetime (if so driven) to pursuing and perusing the multitudes of articles and books, if one can find them.

In the United States, Hooton published a study of the skeletal remains of the Pecos Pueblo people. Kidder was studying Pecos, New Mexico, in the 1920s if not earlier. Following World War II, many studies of prehistoric people in North America and elsewhere have been published. There are too many to list here. They all indicate that length of life among the pre-European Indians was not greater than 20 to 25 years and very likely in the teens. The published diversity is so great that endless debate is possible.

Agriculturalists Lived Longer

People who raised crops lived about 2 or 3 years longer (on the average) than did those who depended entirely on hunting and gathering. And among both populations, males outlived females. We estimate length of life at birth to have been about (see Table 4.1):

	Nonagriculture	*Agriculture*
Males	16 to 17 years	18 to 19 years
Females	14 to 15 years	17 to 18 years

In contrast to these short life expectancies, note that in the late twentieth century, average life expectancy is significantly over 70 years in the economically developed countries.

Some clarification of the terms *agricultural* and *nonagricultural* will help in the following discussion. The growth of agriculture (which we discuss in Chapter 6) was a slow process spread over several millennia. The first hunters and gatherers who tried their hands at primitive cultivation presumably continued to depend on hunting, fishing, and gathering for their main food supply. As cultivation increased, hunting and gathering lost their importance but never completely disappeared as far as we know. These "advanced" agriculturalists had no livestock (except for dogs) and depended on hunting and fishing for their meat. As for gathering wild plants and nuts, we suspect that this continued in

Table 4.1. Estimated Years of Life Expectancy, Prehistoric Amerindians, for Men and Women of Selected Ages[a]

Age	*Nonagriculturalists*		*Agriculturalists*	
	Men	*Women*	*Men*	*Women*
15	19	17	22	20
25	14	12	17	16
35	11	10	13	13
45	8	8	9	9
55	6	6	7	6

[a]See text and Appendix 3.

order to supplement the few (relative to twentieth-century agriculture) cultivated crops and to furnish the ingredients for whatever medicines and religious substances were desired. Hence, when we compare these two groups we are comparing those entirely dependent versus those only partially dependent on hunting, fishing, and gathering of wild plants.

Greater Longevity of Agricultural and Population Growth

The observation that the agriculturalists lived an average of 2 to 3 years longer than did the nonagriculturalists suggests that the rise and development of agriculture contributed to population growth. This is the opposite of the thesis advanced by some[3] that excessive population growth among the hunters and gatherers forced them to "invent" agriculture as a means of increasing the food supply. There is a considerable literature on this topic of which came first, population growth or agriculture? (The academicians' version of the chicken and the egg.) There is no need for us to review this argument in detail. We simply contribute to the debate our thoughts of the relationship of length of life and population growth to the rise of agriculture.

Population growth over the millennia (Chapter 3) was very slow. So slow in fact that no person could have observed increases in population during his or her lifetime. To have felt the need to "invent" agriculture to feed a rapidly growing population, the Ancestors would have had to be aware of a rapid increase in population.

We may also view the "population growth–rise of agriculture" scenario as follows. If population growth was so rapid as to be visible to the unaided eye, why did it require several millennia for agriculture to become an important source of food among all the Indians, and perhaps all other peoples? Judging from the geographic distribution of agriculture about the time of the European arrival and Mooney's population distribution, we estimate that probably not over half of the North American Indians included cultivated foods as an important part of their diet. Evidently, there was sufficient game, fish, and wild plants to feed large numbers. The interrelationship of the growth of population and agriculture is complicated, and we shall explore it further in Chapter 6.

Increases in Length of Life Occurred Slowly

All the Amerindians, just as all hominids, were hunters and gatherers before they became agriculturalists. Those who had agriculture lived 2 to 3 years longer on the average. How many centuries were needed to gain these extra years? Cer-

---

[3] For example: Boserup (1965) and Cohen (1978).

tainly not less than 10 centuries and perhaps 20 or 30 or more.[4] An Indian tiller of the soil who lived in 1492 would have been totally unaware that he or she was living just a bit longer than did some remote ancestor. We may infer that increases in longevity had no psychological impact. In the twentieth century, in contrast, we keep track. We boast about living longer than our parents and bemoan decreases in length of life.

Men Lived Longer Than Did Women

Much of the shorter length of life among the women, both among the agriculturalists and nonagriculturalists, is attributable to childbirth and maternal mortality. Let us compare length of life at the beginning and end of the childbearing years, ages 15 and 45 (see Table 4.1):

	Nonagriculture			Agriculture		
Age	Men	Women	Deficit among women	Men	Women	Deficit among women
15	19	17	2 years	22	20	2 years
45	8	8	0	9	9	0

In the teenage years, the future life expectancy of women was significantly below that of men. Once women reached the end of the childbearing ages, their life expectancy was the same as that of men. This is totally different from that in twentieth-century economically developed countries, where women outlive men by close to 10 years (at birth); indeed, at every age, length of life is greater for women than for men.

This deficit among the prehistoric women resulted from several factors including lack of modern medical facilities, perhaps an inadequate diet, and the very high birthrate. Among the hunters and gatherers, we suggest that excessive physical labor in foraging for wild plants (nature's bounty), and perhaps hunting, also contributed.

OF THE CAUSES OF DEATH[5]

We believe that (a) warfare and other fighting, plus accidents while hunting or on other occasions, were important causes of death, especially for men; (b) among women of childbearing age, childbirth must have claimed many lives;

[4] Much of our sample of nonagriculturalists comes from sites of the Archaic period, some 3,000 years or so before the arrival of the Europeans. That of the agriculturalists is between 500 and 1,000 years prior to Columbus's arrival. The difference is 2,000 years, or about 20 centuries.
[5] The reader who is interested in pursuing this topic can begin with medical texts and follow with materials written by physical anthropologists. See, for example, the writings of Angel (1971a,b), Ubelaker (1978, 1980), Cybulski (personal communication), and Zimmerman (1980).

(c) since the population was young with average (median) age perhaps about 15 years (half the people were under 15 years), childhood diseases must have been widespread; these include diarrhea, enteritis, and related congenital malformations and diseases of early infancy, very low weight at birth, lack of sufficient or appropriate food, and so forth; (d) among the older ages there must have been fewer deaths than at the younger ages, because there were very few older people; only 1 or 2% of the population was aged 50 and over. The older people suffer from diseases of the heart, malignant neoplasms (cancers), cerebrovascular diseases, and the like; and (e) epidemic or contagious disease may have been at a minimum insofar as the people may have lived widely scattered in small groups.

Environmentalists today complain that we are poisoning our environment with chemicals and modern gadgets. But, at least today we have public health and medical facilities; although not perfect antidotes, they do contribute to increased length of life, as we saw previously when we compared that of the prehistoric Amerindians with the twentieth-century population.

The prehistorics instead of living in the fabled Garden of Eden faced a poisonous natural environment and had few facilities with which to protect themselves. Apparently these people had every physical ailment known to modern people insofar as such can be detected in skeletal remains and mummies.

Viral diseases such as AIDS and other potentially deadly lethal organisms appear and disappear and leave no calling cards. Barbara J. Culliton quotes Joshua Lederberg, Rockefeller University president, as saying that great plagues may again descend upon humankind. Bacteria and unknown viruses may suddenly appear and infect people who do not have immunity, and then we have a new virulent epidemic—one that may leave no clues for future physical anthropologists. If there were any such presently unknown diseases among the prehistoric Amerindians, no one can say.

There is a vast published literature in which the analyses of skeletal remains and mummies have been reported. Overviews have been prepared by various authorities, including, for example, Hart, Zivanovic, Brothwell and Sandison, and Cockburn. Here we shall present but a short overview of some of the medical problems faced by the Ancients. Not all of these physical ailments necessarily resulted in immediate death, of course. But many, if not all, contributed to their ultimate demise.

How we know about these diseases or ailments is described in the literature. There are many procedures available, and new ones are introduced even as we write. We cannot begin to summarize this literature but shall simply mention several writers.

Ubelaker (1978, 1980) presents an adumbrated list of ailments and diseases among the Ancients, including porotic hyperostosis (thickening of bone tissue) resulting from iron-deficiency anemia; tuberculosis; gallstones; black-lung disease found in ancient mummies in Peru and Chile (Allison 1976); syphilis of one type or another; arthritis; bone fractures; dislocation of joints; osteomyelitis resulting from infection by *Staphylococcus aureus,* salmonella, and other sources; congenital disorders; tumors; metabolic disorders; endocrine disturbances; and so on.

Pfeiffer (1977) in her study of the Archaic (nonagricultural) population of the Great Lakes region considers trauma to have been the major health problem in that region. "The greater portion of pathological conditions noted among the skeletal remains appears to be the result of external trauma." She suggests that warfare was a contributing cause. "Pending further evidence, it does appear likely that the people of Frontenac Island were involved in warfare, and the women may have been just as active as the men. They may at least have been just as likely victims" (p. 182).

In this study, she found that "osteoarthritic degeneration seen among the Archaic sample is slight" (p. 184). Also the "frequency of dental caries is very low, while heavy wear is common" (p. 198).

Cybulski (1981) believes that the skeletal record indicates but the minimum extent of such problems. Too many afflictions cannot be ascertained from skeletal remains, acute infections for example, even when the entire skeleton is available. Some diseases affect other parts of the body before the skeleton; if the person dies before the bones are affected, all signs of the disease are lost, Cybulski says.

Vitamin deficiencies can result in such illnesses as beriberi, pellagra, megaloblastic anemia, scurvy, rickets, and other bone disorders that are visible in the skeleton. The deficiency or excess of some minerals in the food or water such as lead, iron, iodine, zinc, fluorine, and perhaps a dozen more trace elements can be deleterious to health (see Chapter 6).

Botulin, a toxin that is formed by a spore-bearing bacterium, and salmonella, a naturally occurring bacteria, can lead to death. So also can the ciguatera toxin sometimes found in fish and seafood.

Twentieth-century people, especially those living in the more economically developed countries where there are considerable medical facilities, may be less afflicted by these natural lethal substances—they are not immune—than were the Ancients. Although there are problems with some foods, if one has sufficient food variety, the person is less likely to get sick. However, where people tend to concentrate on a small number of food items such as shellfish or maize or cassava, they may ingest too much of undesirable substances.

Further, present-day medical knowledge can circumvent some of these problems. With proper medication, salmonella, for example, is not invariably fatal. Scurvy can be prevented by eating citrus fruits. Vitamin pills can be added to one's diet if necessary.

The prehistorics, on the other hand, had but little knowledge about the causes of their illnesses and even less knowledge about how to combat these sicknesses. They could do but little more than attribute their health problems to the wrath of the gods.

There are other classes of potentially lethal substances many of which leave no detectable (at present) evidence in skeletal remains and mummies. Wing and Brown (1979) list some of them. Included are the antimetabolites, chemicals that prevent the utilization of normally occurring nutriments in the food eaten. An example—certain plants including soy beans "contain substances which depress the uptake of iodine by the thyroid gland." This will decrease the production of thyroid hormone. It is not certain whether these goitrogens by themselves produce signs of goiter, but they probably contribute to goiter in iodine-poor soils and waters.

Other potentially lethal substances are a variety of naturally occurring toxicants. For example, a steroidal alkaloid that is found in potatoes in some cases has caused food poisoning (p. 69). Naturally occurring cyanide (in one form or another) in certain foods such as cassava (bitter manioc) can lead to trouble.

Two important questions may be asked. What proportion of the population experiences such health problems? What proportion of those afflicted died as a result? We have not found any answers to these questions. Knowledge of the true incidence of various diseases will never be known, in Cybulski's opinion. An important reason for our inability to answer these questions is the inability of investigators always to correctly identify the cause of a disease detected in the remains. Perhaps all that we can say with certainty is that the frequencies of the various causes of death differed among the prehistorics from that of late twentieth century people, if only because of the differences in age composition of the respective populations.

THE PRE-EUROPEAN AMERINDIANS
WERE SIMILAR TO ALL ANCIENT SOCIETIES

Short length of life was common to all ancient societies as our brief summary indicates. Valiant attempts have been made to calculate length of life for many ancient populations. The most inclusive lists of such studies that we have seen are those of Vallois (1961), Hishinuma (1977), and Acsadi and Nemeskeri (1970).

The uncounted numbers of physical anthropologists, archaeologists, actuaries, statisticians, and demographers who have constructed life tables all faced a common problem—lack of good and correct information with which to start their calculations. Prior to World War II, the methods for ascertaining age and sex of skeletal remains were inferior to those subsequently developed. Too many of the reported findings are of pre-World War II vintage. Determination of the age at death from the skeletal remains has been vastly improved in the latter part of the twentieth century, and the techniques are continuing to be improved. The actuarial procedures for constructing life tables, on the other hand, were well established by the beginning of the twentieth century. Accordingly, length-of-life calculations made post-World War II are more likely to be reasonably correct than those made earlier. Nevertheless, even those made earlier are correct in indicating that length of life was considerably shorter than at present.

Information about the Australopithecines who lived 3 to 4 million years ago and may be our oldest ancestors can be derived from the age distribution presented by McKinley (1971). From these data we calculate that life expectancy at birth may have been around 10 years or perhaps less. The uniquely correct figure cannot be ascertained because there were several varieties of Australopithecines and no investigator has compiled a "proven-to-be" correct sample of the entire population. For example, "Lucy," who is classified as *Australopithecus aferensis,* and who lived some 3 million years ago, was estimated to be "only 3½ feet tall, although she was full grown" (Johanson and Maitland 1981).

Australopithecus robustus, first discovered in South Africa, on the other hand, "were certainly hefty fellows, standing close to five feet tall with a generous endowment of weighty muscles. . . . The robust australopithecines that lived in East Africa were significantly bigger—they were hyper robust" (Leakey and Lewin 1978, p. 64).

The great antiquity of these creatures together with the reported variation in the skeletal structures raises questions about the estimates of length of life. Was their physiology the same as that of present-day humans? Do today's criteria for assigning age to skeletal remains apply to these earliest forms? We know of no answers. McKinley (1971) presents an "estimate of 11 years for sexual maturation in australopithecines. This age is the median between chimpanzees and man" (p. 424). If there is a difference in physiology, then the criteria for assigning age are not necessarily the same for the past as for the present. All that we can say, then, about our most ancient ancestors, is that they lived very short lives by twentieth-century standards.

In more recent times, the last 50,000 years or so prior to the twentieth century—all measures of time are indefinite and flexible—the bits of information available suggest that length of life was between about 15 and 25 years until about the seventeenth or eighteenth centuries in Europe. Neanderthal Man and Woman and their children, who lived tens of millennia ago, had an estimated life expectancy of 12 to 15 years. We tend toward the 15-year edge.

With the advent of modern man, *Homo sapiens sapiens,* and while people still lived in the Neolithic Age (before metal came into much use), perhaps 10,000 years ago, life expectancy was in the vicinity of 18 to 21 years. During the early metal period, perhaps 8,000 years ago to around 3,000 years ago, life expectancy may have averaged 19 to 22 years. Note that we present approximations, a 3- or 4-year range of estimate. Any attempt at presenting a more precise length-of-life figure would be a misuse of statistics. Uniquely correct values do not exist.

Hishinuma (1977) provides information for the Jomon period in Japan. "The Jomon Age of Japan started about 10,000 years ago and continued up to the Yayoi Age which commenced several centuries B.C. It belonged to the Neolithic Age and is generally divided into five stages, namely the Earliest Jomon, the Early Jomon, the Middle Jomon, the Late Jomon, and the Latest Jomon eras" (p. 18). Agriculture arose during the Middle Jomon. The average length of life was about 15 years throughout the Jomon Age and varied little from one stage to another as far as can be determined.

Angel (1971) reported age and sex distributions of skeletal material for ancient Greece and Turkey; we estimated length of life from his data. During the Paleolithic Age (significantly older than 10,000 years ago), life expectancy was 15 years at the most. During the early period of metal use it may have been between 14 and 17 years.

In the Roman Empire, length of life varied between 16 and 30 years, depending on the investigator. How was age at death estimated? How did the investigator calculate his life table? Hishinuma collected and presented all the analyses he could find. The best that can be said is that there is great variation among all the reports. Nothing more authoritative can be said.

Between the seventh and seventeenth centuries, length of life as estimated ranged between about 15 and 25 years. The reported length of life depended on the particular geographic area studied, the time period, and the capabilities of the investigator. Hishinuma[6] presents reports for Medieval Europe (seventh to fourteenth centuries), Medieval England, and Tokyo during the Edo period (twelfth to eighteenth or early nineteenth centuries). Much of the reported differences in length of life may simply depend on the time period studied. In

---

[6] An example of diversity that he reports is that for Breslau, at the end of the seventeenth century. Halley had calculated life expectancy of 33.5 years. Hishinuma (1977) recalculated and decided that 23.7 years was more probable. Hishinuma explains: "The numbers of death by age . . . in the years 1722, 1723, and 1724 were added together and is a completely different material from the one used by Halley. However, there is no marked difference for a person aged 20 years and over between (us). However, with life expectancy at birth the figure given by Halley of 33.5 is 10 years longer than that given by me of 23.7" (p. 69). Apparently differences in estimating the death rate of young children (where death reporting is far from complete) was a major reason for the difference in life expectancy at birth.

Perhaps also, the difference is due in part to a difference in timing. Halley used deaths by age and sex for the years 1687–1691. Hishinuma introduced data for the years 1722, 1723, and 1724 with no further explanation.

See also Halley's *Degrees of Mortality of Mankind,* reproduced by the Johns Hopkins Press, 1942, in its series *Reprint of Economic Tracts.* Lowell J. Reed edited the original Halley statement that appeared in the Philosophical Transactions of the Royal Society of London, 1693, vol. xvii. and wrote the introduction to the Johns Hopkins reprint.

times of extended epidemics, warfare, or famine, length of life must have been shorter than in more benign times.

By the latter half of the eighteenth century, length of life surpassed the 30-year mark in some parts of the world. It reached 35 years in Sweden, 1751 to 1790.

SUMMARY

The average length of life in ancient times among the North American Indians who did not have agriculture was 14 to 15 years for women and 16 to 17 years for men. Sometime during the first millennium A.D. many of these people acquired agriculture, and life expectancy rose by 2 or 3 years. The shorter length of life (and higher death rate) among women resulted, in large measure, from childbirth and maternal mortality.

These Amerindians had every disease known in the twentieth century and that can be diagnosed from skeletal remains and mummies. In addition, it is believed that they had many more afflictions that cannot be detected in skeletal remains. Nature was and is replete with diseases and death-causing forces. These Ancients, not knowing precisely what caused their problems, had no way of counteracting Nature.

Length of life of under 20 years among the Amerindians seems to have been but little different from other ancient people around the globe. Even Medieval Europeans probably did not live significantly longer. Apparently, the 30-year mark was not passed until the eighteenth century, and then only in very few countries.

Chapter 5

Glimpses of Ancestral Family Life

INTRODUCTION

Glimpses of family life[1] and society among these Ancients can be obtained from our analysis of length of life (Chapter 4). We can infer the ages of Adam and Eve when they first joined, assuming that they were *Homo sapiens sapiens,* and about how long they lived together before one or the other died. Whether they loved each other, whether Adam helped with the children and the housework, and similar questions we cannot answer. Some answers can be guessed. But the intimate facts that make for a bestseller romance novel are beyond the capabilities of a life table to uncover. We leave such "descriptions, deceptions, and findings" to the writers of bestsellers.

In the following pages, then, we shall infer what we can about marriage formation and the size of the population providing the marriage partners. Next we shall explore the probable frequency of widow–widowerhood. Then we estimate the frequency of orphanhood and from this we infer what we can about the nuclear family versus the extended family. We also estimate their possible birthrates. On the basis of these observations, we discuss the implications of mortality for the size of the group, band, or tribe.

---

[1] For observations on the role of women in addition to childbearing, see Dahlberg (1981).

MARRIAGE AND THE FAMILY

Marriage Formation

Everyone capable of mating, coupling, or marriage and presumably capable of reproduction, must have done so, considering how high the death rates were. The tribe or band could not afford to have any of its members sitting on the sidelines, so to speak, that is, not coupling or refusing to bear children. From this we infer that marriage would take place at the youngest possible age. How old a girl or woman was—12 years, 15 years, older?—cannot be said with certitude because it depended on her nutritional well-being. She must have enough body fat to bring about menarche and maintain ovulation. Menarche is delayed in malnourished girls. Further, when menarche is delayed, menopause commonly occurs early (Cassidy, p. 132). Because we do not know the precise state of nutrition among the prehistoric Amerindians nor the possible variation from tribe to tribe, we cannot specify age of menarche and marriage. We note only that (a) although social marriage can occur before menarche, there is no advantage to the group if children do not result; and (b) the band needed all the births possible if it were to continue to exist.

In our society there is a tendency to equate marriage with monogamy, although recognizing that polygyny and polyandry exist. However, when death rates are very high, a tribe cannot afford to have celibate adults in the reproductive ages. They represent lost opportunities to increase the size of the group. Whether a group "needs" to increase its size is not for us to say. We simply note that virtually every population, nation, band, or tribe wants more people, either for purposes of warfare, assumed international (or intertribal) importance, or some other illogical reason.[2]

Polygyny must have been common among the prehistoric Amerindians. The very high death rates would have led in many instances, to a lack of marriage partners and the necessity to "double up." Driver (1961, p. 276) suggests that the vast majority of North American peoples practiced polygamy. He then qualifies his remarks by noting that exclusive monogamy was the rule among the Iroquois and some of their neighbors.

Marriage Dissolution

Unlike modern times, divorce was not needed to dissolve a marriage. Death of one spouse did it. Whether there were separations in addition to deaths among

---

[2] In the case of ancient China, and perhaps twentieth-century China also, population growth was viewed as an indication that the ruling government was good. So the statisticians, when presenting numbers to the emperor, exaggerated "so as to please the reigning emperor" (Chen 1946, p. 2).

the prehistoric peoples we shall probably never know. But the death rates were so high that few marriages lasted very long. We estimate as follows. If both the male and female—the boy and girl—were 15 years of age at the time of union, only about 8 in 10 couples would still be intact 5 years later; one mate died during this 5-year period. At the end of 10 years, half of the couples would still be intact, and at the end of 15 years we find about one-third intact and two-thirds broken (Figure 5.1).

If one partner is older than the other, the proportion of unbroken unions is likely to be smaller.

Clearly, several consecutive marriages were possible during the reproductive ages of, say, 15 to 45 for women, and 15 to 55 for men. If there was a shortage of teenage brides or grooms, this situation would soon be rectified as an already united person becomes a widow or widower. Or widows and widowers could form new unions and their reproductive potentials need not be wasted.

Orphanhood

What is the probability of a newborn becoming an orphan during its childhood, in light of the high mortality rates of the prehistoric adults? The answer is important insofar as it casts light upon the possible role of the nuclear family as we understand the term, if such families did exist in the past.

Questions: Until what age is a newborn so dependent upon adults that it cannot survive alone? Or, by what age does a child accumulate all the knowledge and experience necessary so that it can take its place as an adult in the community? There is no clear answer except at the very beginning of life. Accordingly, we present estimates of the probability[3] of orphanhood for three ages: 5, 10, and 15 (Appendix 10, Table 10.1). Until the age of 5 or thereabouts, the child needs adult care; it cannot successfully hunt nor gather on its own. By age 15 the child has probably learned and experienced enough so that it can take its place in the adult society. Take your choice as to where to draw the lines designating the beginning and the end of childhood and orphanhood.

Because the probability of becoming an orphan depends on the age of the parents at the child's birth, we show the probabilities for six ages of parents ranging from 15 years to 40 years. For the sake of simplicity of calculation, we assume that both parents were of the same age. Note that if one parent is older, then the probability of orphanhood is increased; how much depends on the difference in age between the parents.

Of the infants who survived to age 10 among the hunters and gatherers, about half become orphans, if both parents were 15 years of age at the time of

---

[3] We can calculate probabilities for every single year of age between 5 and 15 if desired. We do not believe that such work is worth the effort.

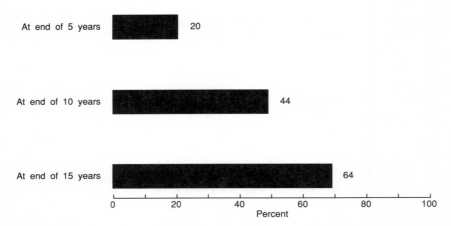

Figure 5.1. Estimated percentage of marriages broken by death with both partners age 15 at time of union (includes both agriculturalists and nonagriculturalists).

birth of the infants. If both parents were 25 years of age, about 7 in 10 of the children are orphaned by age 10. If the parents were 40 years of age, 9 in 10 of the infants will be orphaned.

Among agriculturalists the probability of becoming orphaned is a little smaller. If both parents were 25 years of age at its birth, 6 in 10 are likely to become orphans.

Young children under 5 years of age certainly are dependent on adults. Of these very young children about 2 in 10 among the nonagriculturalists become orphaned by age 5, if the parents were both 15 years of age at its birth. If the parents were in their 20s or older when the infant was born, close to half will be orphaned within the next 5 years. Among the agricultural population somewhat fewer become orphans. About half of all orphanage results from the death of the mother.

The Nuclear Family

From the preceding observations we draw the conclusion that the nuclear family by itself was not viable. Extensive community or group support was needed. We assume that both parents, or proxy parents, or some other parenting system, were needed to sustain the child both physically and emotionally and to pass on the cultural heritage. Because comparatively few children reach age 10 and even fewer age 15, having both parents living, it is obvious that others in the tribe must take on the parents' job or the group would soon disappear. There would be no new generation to replace the previous one.

Clearly these prehistoric peoples must have worked out extended-family systems, a widespread "safety net" that not only furnished food, clothing, housing, and protection but also taught the ways of the group to the youngsters. Because there were comparatively few grandparents alive who could act as the "net," the community as a whole must have done so. Of course the specific situation must have varied from one band to another and must have depended on the size of the band. If it was very small, say 50 people, the entire group may have acted as the family. If it was large, several hundred subdivisions such as clans may have operated. Beyond such suppositions we can say no more.

The practice of women adopting children, or an orphan child "adopting" a mother, persisted into the nineteenth and twentieth centuries among the Cheyenne Indians, for example, according to Moore and Campbell (1989). This type of exchange or adoption reportedly took place among sisters in this tribe. "According to elders, the rights of sisters are aboriginal. . . . Cheyenne children have always had several potential mothers in reserve" (1989, p. 31).

THE BIRTHRATE

Several measures of the birthrate are available. We shall discuss three: (1) the *crude* birthrate, or the number of births per year per 1,000 population; (2) the *total fertility* rate—TFR—or the sum of the age-specific rates (see Table 5.1); and (3) the *net reproduction* rate[4] that combines births and deaths in order to measure the rate of growth of the population in the absence of in- or outmigration.

Crude Birthrate

Among the nonagriculturalists, the births may have numbered about 65 per 1,000 population. As far as anyone knows, this is the highest rate that is physiologically possible. There is no authenticated report for any nation in the world of a crude birth rate above about 60 per 1,000 people per year.

We reason as follows. The crude birthrate refers to live births, not total conceptions. The latter include involuntary fetal mortality (spontaneous abortions and stillbirths) and induced abortions. Hence the live birthrate is significantly lower than is the conception rate. Involuntary fetal mortality may amount to around 30% of all conceptions, according to Jean Bourgeois-Pichat (1973, p. 75). Hence, a live birthrate of 65 per 1,000 population per year implies a conception rate of 90 to 100 per 1,000 population per year. Women in the reproductive ages of 15 to 44 among the nonagriculturalists constituted about one-fifth of the total population. Accordingly, in a tribe containing 1,000 people

---

[4]The net reproduction rate minus 1 equals the currently more fashionable term *intrinsic rate of natural increase.*

Table 5.1. Possible Age-Specific Birthrates per Woman
in 5 Years: Prehistoric North American Indians[a]

Age of mother	Births per woman	
	Nonagricultural	Agricultural
15–19	1.1	1.0
20–24	2.4	2.0
25–29	2.6	1.7
30–34	1.6	1.4
35–39	1.0	0.9
40–44	0.6	0.5
Total	9.3	7.5
TFR, estimated	9	7 or 8

[a]See Appendix 4 for sources and further information.

there would be about 200 women aged 15 to 44. Thus, a conception rate of 90 or more per 200 women indicates a conception rate of one every 2 years per woman. Further, if we take into account the existence of sterility and subfecundity, then the fecund women must have a conception rate of more than one every 2 years in order to produce a live birthrate of 65 per 1,000 total population per year. Because it is difficult to visualize a live birthrate significantly higher than 65, the population must have been reproducing very close to the physiological maximum.

If we may digress for a moment, let us consider as follows. At a live birthrate of 65 per 1,000 population, the average interval between births is about 3 years. If the women had 90 conceptions per year per 1,000 population, the average interval between conceptions is about 2 years. Further, the spacing probably is not of equal length for all age groups; those ages having the highest birthrates must have had shorter-than-average intervals, and those having the lower birthrates, longer-than-average intervals.

Our estimates resemble those reported by Hassan (1981). He reviewed some of the literature on length of time between live births (Chapter 8 in Hassan) and finds that the published estimates vary from about 2 to 3 years. This range resembles the difference that we estimate between conceptions and live births. Two problems stand in the way of more nearly accurate estimates of the time interval. One is the simple fact that many spontaneous abortions occur so early in the pregnancy as to be unnoticed, or unreported. A second is that the line between live and still births is uncertain in some instances. Was the infant dead at birth or did it live 1 or 2 minutes? In many countries today it is legally reportable as a live birth if it lived for any length of time, no matter how little. Other countries count as live births only those that lived for some specified length of time, a day, a week, or whatever. Obviously, the reported birthrate is somewhat lower in these latter countries. These variations in counting confuse the interpretations of the birth statistics.

To return to our discussion of length of life and the birthrate. The increase of 2 or 3 years in length of life among the agriculturalists, in theory, could have led to a crude birthrate of about 55 per 1,000. If this had happened, it would suggest that voluntary birth control measures had been introduced. Whether the birthrate actually fell this much or remained closer to the level of the hunters and gatherers—the nonagriculturalists—cannot be said with certainty. We think that any decrease that may have occurred was less than the 10 points, 65 down to 55. We reason as follows.

If the birthrate had decreased in accordance with the increase in length of life among the agriculturalists, there would have been very little, if any, population growth. The number of deaths would have equaled the number of births. But there is reason to think that the birthrate fell little, if at all.

People do not decrease their birthrate instantly if their death rate falls. If the crude birthrate had remained at the level of bout 60 to 65 per 1,000 population per year, there would have been close to 1% increase in population per year. This could have resulted in doubling of the number of people in 75 years. Over several millennia the increase in population would be too much to contemplate.

If the birthrate had decreased just a little such that the rate of population growth was but 3 or 4 per 1,000 population per year, the population would double in about 200 years. Even at this low rate, a population can increase close to 20 times in only 1,000 years.

It must be remembered also that the time interval over which increases in length of life (or decreases in the death rate) occurred is one or more millennia. An increase of life expectancy of 3 years in a period of well over 1,000 years would not be noticed; no living person in the fifteenth century could be aware that the death rate was decreasing at such a slow rate, and lower her birthrate accordingly. Hence, we believe that the birthrate remained substantially unchanged or decreased very little. The death rate, however, fell just a little more than did the birthrate (if the latter fell) as agriculture was introduced and expanded.

Total Fertility Rate, or Number of Children Born

Among the nonagricultural population, those women who lived through the childbearing ages averaged about 9 births (Table 5.1). Among the agricultural people, the number of children may have averaged about 7, or possibly 8.

Actually, few women would have had as many live births as these averages suggest because so many died long before menopause. We estimate that among the hunters and gatherers perhaps only 1 in 14 survived from menarche to menopause (age 15 to 45), and among the agriculturalists 1 in 4. Quite possibly the average woman among the nonagriculturalists had about 6 children during her short lifetime. Among the latter, the agriculturalists, perhaps the average was 5 or 6. Too many died during the childbearing ages.

Exactly how many children these women had and exactly how many women lived from menarche to menopause we shall never know for certain.

CHILDREN UNDER 5 YEARS OF AGE

Introduction

We look into this topic because some anthropologists have argued that hunters and gatherers had to control their fertility. Male anthropologists have assumed that women were the foragers and hence could not carry two infants simultaneously, breast-feed them, and continue foraging. Therefore, it is argued, some type of birth control (including infanticide) had to have been practiced (Birdsell 1968, p. 236).

We believe that the use or nonuse of fertility controls has but little connection with the problem of collecting wild foods. Consider the following:

1. Infant and child mortality was so high that even if the birthrate was as high as 65 per 200 women in the childbearing ages (annually), not enough infants would survive long enough to prevent their mothers from foraging. We estimate that at least 4 in 10 of the live-born infants died before reaching age 5. Hence it is unlikely that a woman would have two infants to breast-feed and carry around with her, unless they were twins.

2. Children by the age of 3 can walk great distances. Certainly 4-year-olds can. They can toddle along after their mothers. Whether they required breast feeding is a question to which we have no answer. They can be breast-fed, or they can eat "grown-up" food or both. We shall never have definitive information about the child-rearing habits of these pre-Europeans.

3. If a mother had twins, or if an infant was left motherless, there would be enough surrogate mothers available (assuming a large population)—that is, women whose infants died and who were thus available to take care of motherless infants. About twice as many young children died before the age of 5, as mothers died in a 5-year period. Of the children, at least 4 in 10 died and of the mothers, perhaps 2 in 10. Thus, in a large population there is an excess of mothers whose infants died. Of course, in a small group, say 50 or 100 people, this ratio of maternal to child deaths may differ from the averages.

Let us assume that we have a band of 100 people, 20 of whom are women between the ages of 15 and 45. Let us assume that all 20 women gave birth in 1 year to 20 live births. If the preceding average death rates applied, we expect about 4 mothers and 8 infants to die. Four surrogate mothers remain with no infants to take care of. But given such a small population, 20 women, chance alone may result in there being as many as about 7 maternal deaths and perhaps only 4 child deaths. Hence 3 infants may be left with no surrogate mothers, unless the band had exchange rights with the other bands. Another band containing 20 women in the childbearing ages might experience, by chance alone, only 1 maternal death and perhaps as many as 10 child deaths. Women would be available to take care of orphans. Precisely what happened in prehistoric times we shall never know. Suffice to note that the exigencies of life did not make fertility controls mandatory.

Some Numbers

Among the prehistoric nonagriculturalists, the average number of children under age 5 per woman between the ages of 15 and 45, was about 1¼. If we assume that about one-third were 3- and 4-year-olds, then there may have been less than 1 child under the age of 3, per woman, perhaps 9 for every 10 women.

Among the agriculturalists, the number under age 5 averaged about 1.1 per woman. If we assume that about one-third were 3- and 4-year-olds and could toddle after their mothers, then the average of those under 3 years reduces to approximately 7 per 10 women.

How do these numbers compare with underdeveloped countries in the latter part of the twentieth century? For some African and Pacific Island countries we have census information for their rural populations. Because these are agricultural populations—we have no data for hunters and gatherers—we compare them with the prehistoric Amerindian agriculturalists. In 8 of the 10 rural populations for which we have information, the number of children under age 5 per woman was about .9 or slightly higher—definitely under 1 child per woman in the reproductive ages.[5] Included are the rural peoples of Botswana, the Ivory Coast, Libyan Arab Jamahiriya, Morocco, Guyana, Papua New Guinea, Samoa, and the Hebrides. For Fiji and the Gilbert Islands, the number of children under age 5 per woman is about .7. These reported averages may be a little low because census counts of children generally omit some of the little ones. Thus we suspect that there is—or was—not too much difference between the pre-European American Indians and twentieth-century rural people in the underdeveloped parts of the world. Only to the extent that birth control may have been adopted in recent years might the present populations in these economically underdeveloped areas have significantly fewer youngsters than did the prehistoric Amerindians.

[5] In today's economically developed countries, the ratio of children to women is much lower. In the United States, for example (1980), there were only about 3 children under age 5 per 10 women—(one-third of a child per woman)—between the ages of 15 and 45.

SIZE OF THE BAND—ITS SIGNIFICANCE AND IMPLICATIONS

The size of the band or group has a bearing on marriage formation, lifestyle to some extent, and even intergroup trade relations. To begin, *Homo sapiens sapiens* were constructed biologically so that there are almost equal numbers of men and women. In the case of a large population, very many thousands and more, there are almost equal numbers. But if the group is small, the sexes may be greatly unbalanced from time to time. We illustrate. Let us assume a band of 500 people and that the marriage, or pairing, age is 15 to 19 years. About 12%, or 60 people, are aged 15 to 19 (calculated from our life table: see Appendix Table 3.5). We expect that close to 30 would be men and approximately the same number women. However, chance variation, the luck of the throw, can intervene. As a result of "bad luck," there may be 20 women[6] and 40 men at one time, and 20 men and 40 women another time. The sexes of marriageable age will be unbalanced, assuming monogamy. What, then, is the minimum size population that can guarantee enough mates (allowing for polygyny) for all?

Our best guess based on untestable assumptions is that a total population of 4,000 to 5,000 is needed to maintain a reasonable balance of the sexes.

Small groups numbering 25 or 50, even several hundred, were demographically unstable. On the one hand, the hunters and gatherers (according to the anthropological literature) had to live in small groups in order to exploit the natural resources. Large groups of several thousand could not maintain themselves except under extraordinary circumstances as, for example, the fishing tribes of the Pacific coast. On the other hand, small groups could never be certain that they would always have enough people for reproductive purposes. Hence, it was mandatory for small groups to be part of larger networks so that mates could be obtained. The small groups may have lived independently during most of the time, but they had to assemble or otherwise be in contact from time to time.[7]

How large were the prehistoric groups of Amerindians? According to Mooney's information, the majority of the tribes may have been too small to guarantee survival. This may hold for the agriculturalists as well as the nonagriculturalists.

We suggest that there was a continuous process of growth and decay of tribal size. Small groups either grew by a surplus of births over deaths or by amalgamation with other tribes. Or they disappeared either through annihilation

---

[6] This is a simple probability calculation. We assume that 6% of the total population are females aged 15 to 19, as given in the life table (Appendix Table 3.5). The sampling error is $\sqrt{npq} = 5$. Two sampling errors equals 10 plus or minus the expected number of 30. Actually, the calculations for ascertaining the possible extent of imbalance of the sexes in small groups are more complicated than is our simplistic example.

[7] For an example of how the prehistoric Amerindians may have lived, see Gould (1980).

or absorption by other tribes. New small groups were also being formed continuously, either through the decimation of larger groups, or via the budding off from larger tribes. Such budding could have occurred because of economic reasons or because of intratribal conflict.

On the assumption that small groups needed a network of support from other bands, we may deduce that intergroup contact for mating or social purposes was accompanied by intergroup trade and food exchange and perhaps other exchanges. Which need came first, mates or food? In situations where there was no dearth of food, as Rick (1980) describes, or among the Pacific coast Indians, food may not have been a problem. For such small groups, mate exchanges would be necessary and may have come first. For other groups where food may have been a problem, perhaps trading of food and mates arose together at some point in the far distant past, perhaps in Asia.

Finally, if there still is an insufficiency of men or women, the capturing of mates from other tribes could be resorted to.

SUMMARY

The birthrate was probably at or near the physiological limit, especially among the hunters and gatherers. It may have been a little lower among the agriculturalists. Nonagricultural women who survived to the end of the childbearing period averaged about 9 live births, we estimate. Among the agriculturalists, the average may have been 7 or 8.

Little children, those under 5 years of age, may have been but little more numerous than among some rural populations in economically underveloped countries today. Among nonagriculturalists there may have been as few as 9 tots—excluding 3- and 4-year-olds—per 10 women aged 15 to 44. Among agriculturalists, there may have been as few as 7 per 10 women. Among some of the twentieth-century rural populations outside of North America, the ratio may be close to 6 per 10 women, more or less comparable to the prehistoric Amerindian agriculturalists.

Orphanage was very common among the prehistoric Amerindians. Twenty to 30% of the infants who survived to age 5 were orphans by that age, if the parents were under about 25 years of age when the infants were born. The death rates among the parent generation were very high. If the parents were over 25 years of age, perhaps between 4 and 5 of the surviving infants were orphaned; if the infants survived to age 10, some 2 out of 3 were orphaned by age 5.

How large must a band be to assure that all members may have mates? Let us assume that the age of marriage or becoming paired or mated is 15 to 19. In small populations of a few hundred there could be very great imbalances of the sexes in this age range, thus leaving many unmated, under conditions of monogamy. A population numbering 4,000 to 5,000, we think, is needed in order to assure a reasonable balance of the sexes at initial pairing age.

What are the alternatives? Polygamy is one solution. Another is the effects of the high death rate. Marriages were constantly being broken by the death of a spouse; new potential mates, widows and widowers, constantly became available.

The demographic facts of life are all important.

Chapter 6

Following the Food Trail, or What's for Dinner?

INTRODUCTION

The Ancestors went where the food was just as present-day *Homo sapiens sapiens* do; only we speak of going where the jobs are. They found food or moved elsewhere. But did they have an adequate diet? In discussing possible causes of death and the short length of life, we alluded to the possible effects of inadequate diets and food deficiencies. In this chapter we shall delve further into health problems that may be traceable to the foods eaten.

Another question is whether diet affects the birthrate. There is considerable discussion about the answer, and we shall attempt to briefly summarize the arguments.

The reader must be aware that there is no definitive information about exactly what they ate, how much, and how nutritious the food was. Further, these Ancestors may have had preferences and prejudices about various food items, just as twentieth-century people have; we shall never know how the diet actually consumed may, or may not, have differed from the foods available. We shall attempt to present a sketch of their possible food basket, but we are not presenting a comprehensive coverage of this topic.

An interesting and comprehensive overview of this subject is presented by Yesner (1980). Most of the references that he cites are to the Eastern Hemisphere. Nevertheless, we believe that Yessner's comments and inferences are also pertinent to the prehistoric North American Indians. Yesner argues that anthropologists have not cooperated sufficiently with nutritionists. Hence, the former have missed some of the most important aspects of human adaptation to the natural and social environments, over the many millennia since *Homo sapiens sapiens* appeared.

The single most important food event, of course, was the introduction and spread of agriculture. Slowly over the course of centuries and millennia diets changed radically. This change had not been going on very long in North America prior to the European invasion, in comparison with areas south of the Rio Grande or in the Eastern Hemisphere. Nevertheless, where agriculture was most developed, there the diet must have differed most from the preagricultural period.

Although there are many references in the literature to foods eaten, we have seen no compilations and summaries of these that inform us of how much they ate of each type of flora and fauna. With such a compilation for a specific time period and geographic area, one could attempt to judge the adequacy of the diet. The Brothwells (1969) published a very readable worldwide summary that is useful for trying to understand the Amerindian diets. Zivanovic (1980) presents an excellent discussion of how deficiencies in diet may manifest themselves in the skeletal remains. By combining these two sources, we hope to discern more about the influence of diet on length of life.

If we had good, or even fair, information about the foods actually consumed, perhaps the diets could be evaluated. (Such evaluation, in turn, would open an entire new area for disputation.) For example, we know that the "gung-ho" Paleo-Indians hunted and consumed big game, the megafauna. But we do not know how much big game nor what else they ate. Wild vegetation may have been the major part of their diet, for all we know. But picking grasses and digging for roots is not as exciting to twentieth-century anthropologists, writers, and cartoonists, as is hunting mammoths. So the latter is discussed and depicted. See, for example, the publication *Mammoth Trumpet*.

Different physical environments and climates dictate the types and amounts of flora and fauna available. The Inuits hunt Arctic sea mammals. The Western Woods Cree[1] hunt woodland caribou and moose in their subarctic territory. The Anasazi in the semiarid Southwest United States availed themselves of cactus and cactuslike plants. Perhaps the prickly pear,[2] sold today in fruit and vegetable stores, was an important food.

Given such great variation in types of potential foods, the ideal diet study would consider separately each environmental area of Canada and the United States and take into account the food preferences and prejudices of these prehistorics. Unfortunately, such an undertaking is far beyond the limits of our resources. The most that we can do is to point to a few limited generalities:

---

[1] James Smith (1981).
[2] This plant is found in arid areas throughout the west. It is also called "tuna" and "beavertail."

1. The hunters and gatherers selected from whatever the natural environment provided.
2. Those who had agriculture supplemented their home-grown foods with desired wild vegetation as available.
3. In the absence of domestic livestock, except for dogs, practically all meat and all fish were obtained by hunting and fishing.
4. With such a diversified menu, many, an unknown number, unwholesome foods or contaminated water, was probably consumed.

Finally we must note that since the prehistoric people must have increased in numbers between the date of their first entry into the Western Hemisphere and the coming of the Europeans, their diets could not have been all bad.

SOURCES OF INFORMATION ABOUT FOODS

When digging into sites that had been occupied in the days of yore, archaeologists often find garbage dumps. Along the shorelines they sometimes find shell middens, mute evidence that the Ancients had eaten shellfish. The surviving garbage piles contain a large part of our information of foods consumed.

There are several sources of information regarding the foods—wild plants, animals, water creatures, birds, and so on—on the basis of which, with imaginative processing, we try to reconstruct their dinner menus. None of these sources, however, is able to tell us what proportion of the total diet was derived from each of these products, nor how wholesome these items were, or are. Further, and of utmost importance, is the simple fact that the surviving garbage dumps, or explorers' accounts, do not necessarily provide correct samples of all foods consumed. They may be correct samples or not, and we shall never know. If they are not correct samples, then they may maximize the prevalence of certain foods and minimize that of others.

Nevertheless, if it were possible to relate quantities of these food items to the number of people and their age and sex distribution and if today's nutritionists knew the nutritional value of each food item, we might have better knowledge of the quality and adequacy of the Ancients' diets.

Historical Accounts

Many of the early explorers commented about the foods eaten by the Amerindians. The descriptions, however, were often vague and unscientific by twentieth-century standards. Nevertheless, they provide some information. They describe what they saw in the sixteenth to eighteenth centuries. What they witnessed, most likely, were foods that had been consumed for countless generations prior to the arrival of the Europeans. Fowler (1986, p. 64) summarized these explorers' reports (and later accounts) as follows: "Although far from complete, these data allow for some useful comparisons of species distribution and utilization."

Fowler compiled these lists for the Great Basin area: about 150 types of plants consumed, around 75 types of mammals, 75 types of birds, and a large variety of fish, reptiles, and insects. It is not known how much of each was eaten in any particular geographic area. It is not known whether these reports constituted a correct sample of all foods consumed.

Remains of Vegetation[3]

Plants ordinarily do not survive very long except under special conditions such as dry caves. Seeds and nuts, however, can survive even for centuries, under proper conditions. When found at an archaeological site and identified, it is assumed that the people had eaten these plants. Unfortunately, there is no way of estimating quantities consumed from the presence of a few seeds or nuts.

An example is the consumption of wild rice (*Zizania aquatica*) by prehistorics in the western Great Lakes region. Preserved rice grains were found in and around threshing pits and cooking fires in prehistoric sites (Johnson 1969). How much rice was eaten?

Coprolites

These are fossil excrement. When properly analyzed it is possible to ascertain what the person had eaten. Much has been learned from analyses of coprolites found in such places as Hogup and Danger caves (Mehringer 1986). All we can learn, however, is what had been eaten the day or two before the excrement. Only if a number of coprolites extending over a considerable time period are examined, may we begin to get an overall picture. It is probably impossible to reconstruct an entire diet over the course of a year or longer, on this basis. Since many foods are available only seasonally, the findings based on an analysis of one coprolite may depend on the season it was formed.

Heizer and Napton (1969) present considerable information about what can be learned from coprolites. The authors comment on Danger Cave:

> Coprolitic and archaeological evidence from Danger Cave is interpreted as indicating that the subsistence pattern based on exploitation of foods secured from the arid desert biome persisted without significant change for some 10,000 years. (pp. 564–565)

This conclusion was reached after examination of 43 coprolites extending from the ninth millennium B.C. to about 1800 A.D. Question: What else could people

---

[3] Sometimes well-preserved plant remains are found in packrat holes. These remains may indicate changes in vegetation and/or climate over thousands of years. See Betancourt and Van Devender (1981).

have eaten except what nature provided? If the environment remained mostly unchanged over 10,000 years, so would the wild foods served by Mother Nature.

Further, coprolites can provide information on the presence or absence of endoparasites (parasites that live in the internal organs or tissues of the host) and perhaps other aspects of diet sufficiency or diseases.

Bones

Because bones and teeth are the prime survivors of all fauna, large quantities of bones are found in many archaeological sites and are reported in the literature. And the bigger and stronger the bones and teeth are, the more likely are they to survive for millennia. The purpose of studying bones is to estimate the amounts and kinds of animal, fish, or fowl meat actually consumed, from the bones dug from a site.

Some questions: (1) How do we know that the bones indicate type and quantity of meat actually consumed? Perhaps some of the animals were hunted (or scavenged) for industrial uses, for example, skins and furs for making clothing, antlers and bones to be made into tools, and so forth. (2) Were all of the bones found the product of the Ancients' butchering activities as indicated by cutmarks? Or were some of the bones despite their apparent cutmarks the result of natural processes unaided by the human hand (Lewin 1984)?

Let us assume that all of the bones found in a site truly result from butchering for food consumption. We now have another series of problems. It is known that bones are greatly modified between the moment the animal died and the moment the archaeologist dug up the bones. (This study of fossil deposition and change is named taphonomy, meaning laws of entombment.) Gilbert and Singer (1982) list the elements that may be involved in such modification and comment that the quantification formulas currently used by zooarchaeologists (archaeologists who study ancient animal remains) are based on the assumption that the bones recovered are a proper sample of what the Ancients ate. But what the zooarchaeologists find is not necessarily a proper sample of the animals raised or hunted and eaten. Between the hunting (the beginning) and the bones found in the dig (the end) are several possible distortions. Some animals have more durable skeletons so more of their bones survive. Other animals may be hunted or raised only for ritualistic or ceremonial purposes and were not part of the regular food supply. If a large animal is killed far from camp, it may be butchered on the spot and only choice cuts of meat carried to camp and eaten; no bones are evident for the zooarchaeologist to study.

While being buried for centuries or millennia, bones may be disturbed by burrowing animals or soil conditions. Or subsequent to the deposition of the bones, later human inhabitants may disturb the site. Modern agriculture and earth-moving equipment may further distort the remaining bones by smashing them or moving them away from the area of the dig. The final result is that the zooarchaeologist may have only approximate knowledge of what animals were actually eaten.

Milisauskas (1978, pp. 61–62) illustrates some of the problems in estimating amount of meat consumed from the surviving bones, on the basis of Early Neolithic experiences in Europe. Should all animal bones found at a site be counted by type of animal, or should an attempt be made to estimate by type, the minimum number of animals involved? The numbers and distribution are very different. Further, a bovine (or auroch) may furnish 10 times as much meat as a sheep. So how many kilograms of meat were available? There are also differences in the numbers of calories obtainable from various types. A kilo of sheep or goat meat furnishes about 1,500 calories, beef 2,000, and pork about 3,700. Does anyone know how many calories there were in a kilo of mammoth meat? Milisauskas adds: "Different approaches to interpreting animal remains can be used in various ways to support one's favorite hypothesis" (p. 62).

Combine this indefiniteness in amount of meat available with no or little knowledge of amount and type of vegetable matter consumed, and what do we know?

Shellfish Middens

Shellfish, where available, are a nutritious food because they are rich in protein (Erlandson 1988). There is variation among the many types of shellfish, and perhaps in the season of the year, at least in some if not all environments. Nevertheless, overall, shellfish can provide as much protein as deer meat, for example. Further, molluscs are easily obtained. Reportedly, the minimum requirement of 40 grams per person per day can be gathered in minutes, even by novice shellfish hunters.

The shells of molluscs are similar to mammal bones in that they can survive for thousands of years. Great piles of such discarded shells together with fishbones and other debris tell us that people had eaten large quantities of these items. In Denmark, for example, one kitchen midden was about 150 meters (500 feet) long and up to 2 meters (7 feet) deep (*Prehistoric Denmark,* 1970). To determine how important a part of their diet these shellfish constituted, we must know how long it took to accumulate this vast pile, how may people were involved in accomplishing this feat, and what other foods were eaten. All that we know is that these prehistoric Danes ate considerable quantities of shellfish.

Along the coast of southern California and Baja California there are many shell middens. Ancient Amerindians and Danes both gorged themselves on molluscs. Analysis of these middens by Shumway, Hubbs, and Moriarty (1961) led to the following conclusion:

> A study of the food remains in the Scripps Estates Site has provided a basis for several
> inferences regarding the environment and culture as well as the food habits of the

aboriginal population. . . . The type of molluscs eaten, the abundance of tools for grinding plant food, and the great scarcity of vertebrate remains all indicate a simple food-gathering culture, with little or no hunting for larger animals, either on land or the high seas. Some of the fish remains . . . suggest however that boats or rafts were used. (p. 97)

Again we know what items were eaten but not the amount of each type nor the nutritional value of the entire diet. Shell middens are found all over the world where shellfish can be had.

Other Clues to Diet

Analyses of the stomachs of mummies have provided some information. Unfortunately, too few mummies have had the contents of their stomach analyzed. Also, interpretation of diet, that is, inferring diet from contents, is similar to that of coprolites; the contents reveal only what had been eaten recently.

A more esoteric approach involves analyzing the isotopes[4] found in collagen in skeletal remains. Lewin (1983, p. 1369) explains: "The ^{15}N isotope of nitrogen becomes concentrated as it passes up through the food chain." Marine plants have higher concentrations of this isotope than do land plants; hence it is possible to distinguish between people who fed on marine food sources versus those who fed on terrestrial food sources (Schoeninger *et al.* 1983).

Use of the isotope ratio of carbon $^{13}C/^{12}C$ (instead of nitrogen) obtained from skeletal remains provides information about the types of plants consumed (Ericson *et al.* 1981).

Several investigators have shown that the $^{13}C/^{12}C$ ratio of bone collagen reflects that of the diet. The demonstration that the measured carbon isotope ratios conform to expected values of diet in Pliocene mammals opens up a number of possible applications to paleodietary investigations . . . . The technique may be applicable to problems in reconstructing dietary patterns of primates including hominids. (pp. 70–71)

Lewin notes that combining nitrogen and carbon isotope analysis, "a powerful new tool emerges." Problems in applying and interpreting isotope analysis remain.

Another development is a process for identifying blood residues found on prehistoric stone tools. Loy (1983) examined 104 lithic tools between 1,000 and 6,000 years of age from North American sites. He reports having identified human, caribou, Stone Mountain sheep, grizzly bear, snowshoe rabbit, and the like. Perhaps the Ancestors ate well.

---

[4] Dictionary definition: Any of two or more species of atoms of a chemical element with the same atomic number and position in the periodic table and nearly identical chemical behavior, but with differing atomic mass or mass number and different physical properties.

WAS THE FOOD SUFFICIENT AND NUTRITIOUS?

The Brothwells (1969) discuss several aspects of dietary deficiency that we can assume, bothered, or plagued, the Ancients. The authors believe that we shall never be able to measure accurately the amounts of various foods consumed by earlier populations. Nevertheless, some knowledge of the adequacy of the foods eaten can be gained by noting the marks left by food-deficiency diseases on human remains (p. 175). They then list the following categories that we discuss briefly.

Famine Periods

We know that famines occurred in prehistoric times even though we do not know how serious or frequent they may have been. The Biblical 7 fat years and 7 lean years indicate famine. One indication on skeletal remains is the presence of Harris's lines (also known as Milkman's lines and Looser's zones) that result from poor or insufficient nutrition. Zivanovic (1982) describes them as lines that appear on the long bones because of a halt in bone growth during the normal period of growth or because of very poor nutrition that led to stunted growth. When the physical well-being of the person improves, growth continues, leaving a line on the long bone. Many skeletal remains show these Harris lines (see, e.g., Buikstra 1981).

The habits or customs of a people also can indicate that there are, or were, times of insufficient food. For example, Catlin (1984)[5] describes the Buffalo Dance among the Mandan. Buffalo meat was a substantial part of their diet; exactly how much is not known. But buffalo come and go, and sometimes they did not appear where the Mandan could hunt them. The Mandan then began their Buffalo Dance. This involved continuous 24-hour dancing, day after day, until the buffalo appeared. According to Catlin, they believed that their dancing attracted the animals.

Another indication of lack of food at one time or another is the food preservation techniques that evolved (or were invented). There is seasonal variation in the amount available as well as fluctuations from year to year in the size of the crop, animal, or vegetable. Fowler (1986, p. 65) cites the case of wild piñon seeds, an important food in the Southwest United States. Methods were devised for storing the seeds for several years if necessary because the size of the harvest varied greatly from one year to another and could not be predicted.

Other examples of famine, or conditions conducive to famine, can be

---

[5] Although Catlin's (1844) observations were made in the mid-nineteenth century, this dance, or a similar one, probably was part of Mandan culture for untold generations.

presented. Because we cannot specify the frequency or severity of famine periods, however, we shall say no more.

Vitamins[6]

A sufficiently varied diet generally will prevent disabilities and diseases resulting from vitamin deficiencies. Although we know of some of the foods eaten by the Ancestors, we do not have a complete list, nor do we know the quantities consumed. Hence, we do not know just how varied their diets may have been and whether or not they suffered from vitamin deficiencies. Such deficiencies may show up in skeletal remains such as osteoporosis (as discussed below). But osteoporosis can result from several sources and is not specific to a vitamin deficiency. So, did they, or did they not, consume balanced and nutritious diets?

Vitamin A

This is found in animal fats and oils, and the human body can produce it from some fruits and vegetables and honey. Perhaps the most common manifestation of its lack is in night blindness, which does not show up in skeletal remains. Sometimes, however, a lack of Vitamin A

> leads to a suppression of all forms of growth in the epiphyseal cartilage of the bones. The process of remodelling the bones during growth is held back and that part of the bone which would normally be reabsorbed remains as compact bone. This leads to the accumulation of layers of bone along the inner surface of the vault of the skull and to the relative reduction of the cranial capacity. (Zivanovic 1982, p. 121)

Such a result of Vitamin A deficiency can be detected in the skull.

Vitamins of the B Complex

These are found in the outer layers of cereals and fresh meat. Lack of enough of these vitamins can lead to beriberi that may severely affect the nerves or heart. These deficiencies are, as a rule, associated with famines. In such an event, their effects may show up in the skeleton as Harris lines.

Vitamin C (Ascorbic Acid)

This is found in fresh fruits and vegetables, meat, and milk. A deficiency results in scurvy, whose effects can be seen in skeletal remains in the form of osteoporosis. Because this disorder can result from several sources, its presence does not necessarily mean that a deficiency of Vitamin C caused it.

Considering how widespread the sources of Vitamin C are, one might think

---

[6] The following comments are based on the Brothwells (1969) and Zivanovic (1982).

that all hunting and gathering people would have sufficient Vitamin C. But Zivanovic notes that scurvy may occur in areas where people had plenty of green plants to eat but did not know how to prepare the food properly. Simply chewing seeds, roots, and stalks will not necessarily provide this vitamin (pp. 120–121).

Vitamin D

This is present in fish liver oils and dairy foods, and the human body can manufacture it if exposed to enough sunlight. Absence of enough Vitamin D interferes with normal bone growth and may lead to dental problems and loss of teeth (Zivanovic 1982, p. 215).

Other Dietary Disorders

Iodine deficiency,[7] certain intestinal worms, improper infant feeding, naturally poisonous plants, and other natural substances such as insufficient iron can lead to disorders that may or may not be visible in archaeological remains.

An example of a poisonous plant is that of *Cycas circinelis L.* The incidence of amyotro lateral sclerosis (a degenerative fatal disease affecting the spinal cord, also known as Lou Gehrig's disease), Parkinson's disease, and Alzheimer-type dementia was unusually high among the Chamorro of the western Pacific islands of Guam and Rota. Spencer and his colleagues traced this to the eating of large quantities of seeds of the plant *Cycas.* With the Americanization of the Chamorro people after World War II, consumption of these seeds decreased considerably, and the frequency of these diseases reportedly also fell.

Summary

There are very many elements in the foods eaten or omitted from the diet, including insufficient food, which can cause health problems. To what extent they did so cannot always be determined because disorders found in skeletal remains may result from choice of diet or other causes such as infections.

Further, we may ask whether foods lose some of their values as a result of preservation. Consider, for example, pemmican. Dried meat was pounded by the Indians into shreds, mixed with animal fat and sometimes berries, and packed in skin or gut containers. So preserved, it could be kept and eaten over a number of months. Did it retain its full nutritional value all this time?

---

[7] An excellent discussion of the importance of iodine, and the consequences of a lack of it in the diet, is given by Greene 1980, Chapter 10.

ENTER AGRICULTURE—A SHORT NOTE

The first world-shaking invention of *Homo* was the shaping of stone into tools and weapons. With these he was able to conquer the world. Agriculture, or the domestication of wild plants, was the second world-shaking invention. When and how did it all begin?

B. Smith (1989) describes three phases of this transformation from wild to domestic: (a) plant domestication proper, (b) the rise and growth of food-producing economies, and (c) the shift largely to one-crop systems. All writers about the origin of agriculture do not necessarily keep these phases clearly in mind; as a result, the reader finds in the literature various dates for the beginning of agriculture or for specific crops, depending on what point on this continuum the writer chose to start.

Four localized centers of plant domestication are thought to exist: the Near East, North China, Mesoamerica, and eastern North America. In addition, three dispersed noncentral areas of domestication have been proposed: Africa, southeastern Asia, and South America. In each area including North America, the spread of agriculture was accompanied by vast changes in other aspects of life, we suspect. The rise and growth of sedentary societies, building of dams and irrigation works, large population increases, the rise of chieftainships and possibly stratified or class societies, plus an infinite number of other changes of all manner must have taken place. We do not claim that all parts of the original Amerindian cultures were drastically changed by agriculture, but only that enough changes occurred so that fifteenth-century societies were vastly different from those of the Paleo-Indians or their predecessors.

The need for food is biologically mandated. Exactly what foods are eaten and how they are procured, however, in large part are *Homo*-made, that is, culturally determined.

In the following pages we describe briefly the origin and growth of agriculture in eastern North America prior to the European invasion. Indeed, many bands and tribes were still hunters and gatherers at the end of the fifteenth century and some even in the twentieth. But we have not the facilities that would enable us to describe the agricultural history of all of North America.

What, How, and When Is Agriculture?

What?

Previously we wrote of hunting and gathering as somehow distinct from agriculture. This dichotomy was used for the sake of convenience because there is no sharp line of demarcation between the two forms of satisfying hunger. The dictionary defines agriculture thus: "The science or art of cultivating the soil, producing crops, and raising livestock." Those who write about hunters and gatherers define their subject in a negative way—that is, the absence of agriculture.

At some point in the history of "mankind" (and this depends on when one assumes that "mankind" began), *Homo* ate only what he found or caught. At some time in the history of modern people, *Homo sapiens sapiens,* agriculture appeared but not necessarily as a science. Its simplest manifestation was that of "producing crops," and this could have come about without any conscious intent on the part of the Ancestors to become farmers.

Perhaps this process is art rather than science; if so it fulfills two-thirds of the dictionary definition. The last part of the definition calls for "raising livestock." But there were no native animals that could be domesticated, except for the dog. And the dog was domesticated at some unknown time in the past.

Local wild plants may have been domesticated, or semidomesticated, in many localities in North America at various times in the past several millennia. We present Smith's examples of when the earliest domestication may have started in eastern North America in some detail; this includes the area west of the Allegheny Mountains to about Missouri, and south of central Ohio, Indiana, Illinois, and Missouri, to northern Georgia, Alabama, and Mississippi.

How It All Began

Smith, Mason, and others suggest that incipient domestication may have begun simply as a result of hunters and gatherers returning year after year to the same campsite. In so doing, they may have assisted plant development by inadvertently disturbing and enriching the soil. Differential harvesting, particularly concentration on plants bearing observable seeds, would assist in the promotion of one plant over another. One consequence of collecting such seeds was that some of them fell onto the ground around the campsites. Upon returning to the campsite some time later, some of these seeds had grown into new plants with new seeds. After repeating this cycle time after time, they had fields of this cultigen. In essence, this is the story of wild rice that grows in lakes. When it is collected, seeds fall back into the lake and produce next year's crop.

Eventually the people began to give active and intentional encouragement for certain food plants and to the storage and planting of seed stock. This is the stage that we may consider as the beginning of cultivation and when morphological changes associated with domestication can be detected by twentieth-century paleobotanists. This is the period that Smith refers to as a "3-millennium-long (about 5000 to 2000 B.C.) co-evolutionary process."

An alternative model for the origin of agriculture has been suggested by Sterud (1978). He notes that in some parts of Europe pastoralism preceded the raising of crops. Under certain environmental conditions, pastoralism may be a better risk-reducing economic strategy then growing plants. Obviously, in the absence of livestock and wild animals that could be domesticated, the Amerindians could not have used this strategy.

Yet another model, the simplistic or Ajax, suggests that women who presumably did the foraging for edible plants to appease the hunters' hunger attempted to reduce their work burden by raising the plants near their homes. Why walk several miles if it is not necessary?

Probably there are several reasons for the origin of agriculture. No single one can explain the origin in all parts of the world.

When Did It Begin?

Smith (1989) proposes a timetable as follows:

1. Originally there was a "3-millennium-long co-evolutionary process" about 5000 to 2000 B.C. (7,000 to 4,000 years ago, when human and plant processes interacted (p. 246)).
2. Between about 2000 and 1000 B.C., local species were brought under initial domestication.
3. Between about 250 B.C. and A.D. 200, food production economies began to appear, based on local crop plants.
4. Finally, between A.D. 800 and 1100 maize, originally an import from south of the Rio Grande, came to dominate the fields and diets of the eastern North American farming groups.

This time schedule suggests that incipient domestication in eastern North America may have begun some six to seven millennia before the arrival of Columbus.

Further north around the Great Lakes, domestication of indigenous wild plants and the cultivation of imports from other regions may have begun somewhat later, according to Mason (1981). In other parts of North America, agriculture may have started earlier or later then in eastern North America. It all depended on what local wild plants were available, on local climate and soils, and the nature of contacts with other people of North America and those south of the Rio Grande where there were independent centers of plant domestication.

What Plants Were Domesticated?

Gourds (*Cucurbita*) were probably one of the earliest plants to be cultivated. Whether they were valued more for their food or the shells to serve as pots and containers can be argued. Plants of the goosefoot family (*Chenopodium berlandiera*) were also cultivated; this is a wild green. Sunflowers (*Helianthus annuus*) were grown, most probably for their seeds. Marsh elder *(Iva annua)* is another plant that was cultivated early.

In addition, there were three other cultivated seed crops in eastern North America, although Smith states that a convincing case for domestication still remains to be made. They are erect knotweed, a herb *(Polygonum erectum)*; maygrass, a variety of grass *(Phalaris caroliniana)*; and the grain, little barley *(Hordeum pusillum)*. These three crops plus the four mentioned above formed the bases of premaize agriculture.

Enter Maize

Maize, or corn, has the best documented history of all Western Hemisphere cultigens; let us try to trace it from its original home in Mexico.[8] This cereal has been consumed for uncounted millennia; its wild forms were eaten long before domestication began. We shall never know the precise year in which the process of domestication began, but there is reasonable agreement that it could have been a date approaching 10,000 years B.P. We know that maize was modified very considerably in the course of its domestication. The original wild cob was tiny, perhaps as large as a human thumbnail. The modern cob may be 8 inches or more in length. The wild maize was self-seeding; the modern maize must be sown by *Homo*. Other features of the plant also were changed in the process of domestication. Clearly, at the very earliest stages of domestication, it is difficult to distinguish between the wild form and the first steps in domestication because change takes place very slowly; several millennia were required by the Ancients.

The Brothwells (1969) believe that cultivation must have begun some 9,000 years ago. They refer to the "early use and sowing of wild maize in the El Riego Phase (around 7200 to 5200 B.C.)." The true cultivation proceeded during the Coxcatlan Phase (5200 to 3400 B.C.) The equivalent of 7200 B.C. is about 9000 B.P. (p. 204).

Mangelsdorf (1964) dated an early variety of maize to about 7,000 years ago; the start of domestication must have begun significantly earlier. Perhaps a millennium or more was required before the wild plant had been changed sufficiently so as to be recognizable as on the road to domestication.

---

[8] Both the Mexicans and Peruvians claim to have domesticated this cultigen; perhaps both did. Also, maize was grown in the Amazon area (Roosevelt 1980). Because most of the Ancients who settled on the Caribbean islands came from northern South America, and some from Florida (Rouse 1963), there is the possibility that corn entered Florida and then spread northward in the eastern United States and Canada. This South America–Caribbean–Florida route is doubtful in comparison with the routes leading out of Mexico. One reason for selecting the southwest United States as port of entry is that it is within walking distance of Mexico, the origin, or one of the origins.

Several varieties of fully domesticated corn reached the U.S. Southwest perhaps 5,000 years ago (Woodbury and Zubrow 1979). From there maize slowly traveled east and north (Figure 6.1). It may have reached the northeastern states about 2,500 years ago (Whitehead 1965), sometime prior to 1000 B.C. About the same time it may have reached Ohio (Murphy 1971). Maize finally reached southern Ontario, about its northern limit, "prior to A.D. 900" (Tuck 1981). Other cultigens may have required more or less time than the 8,000 years or so of the travels of maize.

Wills (1988) suggests that maize was introduced into the U.S. Southwest between 3,000 and 3,500 years ago; this is 1,500 to 2,000 years later than Woodbury and Zubrow suggest. For our purposes the correct date of introduction from Mexico into the Southwest, if ascertainable, makes little difference. However, as statisticians our first reaction is to ask about the accuracy of the measures of time. This topic was reviewed briefly in Chapter 2—how time of arrival in the Western Hemisphere is estimated—where we discussed the earliest site-dating methods, in particular carbon-14, and noted that different time-measuring procedures produced different dates.

Since maize was first domesticated in Mexico, we suppose that it then crossed what is today the Mexican–U.S. border on its way north. If this border was crossed 3,000 years ago, could maize have reached the northeastern states about 2,500 years ago, and then southern Ontario perhaps 1,000 years ago? In short, are Wills's revised estimates consistent with the time estimates for other areas north of Mexico? We can only raise the question; we cannot answer it.

Why did maize require some eight millennia or more between the first attempts at domestication in Mexico and its final entry into southern Canada? Why did it require perhaps 3,000 years to travel from the Southwest United States to southern Canada? There are several reasons, some of which may be unique to maize and some of which may apply to all cultigens. A general reason is the need to develop a wide variety of any given cultigen. Some varieties will produce bigger and better crops in one locality, and other varieties will do better in other environments. Much time may be required to make these regional adaptations.

Maize, as do some other plants, has an additional handicap—nutritional limitations. Katz et al. (1974) state: "Unless corn is prepared by specific techniques, its nutritional value as a dietary source is at best marginal." Any people who ate it as a major part of their diet, and in the absence of proper preparation, would be malnourished. Alkali processing is the most commonly used technique. An alternative is the supplementation of corn by other foods that are rich in essential amino acids, such as beans. All societies that became dependent upon corn learned the proper processing techniques or acquired supplemental crops.

When maize growing was first introduced into a new area, neither the

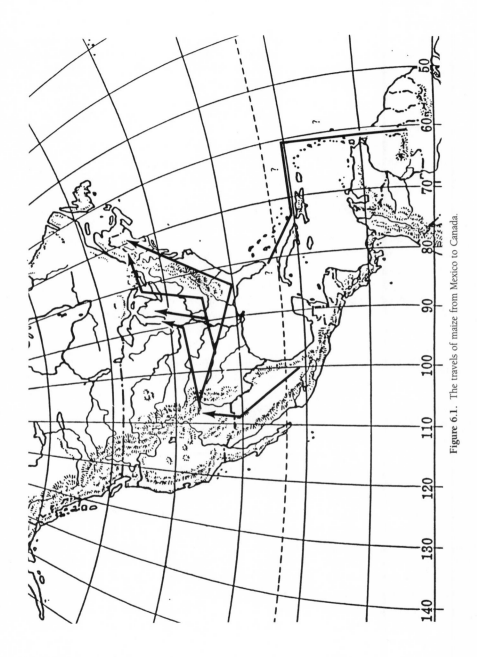

Figure 6.1. The travels of maize from Mexico to Canada.

proper processing techniques nor the needed supplemental crops always accompanied the corn. Sometimes centuries were required to bring these diverse ingredients together, after which maize became an important food item. In the Southwest, it may have required some 1,500 years between the introduction of the corn plant and the time when it became an important item in the diet.

Summary

Agriculture in the Western Hemisphere may have begun almost as early as in the Eastern Hemisphere. But perhaps it took longer in the New World before it displaced hunting and gathering as the main source of food production. Indeed, perhaps half of the Amerindian population were yet hunters, fishermen, and gatherers when the Europeans landed in 1492.

The growth of agriculture was accompanied by growth in population (as we shall see) and vast changes in all aspects of life.

POPULATION GROWTH AND AGRICULTURE

Agriculture permitted a population "explosion." There are probably 1,000 times or more people in the world at the end of the twentieth century as there were 10,000 years ago when cultivation may first have started. And the world's population is still increasing in numbers (United Nations 1973, p. 10).[9]

As for the North American Indians, we have no solid information regarding how much population increase resulted from the introduction and spread of agriculture. The bits of information available suggest that the population increased more rapidly as agriculture became more widespread. We saw previously that the Amerindians who had agriculture had a longer length of life than did those who remained strictly hunters and gatherers (Chapter 4). This increase could have, and probably did, add to the growth of population.

Mason (1981), for example, in writing about the Great Lakes region during the Archaic–Woodland transition (1500 to 100 B.C.) when plant domestication began in this area, emphasized "the accelerating upward population curve." He then commented on the Late Woodland culture (five or more centuries before the arrival of Columbus, p. 297): "The increase in the number of Late Woodland burials, cemeteries, and camp and village locations was due to a growing population." This increasing population depended more and more on agricul-

---

[9] It is estimated that there were between 5 and 10 million people in the entire world 10,000 years ago. By the end of the twentieth century there will be over 6 billion people, assuming that there is no natural or *Homo*-made catastrophe.

ture. "Especially after about A.D. 1000 native agriculture's contribution" to the food supply was greater than ever.

Schwartz (1983) writes in similar fashion about the Havasupai in Arizona. A quite small population first appeared south of the Grand Canyon about A.D. 600. This population is estimated to have tripled by A.D. 800 and doubled again by A.D. 900, "probably resulting from a successful adaptation to an agricultural economy." Note that a sixfold increase in 300 years implies an average annual growth of less than one-half percent per year. This is a very modest rate by twentieth-century experiences of world population growth, which is estimated to be a little under 2% per year.

We can continue presenting testimonials for various parts of Canada and the United States, but by themselves they are not conclusive evidence. To begin, we do not know how much of this increase in any specific area was due to immigrants from other tribes rather than simply the excess of births over deaths. Furthermore, all estimated population sizes when determined from archaeological remains are very uncertain, as described by Frazier about Chaco Canyon (Chapter 8). Nevertheless, these bits and pieces when considered with our estimate of increased length of life among the agriculturalists leads us to believe that there is a good probability of increases in the rate of population growth accompanying agriculture. To present a precise measure we need population counts—censuses—over these many millennia. Such counts are not to be had.

SPIRITUOUS IMBIBITIONS AND TOBACCO

No meal is complete without a drink and a smoke according to Ajax de Smyrna, and many of the Ancients held to this opinion. Alcoholic beverages were produced and consumed largely in conjunction with agriculture, although in some instances these beverages were produced from wild substances. The hunters and gatherers presumably had but little beer or wine. Because wild sources of sugar were not available in large quantities it is thought that honey beer (mead) (if distilled it becomes mead brandy), because of the scarcity of wild honey, was reserved for "important" people—the caciques, the chiefs, and/or the medicine man.

Tobacco was used throughout North and South America where it could be grown or imported. In North America, it may not have reached the cold north and parts of the Northwest Coast until historic times.

Alcoholic Beverages

It is thought that most, if not all, of the beers and wines originated south of the Rio Grande and migrated northward with agriculture. These Ancients did not know of distillation so they produced no hard liquor. Sugar in one form or another, water, and the proper micro-organisms plus a jug to hold the liquid were all that were required. Berries, honey, *agave* (the maguey plant), maize, and many other plants contain the necessary sugars. The micro-organisms float in the air and are available to all. In the case of maize, one of the processes consisted of people first chewing the grains; the enzymes in the saliva started the fermentation.

Cactus and cactuslike plants were and are now used in the Southwest United States. Included are agave (a member of the amaryllis family), dasylirion (*sotol*, a member of the lily family), and various forms of the cacti family. Their saps ferment, and pulque or a similar beer containing 3% to 4% alcohol results. Mescal and tequila are produced by distilling this beer. Pulque reportedly contains vitamins B_1 and C.

Maize beer, or chicha, may have crossed the Rio Grande northward but was never as widespread in the Southwest as in Mexico and Central America. This contains 4% to 5% alcohol, about the same as most modern beers.

Mesquite and screwbean (a close relative of mesquite) also were used for producing a slightly alcoholic beverage, just north of the Mexican border.

In the Southwest United States persimmons were used for making a kind of beer. Whether other fruits and maize were also used in the Southwest or elsewhere in the United States and Canada is uncertain.

With the advent of distilled liquors and modern-type beers, these prehistoric drinks decreased in importance. Having drunk both pulque and chicha, we can attest that the two taste like soda pop in comparison with the "real thing."

Tobacco[10]

The growing and use of tobacco (a relative of the potato and eggplant) was and still is widespread. In prehistoric times *Nicotina rustica* spread to the limits of agriculture, south to Chiloe Island off the coast of Chile (latitude about 43 degrees south) and north to New Brunswick. It is believed to have originated south of the Rio Grande and accompanied maize in the latter's wanderings.

Tobacco was burned in three forms: cigars made by rolling leaves into a shape similar to that of today, cigarettes made by stuffing tubes of reeds or cane with tobacco, and in pipes. One variation of a pipe (if it may be called that) consisted of a tube open at both ends; one end was placed near burning tobacco and the other end in the mouth or nostril and the smoke inhaled. Sometimes a Y-shaped pipe was used. The main stem was held in the smoke and the two arms

---

[10] See Driver and Massey (1957); also Robicsak (1978). For detailed descriptions of the Amerindian use of tobacco as witnessed by the first European explorers, see Fairholt (1976, Chapters 1 and 2).

were fitted into the nostrils. The same type of Y-shaped device was used for snuffing tobacco from a cup at the end of the main stem (Spinden 1950; Wassen 1965). Sometimes, instead of burning, tobacco was chewed or snuffed. Among the Maya and Aztec the fashionable afterdinner smoke was a cigar.

To what extent north of the Rio Grande tobacco was used for social or recreational purposes is uncertain. Smoking pipes was the most common form. The major uses appear to have been ceremonial, as in "smoking the peace pipe," and probably medicinal. If little social smoking was indulged in, we suspect that it was because the smoke was too harsh to be enjoyable. Such harshness could come from the particular tobacco variety smoked and from the way the green tobacco was cured. Stuffing a leaf with dried tobacco leaves would not produce what we would consider an agreeable smoke.

The pipe that was in extensive use in Canada and the United States also produced a harsh smoke. Most bowls were made of stone or clay; as a result, when smoked they became very hot and the smoke very harsh. We can testify to this. To cool the smoke somewhat, very long reed or wood stems were used. Filtering the smoke through water, as in the Near East hookah, also cools smoke, but there is no evidence that the Amerindians used this device.

NUTRITION AND THE BIRTHRATE

Does malnutrition lead to a lower birthrate? Or more precisely, does malnutrition affect fecundity, the reproductive capacity, so as to reduce the birthrate, the actual reproduction? There is considerable argument and debate concerning the answer.

On the surface it would seem logical that malnutrition would contribute to a lower birthrate. It is known that during periods of famine or soon thereafter, the birthrate may fall (Bongaarts 1980). Also known is that poorly fed girls who have too little body fat reach menarche at a somewhat later age (Green and Johnston 1980, p. 123). Further, those who have delayed menarche also have a somewhat earlier menopause. The result is that the reproductive period is shortened.

The major difficulty in trying to answer our first question is that too many factors contribute to the actual and measurable birthrate. Malnutrition, if it occurs, is but one element in dozens. Age at marriage, urban or rural residence, amount of education, and innumerable other cultural elements influence the actual birthrate. How does one disentangle them and measure the influence of each factor? In a real-life situation, this cannot be done because so many of the factors involved cannot be measured. However, even if this untangling could be done, we believe that the level of nutrition *per se* would have but little influence. Except in the case of extended famines.

SUMMARY

As did all ancient peoples, the prehistoric Amerindian hunters and gatherers ate whatever nature provided, such as seeds, nuts, wild plants, shellfish, animals, and the like. Sometimes their diet was nutritious, other times not so. No blanket statements can be made. Nature also provides abundant poisons in some plants. In many instances, the Ancestors learned how to eliminate these poisons; how many died in the learning process we shall never know.

The domestication of maize, beans, sunflowers, and other wild plants extended their food supply. Many millennia were required before these cultigens reached all parts of North America where they could grow, mainly Southwest United States and the lands east of the Mississippi River, and southeastern Canada just north of the U.S. border. For meat, however, they had to continue hunting wild animals and fishing. There were no native animals that could be domesticated as there were in the Eastern Hemisphere. The dog was the only domestic animal, and it did not provide much meat.

Accompanying agriculture were alcoholic beverages. Beers and wines made from corn and cactus or cactuslike plants became available, especially in the Southwest. Tobacco also accompanied the edible cultigens, and the "peace pipe" became famous north of the Rio Grande.

Part II

What Columbus Had Wrought: The Period from 1492 to the 1980s

Chapter 7

How Many?

INTRODUCTION

We shall never know for certain how many people lived in what are now the United States and Canada, at any time before the late nineteenth century. We do not know how many were here when Leif Ericson reached Newfoundland in the eleventh century, nor in October 1492 when Columbus first landed. We can only speculate. The native people of these two countries were never counted in a national census prior to the latter part of the nineteenth century.

In the twentieth century we know approximately how many self-chosen descendants of these original natives there may be, if we can ever agree on a definition of Amerindian that is consistent over time. What we have are estimates of the size of a population that, from one time to another, has been viewed and counted inconsistently by the larger, dominant European-origin society. Further, the Indians themselves have been changing over time, both biologically and in their own views of themselves, their self-identification.

An American Indian is not necessarily forever an American Indian. The twentieth-century people are not identical to those of the fifteenth century. At the time of arrival of Columbus, the Amerindians were obviously different in physical appearance and in way of life from the European and African invaders. Over the following five centuries so much intermingling of Amerindian and Eastern Hemisphere blood and ways of life have occurred that we wonder about the comparability of the native populations in these two time periods. In Appendixes 5, 6, and 7, we discuss further the implications of such changes for ascertaining numbers. As Ajax de Smyrna said, "Give me a definition and I shall give you a number."

We have only an assortment of numbers for the population in 1500 and only approximations in the late twentieth century. We present these numbers

103

gleaned from the literature and census counts so that the reader may select his/her preference. Just remember that none of these can be proven to be uniquely correct. Demographers have devised tests for ascertaining the accuracy of census counts of the total population. From these tests, we have reason to believe that the census count of the total population of the United States and Canada probably is accurate to within 2 or 3%. We have no tests for minority groups such as the Amerindians.

We estimate numbers to be about as follows for Canada and the United States, excluding Inuits and Aleuts:

A.D. 1600	1,200,000
Nadir, A.D. 1920	400,000
A.D. 1980–81	1,500,000

Ubelaker (1988) provides three estimates for 1500 (this seems to be the date):

Minimum	1,200,000
His best estimate	1,900,000
Maximum	2,600,000

The nadir, or lowest point, he places between 1900 and 1925, when he estimates that there were between 500,000 and 600,000.

As of 1980–81 he provides several numbers that apparently add to a total of about 1,700,000.

We can continue to play this numbers game indefinitely, but in our opinion the game is not worth playing. What we feel is more important is a better understanding of when and where the Amerindians were displaced by the Eastern Hemisphere people. And to the extent possible, why such displacement occurred when it did.

But first a word about the relevancy of geography to population growth over the last 500 years.

The climate of North America, going from south to the North Pole, gradually becomes colder and the land less suitable for agriculture. People must eat to survive, and agriculture can support a higher population density than can hunting and foraging. There are limited areas, of course, for example, the Pacific coast of Canada and the United States where fish and other sea creatures are sufficiently abundant so that they provided a steady and dependable food supply in pre-Columbian times. But such areas were the exception.

There are about 3 million square miles of land in Canada and the same in the United States (excluding the Arctic and sub-Arctic areas of Canada and Alaska, where climatic conditions are unfavorable for agriculture). In Canada, the area suitable for cultivation extends only a relatively short distance north of the Canadian–United States boundary. As a result, the area in farms[1] (1986) amounts to 8 or 9% of the 3 million square miles. In the United States, by contrast, farmland constitutes about half of the total land surface (see Chapter 1).

The amount of land actually under cultivation or used for crops (1981) is about 4% in Canada, and about 20% in the United States (Figure 7.1).

Clearly, the amount of cultivable land in the United States is four or five times as great as in Canada. The number of Amerindians in the United States at the time of the first European arrival was four or five times as great as in Canada. Coincidence?

Amerindian population growth after the European invasion was also influenced by these geographic considerations. The Europeans who settled south of the St. Lawrence River and Great Lakes wanted land for farming. They had to get rid of the Indians and killed many, either by warfare or by introducing new disease thus reducing the native population in what is now the United States. In Canada the settlers were less concerned with driving out or otherwise ridding themselves of the Indians because the latter were occupying but little farmland. What little they were occupying the settlers appropriated, of course. However, because the Indians were needed for the fur trade, they were not decimated to the extent that occurred south of the border.

THE UNITED STATES

The First 500 Years: A Short Synopsis

The pattern of change in the numbers of Amerindians in the area now comprising the United States (see Figure 7.2 and Table 7.1) is that of a relatively slow decline during the seventeenth century, and then an increasingly more rapid decline until about the fourth quarter of the nineteenth century. The decline stopped around the turn of the twentieth century. Then the numbers increased slowly to the time of about World War II, and then very rapidly after that war, according to the U.S. census statistics.

Precisely how many Amerindians there are in the 1980s, however, is a matter of definition. The 1980 census requested self-identification, and about 1.4 million people identified themselves as American Indians. However, other possible definitions produce numbers as low as 351,000 (see Appendix 7). For the purpose of describing the general changes over the last 400 years, we

---

[1] Information for Canada from *Britannica World Data, 1989 Book of the Year* and the *1981 Census of Agriculture,* Catalogue 96901, Table 1. Information for the United States from 1989 *Statistical Abstract,* Tables 1,078 and 1,112. These sources are reasonably comparable for the two countries, although possible differences in counting and measuring procedures may have increased or decreased the "true" numbers.

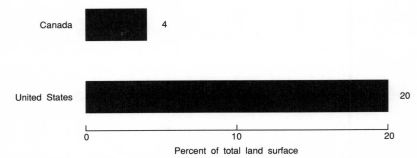

Canada   4

United States   20

0   10   20

Percent of total land surface

Figure 7.1. Land used for crops as percentage of total land surface: Canada and the United States (see footnote 1).

simply use the decennial census numbers when available, plus estimates made by others or ourselves.

Nevertheless, we have reason to believe that the 1980 census number is not comparable to previous census counts (as we explain in a later section dealing with the 1980 census). Briefly, we estimate that there were abut 1 million persons comparable to the number reported in 1970, and some 400,000 or so "new additions."

The Settlers Advance Westward: 1492 to 1850

1492 to 1600

Within a very few years after Columbus's first landing in 1492, Spanish soldiers invaded Florida from their bases in Cuba and Puerto Rico, and the present United States Southwest from New Spain, now Mexico.[2] St. Augustine, Florida, was settled in 1565; De Soto fought his way through what were to be the states of Mississippi and Louisiana in the 1540s and founded or tried to establish several settlements. Before the end of the sixteenth century, the Spaniards founded what ultimately became Sante Fe, New Mexico. The Spaniards were seeking gold.

The French entered the area that now comprises the states stretching from Florida to Louisiana, contesting the Spanish. At the same time, the French sailed up to the St. Lawrence River, founded Montreal and other Canadian colonies, and explored what is now the northeastern United States and the Mississippi River area in pursuit of furs. Adventurers from other European

---

[2] There is a voluminous history of Spanish activities, too large to detail here; see Chavez (1973), Kessel (1979), Clissold (1962), and Day (1964) as starters, plus the *Columbia Encyclopedia*.

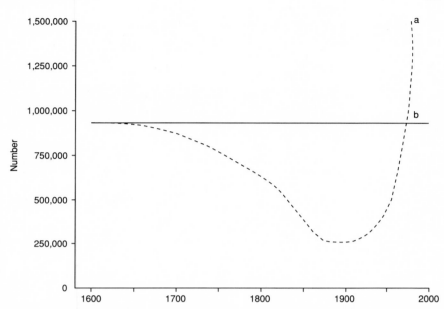

Figure 7.2. Estimated numbers of American Indians in the U.S. territory from 1600 to 1980. At point a, the total as reported by the 1980 Census; at point b, the definition is comparable (more or less) to that of the 1970 Census. See Table 7.1.

countries landed along the Gulf of Mexico and Atlantic seaboards and tried to found settlements.

The number of these traders, adventurers, and protosettlers before 1600 was small compared to the number in the English and other North European settlements and colonies that developed after 1600. Nevertheless, the French and Spanish had some impact on the Amerindian population insofar as early arrivals fought and killed Indians, instigated intertribal warfare over the fur trade, and contributed to the spread of deadly European diseases among the natives. Whether syphilis is one of these diseases is still being argued. Was it introduced into the Western Hemisphere from the Eastern, or vice versa? Several writers have commented that its origin is unknown. Zivanovic (1982) writes that it cannot be detected with certainty from skeletal remains because several diseases besides syphilis leave similar telltale signs.

1600 to 1820

At the beginning of the seventeenth century there were perhaps 1 million Indians and probably fewer than 5,000 people of European or African origin. By 1820 we estimate that there were only about 620,000 indians. By 1820 there

Table 7.1. Estimated Number of Amerindians in the U.S.: 1600 to 1980 (in Thousands)

			Mississippi River					
		Percent change per year	*Numbers*[c]		*Percent distribution*		*Percent change per year*	
	Numbers		*East*	*West*	*East*	*West*	*East*	*West*
1600	1,000	—	320	680	32	68	—	—
1820	620	−.2	120	500	19	81	−.4	−.1
1850	450	−1.1	40	410	9	91	−3.5	−.7
1870	330	−1.6	30	300	9	91	−1.4	−1.6
1890	270	−1.0	30	240	12	88	0	−1.1
1920	270	0	40	230	16	84	+1.0	−.1
1950	360	+1.0	50	310	14	86	+.8	+1.5
1960	520	+4.3	110	410	20	80	+7.2	+2.8
1970	750	+3.7	170	580	23	77	+4.5	+3.5
1980	1,480[a]	+7.0	380	1,100	26	74	+8.9	+6.6
	1,000[b]	+3.0						

[a]Total reported by 1980 Census.
[b]Definition approximately comparable to that of 1970 Census.
[c]East or west of Mississippi River.

were close to 10 million of European and African origin in the area comprising the present—1980—territory of the United States.

The Amerindian population had decreased at a rate of two-tenths of 1% per year. The invaders had increased at a rate too rapid to calculate. Significantly, the rapidity of change for both groups was different east of the Mississippi River as compared to that west of the river, as we discuss later.

During this period, trade with the Indians for furs and hides was important (Viola 1974, p. 9). But the number engaged in the fur trade constituted but a very small portion of all non-Indian workers. In 1820, out of close to 3 million gainful workers, over 2 million were reported to be in agriculture and close to 400,000 were in manufacturing and construction.[3] Clearly, good farmland was more attractive to the settlers than were fur-bearing animals.

East of the Mississippi River. About 320,000, or one in three, of all Indians lived in the east in 1600. By 1820 there were only an estimated 120,000 Amerindians east of the river. By 1820 there were around 9½ million non-Indians, whites, and blacks in the east. Obviously the east was not large enough to hold the natives and invaders (Figure 7.3).

During these 220 years—1600 to 1820—the eastern Indians lost population at a rate of some four-tenths of 1% per year, much more rapidly than west of the river. Let us review briefly the reasons for this decline.

[3]U.S. Bureau of the Census, *Historical Statistics of the United States . . . to 1957*, Table series D 57-71.

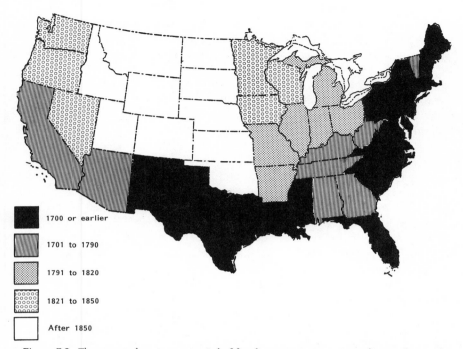

Figure 7.3. The westward movement, period of first known count or estimate for population of non-Amerindian origin: United States.

First to succumb were those natives living along the Atlantic and Gulf coasts because they were the first to have been in contact with the Europeans. Further, they occupied much territory that the colonists considered to be good farmland. As the colonists moved west, they came into contact with more Indians.[4] As a result, the eastern natives moved or were forced to move westward. By 1820 all of the states east of the river except Wisconsin had substantial numbers of settlers, and more were pouring in daily (Figure 7.2). The settlers wanted the land, and every effort was made to induce, or force, the Indians to move, first to Arkansas and then to Oklahoma, the last stop in Indian territory. In addition, the settlers used European-type diseases in lieu of Hitler's "modern" death factories to kill as many natives as possible.

Fighting among Indian tribes had always existed and may have contributed to the decrease in numbers. Intertribal fighting may have increased when the Indians discovered that the fur trade with the whites was a lucrative business.

---

[4] This literature is voluminous. For quick overviews see, for example, Ganteaume (1986) and Viola (1974), especially Chapter 11.

Furthermore, by concentrating on fur and skin hunting and trading for the white man's goods, they became more dependent on whites for life's necessities. In particular, guns, ammunition, and whiskey—the three killers—were in great demand.

West of the Mississippi River. An estimated 680,000 natives may have lived west of the river in 1600. By 1820 there were an estimated 500,000. The population decreased at an average annual rate of about one-tenth of 1%, considerably slower than that of the eastern Indians.

There were only a handful of settlers, mostly Spanish in the Southwest, in 1600. By 1820 there still were relatively few settlers. There were around a quarter million in Missouri, Arkansas, and Louisiana, several thousand in Texas, New Mexico, Arizona, and Colorado, and a sprinkling elsewhere in the west. In California the first Spanish mission and settlement was founded in 1769. In summary, it is probable that the number of Amerindians in 1820 may have been double the number of people of European or African origin.

As long as there was good farmland available east of the Mississippi River there was less incentive for the settlers to move west of the river. In addition, the western prairie lands were difficult to farm until the advent of the modern iron or steel plow, around 1820 (*Columbia Encyclopedia*, "Plow," 1950).

The causes of the decline in the Indian population included killings by the invaders, intertribal warfare, and disease. The Spanish conquistadores wanted the natives' lands and gold, and when they could not find gold their fury was intensified. The Spanish missionaries wanted to convert the Indians, as well as utilize their labor. These two goals were to be achieved via *encomiendas* where the Indians could both learn the Spaniards' religion and work on the mission's farms. "In theory the system of *encomiendas* was not necessarily bad. What in practice it became is well known. It (the system) became slavery and robbery and not seldom it became also murder" (Richman 1965, p. 35). Ajax de Smyrna stated it more directly: "Better a dead Indian than an unconverted one."

Pecos, New Mexico, illustrates what could be accomplished with determination. There were an estimated 2,000 natives in 1616 (Kessel 1979, p. 104), shortly after the Spaniards first settled in the area. The Spaniards, aided by smallpox, Comanche raiders, and famine, reduced the number to a reported 159 in 1799 (Kessel, p. 342). The pueblo was abandoned in 1838 when the last 18 survivors scattered to neighboring pueblos (Kessel, p. 458).

Why was the rate of decline among the western natives slower than among the easterners? One important reason may be simply that the number of invaders was too small to do as extensive damage as was done east of the Mississippi River. The small number of European settlers may have had a less urgent need for unlimited amounts of land. This possible lesser felt need for land may have been influenced by the fact that much of the land was semiarid or mountainous, "fit only for Indians."

Another element undoubtedly was the in-migration of Indians from the east. We know that there was such east-to-west movement but do not know how many easterners ended up alive in the west. No matter how small this number may have been, it helped to slow the population decline in the west.

1820 to 1850

Total U.S. During this period a "30-years war" was carried on by the federal government together with the white settlers against the natives. The result was that by 1850 the Amerindian population declined by almost 200,000 (a rate of about 1.1% per year) to an estimated total of 450,000.

The white and black population numbered over 23 million in 1850, an increase of 13 million since 1820 (about 3% per year).

East of the Mississippi River. The white settlers had fought valiantly to clear the lands east of the Mississippi River and by 1820 had reduced the number of Indians to around 120,000. The whites, aided and abetted by President Andrew Jackson, redoubled their efforts (Foreman 1982) after 1820, and by 1850 only a few Indians remained east of the river. Our best estimate is around 40,000. Foreman described the causes and beginnings of the Removal, reminiscent of Hitler's "Final Solution." How many Indians died or were killed and how many reached the western United States is not known.

West of the Mississippi River. By 1850 the people from outer space had spread throughout the United States (Figure 7.3). The Plains and Mountain states had relatively few settlers, but there were considerable number in the Southwest and Pacific Coast states. There were about 2 million settlers including those in the original New Spain areas, and a little over 400,000 Amerindians. The latter were outnumbered about 5 to 1.

The native population decreased at a rate of about seven-tenths of 1% per year during these 30 years. The decrease may have been most acute in California. At the beginning of the seventeenth century there may have been some 300,000 Indians in this state. The U.S. Census of 1870 reported only 30,000. The same factors as in the east decimated the Indian population: disease,[5] intertribal warfare, and the desire of the whites to get rid of the natives. In addition, the Spanish missions and religious orders followed the principle of "convert or . . . " Only further westward migration did not occur. The Pacific Ocean stopped it.

The invaders increased at an annual rate of between 3.5% and 4% per year. Settlers and traders from the east had reached California early in the nineteenth

[5] The literature on this subject is enormous. See, for example, Mooney (1978) and McNeill (1976).

century, as did the Russians and other Europeans. But it was the discovery of gold in 1848 that resulted in massive migration to the Pacific Coast.

This migration gave further impetus to the urge to rid the west of Amerindians. By 1850 the good farmland just west of the Mississippi River—in Iowa, Missouri, Arkansas—was occupied. Further west, insufficient precipitation and a mountainous terrain made the land less desirable to the would-be settlers. The buried treasures of petroleum, coal, uranium, and the like were still buried. The West Coast had good farmland in addition to gold.

The Settlers Have Conquered: 1850 to 1900

A major activity next to the Civil War, during the latter half of the nineteenth century, was the series of wars carried on by the U.S. Army against the Indians. Such warfare had been going on long before 1850, of course, but the culmination was reached only toward the end of the nineteenth century. All the action took place west of the Mississippi; there were not enough Indians remaining in the east to be worth bothering about. Perhaps the most widely know incident was "Custer's Last Stand" in 1876 against the Sioux in the Black Hills of the Dakota Territory. His last stand was simply the end of much campaigning against and attacking Indians. Another notorious campaign was that which became known as the "Nez Perce War" of 1877 in the Pacific northwest.

At the risk of oversimplification, we may say that the purpose of these wars was to subdue the natives completely and force them onto reservations.[6] By the middle of the nineteenth century, the country was beginning to change from rural and agricultural to urban and nonagricultural (Figures 7.4 and 7.5). The Civil War played an important part in this change. We see the change in the type of work carried out by the inhabitants. The numbers employed in manufacturing, construction, and transportation, industries needed for war, increased from some 2¼ million in 1860 to almost 4 million in 1870. The United States was started on the road to becoming a modern "great power."

Additional farm land *per se* was not as pressing a "need" as earlier. Instead, resources suitable for manufacturing and other nonagricultural pursuits were becoming more important. Gold was discovered in California in 1848 and in 1874 in the Black Hills on the Great Sioux reservation. Gold seekers flocked in like vultures and the rights of the Indians, "guaranteed" by treaty, were disregarded.

This scenario, in which newly discovered resources took precedence over the rights of the natives, is repeated many times in the future years.

As part of this national change, four intercontinental railroads, plus many

---

[6] This account is based on information in the *Columbia Encyclopedia,* "Railroads," and *Handbook of the North American Indians,* Vol. 4.

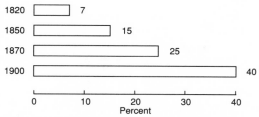

Figure 7.4. Percentage urban for total United States: 1820 to 1900.

short lines, were built between the end of the Civil War and 1890. There were many raw materials to transport and farmland that could be sold to settlers. An immediate by-product of railway construction was the near-elimination of the buffalo herds. How could you operate a train if a herd of buffalo may want to cross the tracks at any moment? A by-product to appear a half century later was the famous Dust Bowl of the 1930s.

The Indians, like the buffalo, were in the way of the railroads and the new settlers. So they were forced onto reservations in the hope that they would not interfere with the operations of the railroads. For some reason that is not clear, they were not all slain as the British did to the aborigines of New Zealand. They were simply harassed and many, but not all, were murdered. To complicate the situation, many railroads were laid through reservations despite the treaties signed by the Great White Father.

The United States continued to undergo social and economic change in future years, and with each change the situation of the Amerindians changed, as we shall see in following chapters.

By 1890 there were about 270,000 Amerindians in the United States or about one-quarter of the estimated number in 1600. Between 1890 and 1900 the population remained largely unchanged in size. The rate of decrease for the entire period 1850 to 1900 was about 1% per year.

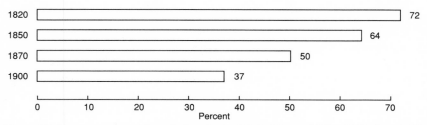

Figure 7.5. Percentage engaged in agriculture for total United States: 1820 to 1900. Source: *Historical Statistics to 1957* (see Chapters A and D).

By 1900, the non-Indian people had settled in all the 48 contiguous states, from Portland, Maine, to Portland, Oregon.

Life on the reservation was difficult. The Commissioner of Indian Affairs often had to supply food and other necessities and some medical service. Gidley (1979) describes life on the Colville Reservation around the turn of the twentieth century, with photos taken by Dr. Edward H. Latham, the Indian Agency physician. The difficulties of life on the reservations—by 1900 very few Indians lived away from reservations—may be captured by noting that life expectancy was around 30 years (see Chapter 9). This was significantly higher than we estimate for the pre-Columbian period, probably because intertribal warfare was stopped, and the white man no longer deliberately spread epidemic diseases (e.g., smallpox) among the natives.

We summarize by noting that the decrease in the Indian population since Columbus arrived had ceased sometime close to the end of the nineteenth century, perhaps by 1870. For the next 50 or 60 years to the time of World War I, the population changed but little in size.

1900 to 1920

Population size remained almost unchanged, around 300,000. Most natives continued to live on reservations and were isolated from the mainstream of the nation. In these years, the non-Indian population increased from 76 to 106 million, or close to 2% per year.

1920 to 1950

The native population increased significantly in the period between the two World Wars and reached about 360,000 by 1950. Service in the Armed Forces during both wars and jobs off the reservations, together with increased "white man's schooling," began to draw some of the Amerindians into the national economic and social sectors, or at least, to approach these sectors. Population increased as much as it did due to the falling death rate.

1950 to 1980

The Amerindian population increased over four times, from about 360,000 in 1950 to a reported number of about 1,400,000 in 1980. This much increase is far too large to have resulted from the natural increase of the population, that is, excess of births over deaths. The fourfold increase indicates a rate of growth of over 4% per year. So high a rate without the aid of foreign immigration is unbelievable. From what countries would Native Americans migrate to the United States? Perhaps a sprinkling from Canada or Mexico, but no more. We believe that about 3% to 3½% increase per year is the highest growth rate achievable by excess of births over deaths, and without immigration.

What Happened to the 1980 Census Count?

We think that the 1980 census count is too great by about 400,000 Amerindians, in comparison with the 1970 count. This is the estimated number of people who, we suspect, shifted their reported race from non-Indian in 1970 to Indian in 1980. If we assume that the number of about 1 million Indians in 1980 is approximately comparable with the 750,000 reported in the 1970 census, then the rate of increase (1950 to 1980) is just under 3% per year. This is a more believable rate of increase than is a growth rate of over 4% per year. Further, the Bureau of Indian Affairs (BIA) reported that in 1980 there were only about 750,000 Indians who were eligible for its services. In short, 1 million may be a reasonable figure between the BIA and census counts.

What happened in 1980 with the census count? Perhaps the earlier censuses missed large numbers. All that we can say is that the BIA numbers in the latter part of the nineteenth century and the first part of the twentieth were very close to the census numbers.[7] After World War II the census reported significantly more Indians than did the BIA.[8]

This numbers comparison leads into what we think is another possible reason for the huge increase in reported population. During the twentieth century, and perhaps especially after World War II, the attitudes of the general American population became more tolerant of other ethnic groups, including Amerindians. This is indicated in such legislation as Equal Employment Opportunity, voting rights, and so forth. Perhaps increased tolerance on the part of the dominant group permits people to change their announced ethnicity as they desire, at least insofar as the census is concerned.

Gibson (1980) in describing the post–World War II period points out that the immediate reaction of the federal government and some influential Congressmen was to "liberate" the Amerindians from assistance by the federal government. The Indian Reorganization Act (passed by Congress in 1934) had "coddled" them too much, these anti-Indian advocates argued. Others rose in defense of the Indians and by 1958 Secretary of the Interior Fred A. Seaton (the Bureau of Indian Affairs is part of the Interior Department) promised that federal

---

[7] For a quick check, look into the *1916 Statistical Abstract of the United States*. Table 8 presents the Commissioner of Indian Affairs' numbers for 1880, 1890, 1900, and 1916. Compare these with the census numbers.

[8] The 1960 U.S. census reported 520,000 Amerindians. The Bureau of Indian Affairs reported 345,000. See the BIA annual reports on population and labor (photocopy). In subsequent years the census count consistently is greater than the numbers released by the BIA.

Indian policy would provide improved health services, education, and assistance for economic development. President John F. Kennedy came out strongly in favor of the Amerindians and helped create a more favorable climate. Commissions and committees issued reports, and gradually some of the rights of the Indians were restored to them.

This transformation of the social scene is explained by Gibson in terms of increased urbanization following World War II, increased education for the Indians, and increased activism on their part. But these, in turn, were part of the general changes, the social trends, taking place in U.S. society through much of the nineteenth and twentieth centuries, if not longer.

Furthermore, the number of mixed Indian and non-Indian ancestry in 1980 is large (Chapter 10). Hence, an unknown number can report themselves to the census either as Indian or some other "census race." Perhaps significant numbers who previously had reported themselves as non-Indian reported Indian in the recent censuses now that it is almost fashionable to be a member of a minority group. (Of course, some groups are more fashionable than are others.)

Also, marriage of Indians with non-Indians, particularly whites, increased in the last couple of decades (see Chapter 10). This indicates increased tolerance of minority people and in turn probably increases the level of tolerance. Offspring of such marriages may report themselves to the census as Indian or non-Indian. Perhaps more have opted for Indian in the post–World War II years, thus adding to the rate of growth of the Amerindian population as reported by the census.

Question: Should such people of mixed ancestry be counted as Indian or non-Indian, or placed in a separate category? When using census statistics we have no choice. You are what you say you are, within the classification limits allowed by the census. The census, consciously or not, reflects what the officials think are the "sacred beliefs" of the dominant white society: A person who is a mixture of white and nonwhite must never be included with the white.

In summary, the numbers game is too tricky for novices to play.

Summary

After losing about three-quarters of the estimated number of people in 1600, the Amerindians increased their numbers during the twentieth century. The official 1980 census count is about 1,400,000, a full 50% larger than when the Pilgrims landed (1620). However, if we accept 1 million as a more plausible number for 1980, then the Amerindian population just about equaled that at the time the Pilgrims landed.

But so many of them are not of 100% Amerindian ancestry. Very many are of mixed ancestry. And as long as non-Indians of mixed ancestry can report themselves to the census as "Indians," the census Indian population will continue to grow rapidly. If these persons of mixed ancestry should report themselves as other than Indian, the census-reported Indian population can decrease. Further, insofar as children of mixed ancestry in turn marry non-Indians, their children's Indian component becomes less and less. Eventually, perhaps after two or three or four generations, the grandchildren become non-Indian—probably white—for census reporting. In such an event, the census Indian population need not continue to increase indefinitely.

CANADA

A Very Short Synopsis

The patterns of population change in Canada (Figure 7.6) and the United States were generally similar—a slow decrease in the seventeenth century followed by a more rapid decrease through the eighteenth and nineteenth centuries. By the latter part of the nineteenth century, the Canadian Amerindian population reached its low point, about half of what it was at the start of the seventeenth century, as best as can be ascertained. During the twentieth century, the population increased, especially after World War II.

In the United States the low point was reached at about the same time. But the U.S. Amerindian population had decreased to about one-fourth of its original number at the beginning of the seventeenth century. Whether a 50% decrease is "better" than a 75% decrease we leave to the reader to decide (Table 7.2).

Decreasing Population, Seventeenth through Nineteenth Century

1492 to 1601

The larger decrease in the numbers of Indians in the present U.S. territory in contrast to Canada is attributable to the basic geographic-economic differences between the two countries. In Canada, geography and climate worked against much successful agriculture, at least until the middle or later nineteenth century. The amount of good farmland in the eastern provinces was very limited so that there was less incentive for the invaders to kill or drive away the Indians in order to appropriate the latter's lands, as was the case in the United States.

Geography favored Canada, on the other hand, insofar as the fisheries are involved. "No part of the world has ever been so rich in edible fish and other products of the sea as the Newfoundland Banks, the coast of the Labrador, and the Gulf of St. Lawrence" (Morison, p. 470). Europe and later the Caribbean islands provided an insatiable market for salted and dried fish, in particular cod. John Cabot on his 1497 expedition presumably "took plenty of codfish simply by letting down and drawing up weighted baskets" (Morison, p. 180). The

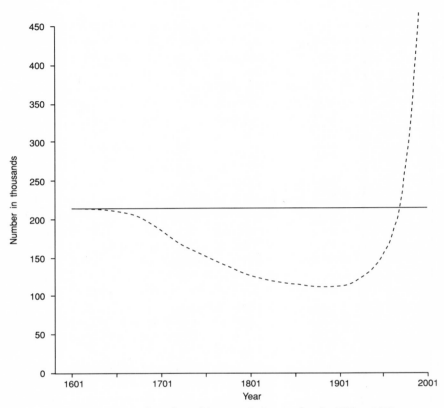

Figure 7.6. Estimated numbers of American Indians in Canada: 1601 to 1986.

Portuguese fishermen had preceded the French and between 1502 and 1524 "ruled" the fisheries.

The first recorded French fishing voyage was in 1504. Spanish and English fishermen soon followed. By 1578 "English fishermen were lording it over all others in Newfoundland harbors" (Morison, p. 471). And the Canadian Maritime Provinces have been British ever since. The Spanish bowed out of the picture by 1603. During the sixteenth century, fishing was a prosperous industry for a few Europeans, and an important source of food for many more.

But the Amerindians were barely, if at all, involved during the sixteenth century. The European fishermen either heavily salted or dried their catch and took it back to the east. For salting, the fishermen did not even have to leave their ships, for they brought the salt with them from Europe. For drying, they had to land where they could sun-dry the catch; this involved but a minimum of contact with the natives. Morison (1971) quotes Parkhurst, an Englishman, who wrote in 1578:

> Not only did the fishermen make about double what they could get on a summer's coasting voyage; they were free of temptation from wine and women, unobtainable in Newfoundland. Thus damsels of the West Country looking for a husband much preferred a fisherman to an ordinary mariner. (p. 478)

Perhaps the situation was not quite as bleak as Parkhurst visualized it to be.

Fishing led to fur trading. Canadian geography is superb for fur-bearing animals. And there was a great demand in Europe for furs, more than could be supplied by trappers in Eastern Europe. The French dry-shore fishermen (fishermen who came on shore for whatever reason), as a sideline, began trading European manufactured goods for furs. The French fishermen were not alone. As early as 1534, Jacques Cartier began trading for furs and established trade agreements with the Indians. Toward the end of the sixteenth century Frenchmen began organizing fur-trading companies (Morison, p. 477). And now the Amerindians began to become involved on a large scale.

We accept the figure of about 210,000 Amerindians (excluding the Eskimos or Inuits) at the beginning of the seventeenth century (Table 7.2). We think that the population size about a century earlier—the beginning of the sixteenth century—was about similar, at least in the same ballpark.

Table 7.2. Estimated Numbers of American Indians in Canada by Regions, 1601 to 1981 (in Thousands)

			Regions					
		Percent		*Numbers*			*Percent change p.a.**	
	Total	*change*						
Year	*number*	*p.a.**	*East***	*P.P.****	*B.C.*****	*East*	*P.P.*	*B.C..*
1601[a]	210	—	70	20	120	—	—	—
1701[b]	170	−0.2	40	20	110	−0.6	0	−0.2
1881[c]	110	−0.2	30	40	40	−0.2	0.4	−0.6
1921	120	+0.2	45	45	30	+1.0	0.6	−0.8
1951	170	+1.2	62	66	42	+1.0	1.2	1.1
1961	210	+2.1	75	84	51	+1.9	2.4	0
1971	300	+3.6	110	140	50	+3.9	5.2	6.0
1981	470	+4.6	170	210	90	+4.4	4.2	6.1
1986[d] census	660	+7.0	—	—	—	—	—	—
estimate	544	+3.0	—	—	—	—	—	—

*Per year.
**East: Atlantic Coast to and including Ontario.
***P.P.: Prairie Provinces: Manitoba, Saskatchewan, Alberta, Northwest Territories, and Yukon.
****B.C.: British Columbia.
  [a]Ubelaker (1988).
  [b]Mooney (1928).
  [c]Census reports, 1881 to 1986.
  [d]1986 count. See Appendix 5, "The New Canadian Amerindians." The census count is 660,000. We suspect that a more reasonable figure is 540,000 to 560,000.

At the beginning of the seventeenth century there were almost no Europeans in Canada. There was a sprinkling of settlers in the Maritime Provinces, the transient fishermen, and a handful of traders and explorers. (See Appendix 11, "Population of Canada by Provinces, 1701 to 1981.")

1601 to 1701

The seventeenth century was the "century of the fur traders." More Europeans arrived to trade for furs and to service the traders (Figure 7.7). With them, if not earlier, came the white man's diseases, especially smallpox, which killed large numbers of Amerindians. Also, intertribal warfare over the fur trade resulted in the killing of more Indians by Indians than was the case before the fur trade began in earnest. We do not know how large the excess of deaths from European disease and warfare may have been. We can only estimate that there was a decrease of perhaps 30,000 to 40,000 natives during this century, an average loss of about 2 people per 1,000 population, each year.

There were about 210,000 Indians at the beginning of this century, and perhaps 170,000 at the end (Table 7.2). There were almost no Europeans at the beginning and about 20,000 to 25,000 at the end.[9] The natives outnumbered the invaders about 10 to 1 at the start of the eighteenth century.

The Eastern Provinces. Practically all of the decline of the native population occurred in the area from the Atlantic Ocean, to and including the province of Ontario. This is where the action was. This was the main fur-trading area and where the Europeans settled. Nevertheless, despite the fact that Indian men were needed to supply the furs and the Indian women were needed to produce the Metis, there was a decline of some 30,000 in this part of Canada.

Jacques Cartier explored much of the St. Lawrence River system between 1534 and 1541 but had not settled in New France. Samuel de Champlain explored between 1603 and 1615, and founded Port Royal (in present-day Nova Scotia) in 1605 and Quebec City in 1608. The Sieur de Maisonneuve and Paul de Chomeday founded Montreal in 1642.

The Company of New France was founded in 1627 to conduct the fur trade. In 1663 it was disbanded, and New France became a colony with a royal governor.

The Hudson Bay Company was chartered by the British government in 1670 to trade for furs and given ownership of Rupert's Land (Figure 7.8), a large part of Canada around Hudson Bay. Those were busy times.

---

[9] For an interesting account of census taking in seventeenth century New France (Lower Canada) see Pelletier (prior to 1931). Note that even in those days census officials were criticized by high-ranking government officials for not enumerating "enough" people, pp. 28ff.

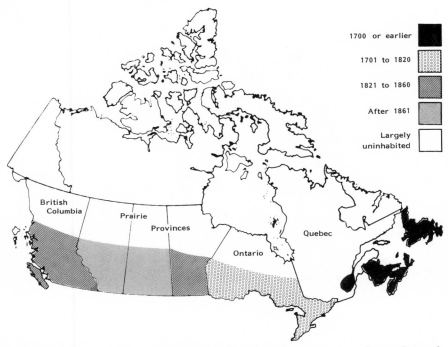

1700 or earlier

1701 to 1820

1821 to 1860

After 1861

Largely
uninhabited

British
Columbia

Prairie

Provinces

Quebec

Ontario

Figure 7.7. The westward movement period of first known count or estimate for population of non-Amerindian origin: Canada.

The Beothuks in Newfoundland were wiped out by the French and British fishermen. A number of tribes were seriously decimated by the Iroquois, who tried to control the fur trade. The Indian wars that began toward the end of the seventeenth century and continued well into the eighteenth contributed to the general mayhem; the Algonquins sided with the French and the Iroquois with the British. Other conflicts with the Europeans resulted in Indian deaths, for example, the Peach Wars of 1655–1664 between the Dutch and the Hudson River Indians. We do not know how many were killed in such warfare with the European invaders, but whatever the number many Indians were killed.[10]

Finally we may ask but cannot answer: How many Eastern Provinces Indians went elsewhere in an attempt to escape the invaders?

The Prairie Provinces. Manitoba, Saskatchewan, and Alberta, or at least their southern parts, were buffalo country at this time. The Yukon and Northwest

[10] For a summary of some of these conflicts and wars, see Waldman (1985), Chapter 5.

Figure 7.8. Approximate area of Rupert's Land in the Hudson Bay territory.

Territory that we include with the three Prairie Provinces had comparatively few inhabitants. The number of Amerindians, we estimate, was about the same, perhaps 20,000, at the beginning and end of the seventeenth century. Except for a few fur traders, there were very few or no Europeans here, for several reasons. At that time the geography together with the available technology was not conducive to agriculture. The topsoil was deep and had been covered for many years with a dense growth of grasses. Many layers of decaying vegetation had produced a fertile and water-holding soil, best for growing wheat (*Atlas of Canada* 1981, p. 44). But such soil could not be worked with the wooden or stone implements available at that time. Iron plows and other, more efficient equipment became available only in the nineteenth century. Hence the Indians depended for their subsistence on hunting buffalo and other game, fishing (where possible), and gathering wild crops. But a hunting and gathering economy cannot support as dense a population as can agriculture. (In certain areas fishing can support a very dense population.) Further, apparently even the buffalo herds could not be employed to their full food potential (at this time) because the prairie Indians did not get the horse until the middle or latter part of the eighteenth century (Waldman 1985, p. 56).

In summary, the natives had no economic base conducive to population growth. For the Europeans, except for the fur traders, there was little incentive to enter the Prairie Provinces.

British Columbia. Half or more of the Canadian Indians lived in what is now British Columbia at the beginning of the seventeenth century. The rather easily procurable fish, especially salmon, and other water creatures supported a very dense population. Indeed, fishing on the Northwest Coast supported a larger population, according to Mooney (1928), than the primitive agriculture could support in the east.

By the end of the seventeenth century there may have been no change or a very small decrease in the Amerindian population.

Very few Europeans had reached British Columbia during this time. Juan de Fuca (1592, Spain), Thomas Button (1612–13, England), and William Baffin and Robert Bylot (1615–16, England) were some of the explorers who visited western Canada and had contact with the Amerindians. The big invasion of people of European origin was to occur in the eighteenth and nineteenth centuries. The great smallpox epidemics and other white man's diseases were delayed until the Europeans arrived. The first very destructive epidemic recorded was in 1781–82 (Mooney 1928, p. 27).

1701 to 1881: Approaching the Nadir

This period of almost two centuries is most important for the Canadian Amerindians. At the beginning they were their own masters in their own lands. At the end, they were the lowest of the low, completely subservient to the invaders. The white man did them a "favor" by allowing them to continue living in their own land.

Unfortunately we cannot document the changes as they occurred. We have reasonably acceptable information for the Indians only for the end dates. All of the years in between are "tiempo incognito." Nevertheless we shall try to infer what happened when, from the bits of Canadian history and statistics that we could locate.

At the beginning of the eighteenth century there were an estimated 170,000 Amerindians and over 15,000 of European origin, 10 or more Indians per single European.

In 1881 there were about 110,000 Indians and 4½ million Europeans. Now there were about 40 Europeans for every Indian. The tables were completely reversed. Not only did the number of Indians decrease, but very many had lost their land and were living on reserves, at the sufferance of the whites.

In 1701 there may have been only some 40,000 Amerindians left in eastern

Canada. By 1881 there were only an estimated 30,000. The number in the Prairie Provinces increased from an estimated 20,000 to about 40,000.

In British Columbia the number of Amerindians decreased from an estimated 110,000 to a reported 40,000 (1881). The Russians greatly assisted by bringing in diseases, whiskey, guns, and ammunition. The Russians finally left North America when they sold Alaska to the United States in 1867.

This geographic redistribution of the Indian population, we suggest, was at least partly attributable to the location of the reserves in the mid- and later nineteenth century. Very many were located in the Prairie Provinces because this area apparently held few economic inducements for the whites. This was the main reason why, in the United States, so many reservations were established in the Great Plains and Great Basin areas in the nineteenth century, areas that apparently offered but little economic opportunities for the whites. Throughout these 180 years, imported diseases may have been the main killer. Epidemics of smallpox, measles, influenza, typhus, and typhoid were recorded. No one kept vital statistics on the precise numbers of deaths; we only know that there were very many.

Deaths resulting from warfare with the whites may have been far less in Canada than in the United States. Waldman (1985) states: "There was little warfare between Indian and White, as compared to events south of Canada . . . in the U.S." (p. 159).

Let us now look at smaller time segments of Canadian history for additional insights.

1701 to 1821. The Europeans continued to settle in the Maritime Provinces and in southern Ontario (Figure 7.7). Toronto was first settled by the French in 1749 and then occupied by the British in 1759. After the American Revolution, many Europeans from south of the border migrated there. (Ottawa was founded in 1827.) By 1821 Ontario probably had about 125,000 Europeans and total eastern Canada (including Quebec and the Maritime Provinces) about three-quarters of a million—the total non-native population of what is now eastern Canada (see Appendix 11).

1821 to 1861. The European population in the eastern provinces continued to increase rapidly to over 3 million by 1861. Except for the fur traders, there were very few Europeans in the Prairie Provinces (plus the Yukon and Northwest Territory) or British Columbia in 1821. Harison (1985) refers to "a couple of hundred white traders living in forts and a growing number of Metis" in Central Canada (p. 18). Early in the nineteenth century, a group of Scottish farmers settled the Selkirk Colony in Manitoba's Red River Valley. By 1861, there were probably under 10,000 non-natives in the Prairie Provinces, almost all of whom were in what is now Manitoba. It was not until late in the nineteenth century that waves of immigrants moved in and agriculture boomed. The settlers now had the agricultural implements needed to work the prairie soil.

The Pacific coast and British Columbia were explored and settled by Europeans late in the game. During the sixteenth century Spanish ships explored the California coast. In 1542 Juan Rodriguez Cabrillo reached what is now San Diego (Richman 1965, p. 6); Spanish expeditions reached and founded a mission at present-day San Francisco about 1774 (Richman, p. 103).

In the meantime, the Russians[11] were exploring the coasts of Alaska and Canada. Vitus Bering in 1728 ascertained that there was no land bridge between Siberia and Alaska. Bering's second expedition was in 1741. When the survivors of this expedition returned to St. Petersburg with valuable furs, the Russian empire immediately entered the fur business. By the end of the century, traders from England, France, Spain, and the United States were in these northern waters.

The Russians continued south, exploring, trading for furs, and killing the native inhabitants. By 1812 they had a post as far south as Fort Ross, close to present-day San Francisco. The Spaniards, in response, sailed north in an effort to halt the Russians and reached as far as Vancouver Island. Finally, in 1795 the Spaniards withdrew.

The fur game on the Pacific coast was becoming bigger and bigger. England, with Captain James Cook, became a player in 1776. At about this time traders and explorers were approaching British Columbia overland from eastern Canada. John Jacob Astor of the United States entered in the early nineteenth century. Finally, in 1846 following the battle cry of "54-40 or fight," a settlement was reached and the forty-ninth parallel became the boundary between British and American territory from west of Lake Superior to the Pacific Ocean.

By the middle of the nineteenth century, settlers were beginning to pour into British Columbia, and the Indians really became involved. There was little good farmland that the settlers wanted. Nevertheless these Europeans could and did give their European-type diseases to the natives.

1861 to 1881. The white settlers only had to populate Alberta and Saskatchewan, settle Vancouver City, and complete the transcontinental railroad that arrived in Vancouver City about 1880. Canada was now "filled" insofar as the Amerindians were concerned; the latter had no course of action left to them.

The areas which are now the Yukon and Northwest Territory were skipped over by the invaders, except for furs and minerals. It made little difference, because very few Indians lived in these areas.

---

[11] Lower (1975); also *Encyclopedia Canadiana;* Kalbach and McVey (1971).

A Century of Increasing Population

1881 to 1921

Sometime in the latter part of the nineteenth century the Indian population reached its low point, probably about 110,000. There was a slow increase (or improved census enumerations) in the first part of the twentieth century, and the population reached about 120,000 by 1921. The growth of the Indian population averaged one-fifth of 1% per year. The total Canadian population grew at an average rate of 1.6% per year.

By the end of the nineteenth century, most persons who were legally designated as Indian in Canada lived on reserves or Crown lands (Patterson, p. 39). World War I attracted many Métis and Indians out of their communities (or reserves) and into general Canadian life. Many moved to growing urban centers. The native population was beginning to revive.

1921 to 1951

The Amerindian population increased by about 50,000 in these 30 years—a rate of 1.2% per year. This average annual rate of growth was only slightly below that of the total Canadian population, which averaged 1.5% growth per year. The Amerindians were beginning to make up for lost time. All three areas of Canada participated in this growing population. We think that the same factors, including World War II, that were attracting the Indian population into the U.S. economic and social sectors were operating similarly in Canada. Patterson describes this change as "the creation of a new synthesis [of Indian and white cultures] rather than assimilation of the natives" (p. 40).

1951 to 1981

These were the booming decades, just as in the United States. The Indian population (including Métis) increased almost three times, from 170,000 to 470,000 in 1981. The rate of growth (average percentage per year) increased from one decade to the next:

	Amerindian	Total Canada
1951–61	2.1% per year	2.7% per year
1961–71	3.6%	1.7%
1971–81	4.6%	1.1%
1951–81	3.5%	1.8%

It is not surprising that the growth rate of the native population was so much more rapid than that of the total Canadian population because the former's birthrate (as measured by the total fertility or gross reproduction rate) is so much higher than the latter's (see Chapter 9). Decreasing mortality accounts for some of the increase in population; life expectancy at birth among the status Indians increased between 2 and 3 years, from 1971 to 1981 (see Chapter 9). Nevertheless, as was the case in the United States, we doubt that an overall rate for 30 years of 3.5% per year, and especially a rate of 4:6% per year between 1971 and 1981, could have occurred via an excess of births over deaths. Instead, we suggest that the entire social milieu changed in such a fashion as to present an apparently large population increase in the latter twentieth century.

This changing social milieu is described by Patterson (p. 40) as follows:

> In the late 1940's and 1950's a fourth phase [began] which was characterized by a sharp upturning of the Indian population, greater organizational activity and the emergence of new leaders, not all of whom thought in terms of assimilation.

Some Indians had begun to view themselves differently. Indians began asserting themselves in an effort to control their lives.

Keeper adds another element similar to that in the United States: the switching of reported ethnicity between Indian and non-Indian by those who could do so. There is considerable intermarriage of Indians with non-Indians in Canada as well as in the United States, and many of mixed ancestry can switch identity easily. People of mixed ancestry were becoming associated voluntarily with the dominant white society. Scottish-Indians became whites of Scottish descent; French-Indians became French Canadians. These people felt that it was undesirable to be Indian and covered their Indian identity with the identity of their white forebears (p. 116).

Keeper continues: "It has become fashionable in the last few years for some people . . . to begin admitting their Indian ancestry." The Canadian public recognizes the Indians and Métis as more than ignorant savages, and an effort is being made by white society to come to an understanding with the Native Americans (p. 117).

Cardinal (1977) is emphatic. "For this rebirth to be meaningful anything short of true independence and complete freedom will not be acceptable" (p. 222).

Evidently change is in the air, although we cannot measure it precisely. Some people can shift between being Indian and non-Indian. We do not know how many shifted which way, and why. We can but suggest that enough did switch from non-Indian to Indian between 1971 and 1981 to provide a higher than natural amount of increase (i.e., excess of births over deaths) for this decade.

An alternative explanation for the large increase, especially from 1971 to 1981, is improved coverage in the 1981 census enumeration. It is possible that many Indians were missed in the 1971 census and then enumerated in the 1981 census. We cannot ascertain precisely what happened. Finally, may we suggest that the high rate of growth between 1971 and 1981 resulted from a combination of switching to Indian identification and improved census enumeration.

Over the last four centuries the number of Canadian Amerindians probably doubled. At the beginning of the seventeenth century, there may have been a little over 200,000. By the end of the twentieth century, there may be in the neighborhood of a half million. Did the Canadian Indians make a better comeback than did their U.S. sisters and brothers, or are the statistics illusionary?

SUMMARY

In both countries the fate and fortunes of the Indians were greatly affected by changes in the nations' technological, economic, and social conditions. The single most important overall change was the shift from agricultural to nonagricultural conditions and the enormous technological innovations that accompanied, or caused, these changes. All the technological, economic, and political changes, in turn, influenced the attitudes of the dominant whites toward the Indians. These attitudes tended to shift from "get rid of them by any means" to "they are one of us."

Because Canada and the United States had more or less the same types of changes, the Indians in both countries responded in similar fashion. The population decreased considerably from the beginning of the sixteenth century until close to the end of the nineteenth when they began to increase slowly. With the advent of World Wars I and II, the Indian population, as counted in the national censuses, increased much more rapidly; by the end of the twentieth century there may be as many, or more, than there were before Columbus landed.

Prior to the mid-nineteenth century, Amerindians were killed or forced out of the lands deemed most valuable at that time; they ended up in those areas of Canada and the United States that the Europeans at one time deemed to be of little value.

Chapter 8

From Exile to Convergence

INTRODUCTION

Prior to the arrival of the Europeans, each tribe was a separate nation beholden only unto itself, as was the situation among all people during most of mankind's history. Each tribe controlled whatever territory it could, for hunting and fishing, gathering wild plants, and agriculture. As a result, territorial boundary lines were probably always in flux as military adventures succeeded or failed. Some tribes disappeared, and new tribes appeared. A constant theme, as nearly as history can be reconstructed, was intertribal warfare.

Each person was a member, or citizen, of his/her tribe of birth. There were no "detribalized" people, that is, people who participated in a larger society. There were no larger societies above the tribal level, until kingdoms arose. Language, customs, religion, and beliefs all differed much or little from tribe to tribe. These tribal differences were not always great because often several tribes had a common background. With respect to language, for example, there may have been hundreds or thousands of languages or dialects among the Amerindians. But it is thought that there were only about a half-dozen phyla (a group of languages related more remotely than a family or stock) (Waldman 1985, pp. 67 ff.). Joseph Greenberg suggests that most of the 1,000 or so languages spoken by the American Indians derive from one ancestral superfamily that he named Amerind (Lewin 1989).

Above all, each tribe was a free nation. Once the Europeans arrived these freedoms were lost.

By being confined to reservations and reserves, the Indians lost much of their pre-conquest freedom; they became wards of the Canadian and U.S. governments. On the other hand, the reservations probably served as depositories of Indian culture. The tribe, or what remained of it, was able to carry on some if not all of its traditions and customs. The native languages continued to be spoken; ancient religious ceremonies, for example, the Corn Dance among the Pueblos, continued; even some hunting and fishing and perhaps agriculture could be pursued.

(The average size of a reservation in the United States in the latter twentieth century is close to 300 or more square miles.[1] This average is larger than some independent nations that are members of the international community, for example, Barbados, Malta, Andorra, etc.)

The effects of the reservation–ghettos upon the Amerindians were similar in many respects to the effects of large city ghetto life upon the European immigrants in North America. Initially the immigrants congregated in ghettos and retained their languages and customs. Subsequently, as they or their children moved out of the ghettos and became acculturated to the larger society, they gave up, or lost many of their distinctive European characteristics. This is true with the present-day descendants of the First Immigrants from Asia.

Before the European invasion, all inhabitants were rural dwellers as we understand rural life.[2] Obviously, raising crops, hunting animals, fishing, or gathering wild plant food are awkward operations to carry on in a city of the twentieth century. By the 1980s the majority of the Amerindians were urban dwellers.

The nearest approach to a metropolis prior to the arrival of the Europeans was Cahokia in what is now southern Illinois (Folsom and Folsom 1983, pp. 258–259). It is uncertain whether this was a contiguously built-up area as we are accustomed to in a modern city, or a cluster of smaller places or villages built around a central city, or religious site, as many of our present great cities were prior to the twentieth century. Cahokia was founded about A.D. 700 and continued until about 1500. Some archaeologists think that it may have contained as many as 40,000 people; others think that this number is greatly exaggerated.

Cahokia was not truly urban in our understanding of the term. Agriculture was the main industry of the inhabitants. Nonagriculture that we equate with urbanism, consisted of trade, the carrying out of civic and religious affairs, and perhaps such craft industries as pottery making, weaving cloth, and the like. Such manufacturing most likely was carried on in homes or small (by our standards) businesses. Further, in light of the considerable number of large

---

[1] All Indian reservations contain about 50 million acres (*U.S. Statistical Abstract, 1976*, Table 346). There are about 200 reservations as nearly as we can ascertain, from the BIA 1982 *Population and Labor Force Estimates*. BIA uses at least three terms: reservation, agency, and rancheria. We were unable to find an "official" number of reservations issued by the BIA.

[2] The most general definition of *urban* as used by the U.S. Census is: a contiguously built-up area containing 2,500 people or more; all other areas are *rural*. In Canada, the minimum population to be classified as urban may be as low as 1,000. Each census has its own specifications tailored to local conditions, but follow the general definition as given above.

mounds they built, we include construction as another industry. Mining may be added to the list of nonagricultural activities if digging down about 30 feet for flint nodules, the iron ore of that time, is so considered. Altogether, a far cry from the nonagricultural activities carried on in today's cities and urban areas.

Poverty Point is another place that may have been an "urban area" (Folsom and Folsom, p. 232). At its height perhaps several thousand people lived there at any one time. And perhaps far fewer. Located in present-day Louisiana, it is thought that it may have been started around 3,500 years ago and continued for some 1,000 years. Basically it was a hunting and gathering and possibly agricultural society. As in Cahokia there was considerable trade with other tribes, presumably the carrying on of crafts, and the building of mounds. Archaeologists estimate that over the centuries the Poverty Point citizens (or did they have slaves?) carried some 50,000 tons of earth, 50 pounds at a time, to build all the mounds.

Estimating the probable population size of a "contiguously built-up urban area" (see footnote 2), long before any censuses were ever taken, is tricky. For several reasons, we opt for minimum estimates for ancient "cities," reasons too involved to explore in detail in our present study. Some previous estimates have been based largely on conjecture. The United Nations (1973) reports:

> Where archaeologists have been able to gauge the area of ancient sites and the type and proximity of dwellings, an assumed average density may indicate the number of inhabitants. Estimates of the labour required to erect the characteristic monumental structures, written records on clay tablets and extent of cemeteries. . . . (p. 14)

"Assumed average" density is pure conjecture; even small differences in the assumptions can result in vastly different population estimates. The same is true of the "labor required"; how many people labor for how long? As for the clay tablets, who took censuses and measured the land surface? The "extent of cemeteries" means nothing without knowing for precisely how many generations (or years) the cemetery was in use.

According to Analect Number 53 of Peng Shun Lu, he was asked, "How do you make assumptions?" Peng replied, "By playing the probabilities, the same as I would at a horse race."

Only very carefully thought-out analyses may produce more nearly correct population estimates. Frazier (1986, pp. 153–159) reports such a study of Chaco Canyon in New Mexico. Earlier analyses and writings by others produced population estimates of 6,000 to 20,000. Frazier reports that Thomas Windes, supervisory archaeologist at the Chaco Center in Albuquerque, after reviewing all of the evidence, concluded that the maximum population of Chaco Canyon may have been no more than 2,000.

Following in this chapter we shall describe the forced nineteenth-century movement to reservations and reserves, the natives' original rural ghettos, in both countries. Subsequently, the movement out of the rural reservations to urban areas together with other social and economic trends of the nineteenth and twentieth centuries led to convergence toward the dominant European-origin culture. However, detribalization, convergence, or even assimilation (if that word may be used) is of interest to us only as part of an overall explanation of changes in population characteristics. In this study we are concentrating on how the interrelated social changes interact with population; study of the problems and tribulations of changing cultures is of secondary interest. Previously we expressed our opinions on cultural change in the *Changing Demography of Spanish Americans* (Jaffe *et al.* 1980, Chapter 2).

UNITED STATES

Reservation-Ghettos

Creation

Prior to the mid-nineteenth century and before the brutal and forceful removal of the population living east of the Mississippi River to west of the river, over one-third of the Amerindians lived in the Historical Reservation Area (HRA) (see Appendix 6). Two out of three lived elsewhere. These proportions were derived from the information collected by Mooney (1928; Figure 8.1). By 1870 the

Figure 8.1. Mooney's (1928) areas (approximate).

removal of the easterners was substantially completed, and in that year the census reported that over 8 in 10 were living in the HRA. This proportion remained virtually unchanged until the end of World War II, almost a century later (Figure 8.2). Following World War II, as many of the people began leaving the reservations, the proportion in the HRA declined and reached short of 6 in 10 by 1980.

Between about 1500 and the mid-1900s, those who had lived east of the Mississippi River were gradually forced westward by the federal army. At first they were pushed just west of the river; as the settlers crossed the Mississippi, the Indians were pushed further west (Foreman 1982, Chapter 1). Simply forcing them westward, however, was considered insufficient by the settlers; the Indians had to be assigned to specific territories. And so reservation-ghettos came into being. The present state of Oklahoma, called Indian Territory in the nineteenth century, was, in effect, one huge reservation and became the end of the line for many easterners during the first half of the nineteenth century.

As long as there were comparatively few whites in these western areas prior to the Civil War, the Amerindians could continue their customary lifestyle more or less—hunting, gathering, agriculture in some areas; above all they had the freedom to move about in the allotted territory. "Big brother/sister" did not bother them as long as their lands were not coveted by the whites.

By 1870 the federal government had opened a system of reservations and agencies that included at least 13 states plus Alaska. The 1870 census reported

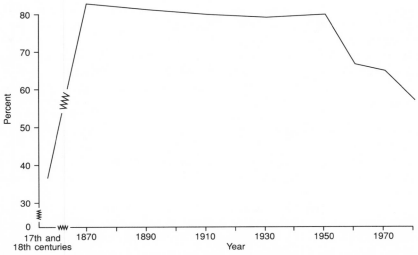

Figure 8.2. Percentage of Indians living in Historical Reservation Area: United States, 17th and 18th centuries to 1980.

on the number of Indians in every state and territory. However, only about 13 contain data under the heading "On reservations and at agencies." Because a population number is given for each state and territory, however, we assume that there was some collection system or government office in each state. For example, for Montana, 19,457 Indians are reported of whom 157 are listed as "out of tribal relations," and 19,300 as "nomadic (estimated)." We have been unable to learn how this table was constructed. The only information we found was to the effect that the 1870 census was aided by the Office of Indian Affairs.[3]

The Spaniards had been in the Southwest long before the east-of-the-Mississippi River settlers reached the river. Large numbers of Indians had lived in California, Arizona, and New Mexico, but the Spaniards decimated them during the seventeenth and eighteenth centuries. Mooney estimated that there had been over 300,000 sometime during the eighteenth century; by 1870 there were well under 100,000. Unlike the Indian population in the east, these southwestern people had no west to which to flee. A few may have fled north, but most seem to have simply been killed or disappeared.

Deloria and Lytle (1983), in their discussion of removal and relocation during the years 1828 to 1887, point out that during the early years of European settlement, some whites felt that they could live peacefully with the Indians. But they were in error. The cultural gap was too broad and too deep to inspire mutual trust. By the time of Thomas Jefferson's administration, the policy of removing the natives was being formulated; the whites felt that they and the Indians could not live together peacefully. So off to the reservations the latter were sent, with Andrew Jackson's blessings.

But settling the Indians on reservations did not solve Indian–white relationships. The whites still dominated. The Indians were now dependent on the white federal government for at least part of their sustenance. Between the army and Christian missionaries and teachers, the Indians were effectively removed from participation in either their own economy and lifestyle, or that of the country.

Leaving the Reservations

For a century, from the mid-nineteenth to the mid-twentieth centuries, the native population remained locked in its reservation-ghettos. About 8 in 10 lived in the HRA until about World War II. For all practical purposes the large majority were effectively isolated from mainstream United States economic, educational, and cultural life.

World War II and the federal government's "American Indian Relocation Program" induced a liberating effect, far more than World War I had induced. In 1930 close to 8 in 10 lived in the HRA. By 1970 about 2 out of 3 lived in

---

[3] 1870 Census, p. xvii; and 1910 Census, p. 253.

this area. There may or may not have been a further decrease by 1980, depending on how Amerindians are defined. Of all persons who reported themselves as Indian to the 1980 census, a little less than 6 in 10 resided in the HRA. Among those who reported having only Indian ancestors, about 2 in 3 resided in the HRA, about the same proportion as in 1970. However, of those who reported mixed ancestry, Indian and non-Indian—should they be classified as Indian and are they comparable to the people who reported themselves as Indian to the 1979 census?—only 4 in 10 resided in the HRA (Figure 8.3).

The American Indian Relocation Program (Madigan 1956), begun in 1952, offered financial assistance, advice, and limited social services to Indian individuals and families who agreed to permanent removal from reservations. Supposedly this was a voluntary program on the part of the natives. Nevertheless, considerable propaganda and promotion were carried on in an effort to induce "volunteerism." In the four years, July 1, 1952 to June 30, 1956, 12,625 people officially volunteered.

Why this program was instituted by the Great White Father–Mother is debatable. One school of thought believes that it was an effort to eliminate tribes and whatever financial benefits accrued to tribal members. Hence, if successful, the federal government would be saved much money, and the tribal lands could become available to whites, especially the mineral-bearing lands. The other school holds that it represented an attempt to bring economic development and success to the poor unemployed reservation dwellers. It is true that economic conditions on many reservations were deplorable. The volunteers were to be sent to a select group of cities where (it was hoped) they would find steady, year-round employment. Relocation offices were opened in these cities in order to help the volunteers settle. The Feds washed their hands then and allowed the local communities to pay for any further welfare programs.

Only a few thousand reservation dwellers were induced to leave their homelands. We do not know how many volunteered before the program was discontinued. Of these volunteers, a quarter or more returned to their reserva-

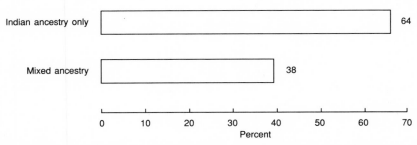

Figure 8.3. Estimated percentage of Indians by reported ancestry living in Historical Reservation Area: United States, 1980.

tions. Nevertheless, the publicity generated by this program during the 1950s together with the increasing levels of official schooling (Chapter 11) may have stimulated urban-ward migration. Between 1950 and 1970, large number left the reservations for urban life without losing their tribal affiliations. Once people become aware of El Dorado, they venture forth seeking it.

Who leaves the HRA and where are they going? We noted that few of those of mixed ancestry lived in these HRA states (Figure 8.3). Does this imply that the latter were the ones who were more likely to have left the reservations following World War II? Or is there the possibility that many of those having mixed ancestry and who did not live on reservations had reported themselves as non-Indian in the census of 1970 and earlier, and as Indian in 1980?

Where They Went

Where did they go? To the cities, of course. Large numbers went to urban areas; this was a profound change for many previously rural dwellers. Living on reservations in isolated rural areas effectively isolated them from the non-Indian population. Once people left the reservations and moved to urban areas, they began to mix with non-Indians and enter, or approach closer to, the mainstream of schooling and jobs, and there was increased frequency of marriage with non-Indians.

As recently as the beginning of World War II, at the time of the 1940 census, fewer than 10 in 100 throughout the United States lived in urban areas, places containing at least 2,500 dwellers. By 1950 about 15 in 100 were urbanites. By 1970 almost half were reported as living in urban areas.[4] Most of these city folk lived in Standard Metropolitan Statistical Areas, that is, in or adjacent to large cities (Figure 8.4).[5]

Detribalization or Convergence

Urban life favors social and cultural change and most likely contributed to detribalization or convergence. Webster defines *detribalization* as the noun form of "to cause to relinquish tribal identity." *Convergence* is "movement toward

---

[4] The 1970 Census reported 750,000 Indians in the 48 coterminous states, of whom 335,000 lived in urban areas, and 415,000 in rural areas (Population Census (2)—1F, Table 1). The number 415,000 is close to that reported by the BIA as living on or adjacent to reservations (1971 report).

[5] The U.S. Census Bureau defines Standard Metropolitan Statistical Areas as follows: "The general concept . . . is one of a large population nucleus, together with adjacent communities which have a high degree of economic and social integration with that nucleus. . . . Each SMSA has one or more central counties containing the area's main population concentration: an urbanized area with at least 50,000 inhabitants" (PC 80-1-C1, p. A.3).

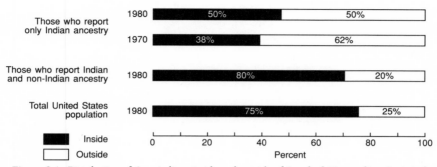

Figure 8.4. Distribution of Amerindians inside and outside of Standard Metropolitan Statistical Areas: United States, 1970 and 1980.

union or uniformity." Each definition is largely the obverse of the other. Neither definition is very useful, however, for the measurement of the rate at which the native cultures may have changed. We suggest that this process during the historical, or post-Columbus, period began slowly and then picked up speed, especially after World War II. Figure 8.5 illustrates the possible speed of this change as we judge from reading the literature. Since we have neither a statistically workable definition of change nor the proper statistics to measure this process, we must use whatever fragments of information can be found and try to visualize change over time. In the pages and chapters that follow, we present the information which we believe contributed to social change and which led to Figure 8.5.

Influence of the Whites

Missionaries were active in Indian affairs since at least the beginning of the nineteenth century, and probably earlier. It appears that there was a conflict of interests among some, if not all, whites and among the U.S. government officials—on the one hand the desire to eliminate the Indians and make room for the settlers, and on the other, to save the souls of the Amerindians. Might it be that saving souls was the rationale, conscious or otherwise, for the former? Without public opinion polls around the end of the eighteenth century we have no definitive information on what the white public thought of the Indians, if the former thought at all.

The church officials—the religious—however, were continuous and vociferous lobbyists, and there is an extensive existing correspondence between them and federal government officials. One such government correspondent was Thomas L. McKenney, who was superintendent of Indian trade, 1816 to 1830; as such he was a one-person precursor of the present-day Bureau of Indian Affairs. Viola analyzed his correspondence and official papers and concluded that

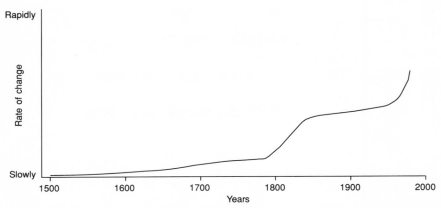

Figure 8.5. Hypothesized rates of change in detribalization of U.S. Amerindians: 1500 to 1980.

McKenney and his fellow "humanitarians" believed that agriculture would be the savior of the Indians when accompanied by conversion to Christianity and regular school and church attendance.

It did not take long for McKenney to understand the situation. He soon realized that the Indians' ability to acquire the white man's vices was very great. Therefore, he accepted the Indian removal as necessary for the Indians to avoid the vices of the whites. Other pressures for Indian removal were older and less humanitarian. White planters wanted the large tracts of rich land held by the southern Indians (Viola 1974, Chapters 3 and 11).[6]

Were God and Mammon in conflict or was God simply serving Mammon? Whatever the answer may be, the result is the same—Amerindian people and cultures were changed in response to these pressures.

Religion

By the nineteenth century the several churches and hordes of missionaries brought about some degree of change in native religions. Obviously Christianity was not present in the Western Hemisphere before the arrival of the Europeans, and by the twentieth century most of the Amerindians are at least nominal Christians.

Indians Not Taxed

The U.S. Constitution specifies that Indians who are not taxed are not to be counted for the apportionment of Congressional representatives among the states. Hence, at first the decennial censuses only counted those few who lived

---

[6] See also L. C. Kelly 1983, pp. 141 ff.

among the general population and presumably paid taxes. If paying taxes is one indicator of convergence, then this process was underway since at least the mid-nineteenth century. The "tax collector" (1910 Census, p. 283) succeeded as follows:

	Number	Percentage of Indians who presumably paid taxes
From 1500 to mid-nineteenth century	Almost none	0 or close to it
1870	25,700	8
1880	66,400	22
1890	58,800	24
1900	107,700	45
1910	194,000	73

If we equate paying taxes with voting rights, then it was not until 1924 that all Indians were finally converged. In that year the Indian Citizenship Act was passed [8 U.S.C.A. 1401 (a)(2)] (Deloria and Lytle, Chapter 9). We do not know how many actually voted or were allowed to vote; we only know that now they are officially citizens.

Out of Tribal Relations

Presumably a few Amerindians had left their tribes as early as the eighteenth century and possibly earlier. Did Pocohontas converge and leave her tribe when she became a Christian and married John Rolfe in the early seventeenth century? There must have been considerable sexual intermixture of Indians and non-Indians judging from the large number of 1980 U.S. inhabitants who claim to have Indian ancestors. But did all such intermixture lead to detribalization or convergence?

In 1870 the United States census reported that 1 in 10 Indians were "out of tribal relations."[7] This is close to the proportion of Indians who presumably were taxed. Significantly, in the HRA where the natives were isolated, only about 1 in 35 was reported as being "out of tribal relations." In the other states 1 in 3 was so reported. We infer that many of those who were left alive in the other states (mainly those east of the Mississippi River) managed to do so by adapting themselves (to some extent at least) to the white civilization.

In the HRA, on the other hand, detribalization and convergence were not absolutely necessary for survival, at least during the nineteenth century. Efforts had been made by government and missionaries to change the Amerindian

[7] We assume that this means "detribalization," however that word may be defined, but have not found any specific definition that the census may have had.

lifestyle, but they were not very successful. The federal government continued to supply the Indians with the minimum food needed to prevent wholesale starvation. So why converge? (See Deloria and Lytle 1983.)

Between 1870 and 1930 about 1 in 10 were reported by the censuses as "out of tribal relations" (or some similar-sounding heading). In 1930 the subject was referred to as "tribe not reported"; this included those Indians who failed to specify the tribes of which they may have been members. This ratio of 1 in 10 is but an approximation and does not tell us how many may have forsaken their Indian culture for that of the Europeans. But it does suggest that the extent of detribalization was neither increasing nor decreasing over this 60-year period.

By 1970, following World War II, about 2 in 10 were classified under the heading "tribes not reported." This apparent increase between the 1930 and 1970 censuses resembles the increase observed previously in Indian urbanization. This parallelism suggests that whatever social and economic changes contributed to leaving the reservations, especially those in the Historical Reservation Area, and going to cities, also contributed to converging with the European-derived culture.

In 1980 about 2 in 10 were reported as "not enrolled in tribe" (Population Census, 1980, Volumes 2–10, Tables 4 and 13). There has been no change since 1970.

Language

Forsaking the traditional language indicates changes in at least part of the original culture. The Amerindians were rapidly forsaking their native languages by the latter part of the nineteenth century or at least becoming bilingual. We have numbers for those listed as "unable to speak English." We suspect that most of those who could speak English also knew their mother tongues, but the census furnishes no direct evidence on extent of bilingualism.

In 1900, 42% were reported as unable to speak English, in 1910 about 31%, in 1920 some 21% and in 1930 about 17% (Census 1930, Table 46). In 1980 the census asked two questions: What language is spoken at home? And for those who said a non-English language they were asked: How well do you speak English? One in 4 claimed to speak a native language at home. But almost all stated that they spoke English "well" or "very well." Between 3 in 4 in 100 Amerindians (in total United States) replied that they spoke English "not well" or "not at all." Evidently by the beginning of the twentieth century very many spoke English and perhaps were bilingual. We suggest that those who spoke only English have forsaken more of their traditional culture than have those who speak their native language plus English.

When most lived on reservations (in 1900 and 1910) there were many more who were unable to speak English, particularly in the Historical Reservation Area. In 1900 half of those living in these states were unable to speak

English; in the other states only 1 in 5. In 1910 the "unables" were almost 4 in 10 in the Historical Reservation Area, and only between 1 and 2 in 10 in the remaining states. It is apparent that leaving the reservation and moving to cities or otherwise coming into contact with the great outside world contributed to increased use of English. On the other hand, perhaps those reservation dwellers who could speak English were the ones most likely to leave.

Great changes took place during the last couple of decades of the nineteenth century and the beginning of the twentieth. When we compare the two (published) age groups, 10 to 19 years, and 20 and over (in 1910), we find the following pattern:

	Percent unable to speak English	
	Age 10–19	*Age 20 and over*
Historical Reservation Area	20	45
Other states	6	16
Total United States	17	38

Comparison of these two age groups highlights what may be a turning point in convergence—toward the adoption of English, if not other characteristics. The younger age group was born in the last decade of the nineteenth century and was of school-attendance age (whether they attended school is another question) in the first decade of the twentieth. The older generation, those 20 and over, had an average (median) age of almost 40 years; all of them were born and of school-attendance age in the last half of the nineteenth century. Between these two generations, the proportion "unable" to speak English was cut in half.[8]

Prior to the middle or latter part of the nineteenth century considerable English language convergence must already have occurred. If by the latter part of the century about one-third or more were "unable" to speak English, then one-half to two-thirds must have acquired some English since the original landing of the first Europeans. And all this was going on while the Great White Father–Mother and his/her henchmen persecuted the natives.

CANADA

Introduction

The experiences of the Canadian Indians were similar to those of their United States relatives. The white man's legal structures, the timing of events, and other

---

[8] The proportion who were able to speak English increases from about 62% among the older generation to about 83% among the younger. The 1910 census (pp. 232 ff.) provides no numbers for "able to speak English."

details varied, of course. Nevertheless, if we were to draw a chart showing probable rates of cultural change over the last five centuries as we did for the United States Amerindians (Figure 8.4), we should expect to see very little difference between the two countries.

When the Europeans were interested in furs almost exclusively, the Indians were necessary allies. But as the number of Europeans increased in eastern Canada, particularly along the St. Lawrence River, and the fur trade in this part of Canada diminished, displacement of the natives began. Also, many of the Indians had been allies of the British during the U.S. Revolutionary War. After this war and the War of 1812, however, the British no longer feared an invasion from the south. Indians were no longer needed as military allies.

Hence, by 1830 native settlement on reserves began in earnest (*Canadian Indian* 1986, pp. 54 ff.). Presumably, these reserves were to be their permanent homelands. But the Indians were beset continuously by troubles with the whites—squatters, loggers, poachers, would-be farmers, and other vermin who wanted the Indians' lands. Innumerable government commissions investigated and recommended on what to do about the Indian problem. (The Canadian government is no different from all other governments.) Sometimes complete assimilation into the mainstream was stressed. Sometimes isolation from the mainstream and the creation of more reserves was stressed. Innumerable treaties and other "legal" documents were signed with the Indians. With every official document, insofar as we can determine, the Indians lost more territory.

Now the Métis enter the picture, in the mid-nineteenth century. These Indian–European mixtures had been in Canada since the beginning of the sixteenth century, and by the nineteenth century were most populous in the to-be Prairie Provinces—Alberta, Manitoba, and Saskatchewan. The Canadian government had largely ignored these people; they were neither Indians nor Europeans. But by the mid-19th century white settlers wanted the land, described in the *Canadian Indian* as "the area of prime agricultural land north of the American border between Lake Superior and the Rocky Mountains" (p. 57). The Canadian equivalent of the U.S. Indian Wars was carried on against the Métis, albeit on a much reduced scale. Finally in 1982, the Constitution Act officially recognized the Métis by stating "the existing aboriginal and treaty rights of the Indian, Inuit, and Métis people of Canada" (p. 95). The 1981 census of Canada anticipated this recognition by including the Métis with the Inuits and Indians in the category of "Native People."

The final product of all this government activity was to deprive the Amerindians and the other Native People of most of their land, locking them into reserve–ghettos and keeping "the Indians in a state of wardship regulating all aspects of existence on and off the reserve" (p. 61).

Reserves versus Reservations

The reserves in Canada are located all over the country, except for the far north, as shown in Figure 8.6. In contrast, in the United States the reservations are concentrated in the western states. This difference in distribution resulted from the fact that most of the land not desired by the Canadian whites is in the colder north. In the United States, on the other hand, the undesirable land was that west of about longitude 100 (extending from central North Dakota to Laredo, Texas[9]) with the exception of the Pacific Coast states. So the Canadian Amerindians, insofar as they were displaced from the south, were moved northward, and the U.S. Indians westward.

Further, the 13 provinces and territories in Canada are so extensive that moving the Indians northward did not necessarily require crossing a province boundary line. Hence, there was relatively little measurable redistribution of population among the provinces and territories. South of the border, however, the 48 coterminous states geographically are so much smaller that moving even a relatively short distance may take one to a different state.[10] Consequently there is no analytical purpose to be served by designating a Reserve Area as we did for the United States. Accordingly we cannot describe the redistribution of the Canadian Amerindian population accompanying the designation of reserves, if there was a significant redistribution, and the presumed reredistribution in the twentieth century as many people left the reserves.

Nevertheless, fragments of information suggest redistribution patterns similar to those in the United States. (1) Canadian Indian population was densest in 1500 in the area just north of the international boundary (excluding the Rocky Mountain area) and along the Pacific Coast. Further north, around Hudson Bay, the Yukon, and the Northwest Territory, density was at the lowest (Waldman 1985, p. 30). We think that many natives including Métis were displaced from the south and then moved north. Subsequently, especially after World War II, many who left the reserves (or other territories) went south to cities located just north of the Canadian–U.S. border. (2) When once assigned to reserves the Indians were not allowed to leave the reserves even temporarily without a pass issued by the government Indian agent (see Appendix 3). This restriction was dropped in the mid-1950s. (3) The proportion of status Indians who lived off the reserve or crown land increased rapidly since 1961, as we shall

---

[9] Rainfall west of this line is too little to have attracted settlers as long as better watered land had been available.

[10] A migrant is one who crosses a boundary line. The closer the boundary lines are to each other the greater is the "volume" of migration. And the smaller each unit is—for example, a state in the United States as compared with a province in Canada—the more boundary lines there are. All data on migration are fictitious.

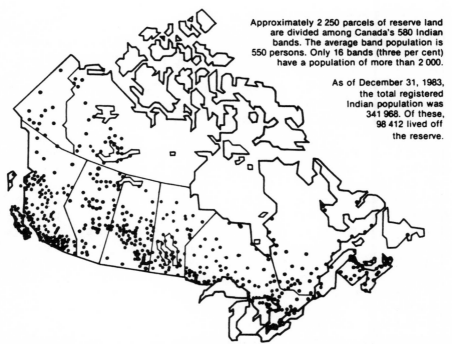

Approximately 2 250 parcels of reserve land are divided among Canada's 580 Indian bands. The average band population is 550 persons. Only 16 bands (three per cent) have a population of more than 2 000.

As of December 31, 1983, the total registered Indian population was 341 968. Of these, 98 412 lived off the reserve.

Figure 8.6. Distribution of Indian bands and reserves: Canada, 1983. Source: *The Canadian Indian*, p. 89.

see. (4) The proportion who lived in urban areas—most reserves are in rural areas—increased greatly since 1931, and especially since 1951 as restrictions against leaving the reserves were removed.

Leaving the Reserves

By 1881 the Indians were securely confined to their reserves. Beginning with that year and extending to the end of World War I, the number of Indians reported by the Department of Indian Affairs was almost the same as that reported by the decennial censuses. This suggests that relatively few left the reserves during these four decades, unless one government agency simply copied numbers from the other. There are several other problems with these numbers. Presumably the Métis are excluded from both counts, but we cannot ascertain this. Also, the Indians had been separated into *status* Indians who were under the jurisdiction of the Department of Indian Affairs and the *nonstatus* Indians whom the department does not recognize.[11] Are the nonstatus included or not included in the population statistics published by Indian Affairs? We should not expect them to be included in the Indian Affairs reports if the latter had no jurisdiction over them. On the other hand, we assume that they are included in the census counts. So why do the two sources provide such similar numbers from 1881 to 1921? Or were there virtually no nonstatus Indians in 1881 and earlier? If there were none or very few, why then did the first Indian Act of 1876 distinguish between the two categories? More questions without answers.

From 1931 to 1971 the census reported more Amerindians than did Indian Affairs. This census surplus suggests that more left the reserves during these four decades than earlier. The Indian Affairs count was only about 90% of that of the census.

By 1981 the number reported by Indian Affairs was only about 70% of the census count—if the Métis were included in the earlier censuses. If the Métis were excluded from earlier censuses and we exclude them from the 1981 census count, then the number reported by Indian Affairs amounts to about 90% of the census count. Where were the Métis prior to 1981?

Not all Indians under the jurisdiction of Indian Affairs lived on reserves or crown lands.[12] The proportions who did not are as follows: 1961—17%; 1971—27%; and 1981—30%. These increasing proportions suggest that many left the reserves during these 20 years. Where may they have gone?

To the cities and on the road to convergence, naturally. From the very beginning—when the Ancestors still lived in northeastern Asia—the natives were rural dwellers. The establishment of the reserve system in the nineteenth century guaranteed the continuation of this state of affairs even as in the United States. From 1881 (the earliest date for which we have information) to 1941 and World War II, only about 1 in 25 lived in urban areas (according to the decennial censuses). Beginning in the 1940s the proportion who were city folk rose rapidly and reached 43% in 1981.[13] These increases in urbanism parallel the large increases in population of those who were under the jurisdiction of Indian and Northern Affairs and who lived off the reserves and crown lands. Evidently there was a significant post–World War II movement to the cities.

Until World War II, the natives were largely isolated from mainstream Canadian life. Then, during the war, movement to urban areas and convergence began in earnest. By 1981 about 43% of the natives were living in cities containing 2,500 or more people (Figure 8.7). This is less than the 55% reported in the United States in 1980 (for places of 2,500 or more population).

---

[11] The distinction between status and nonstatus was promulgated in the First Indian Act of 1876 passed by the Canadian Parliament.

[12] There is a legal distinction between these two types of Indian "homelands," but both are equally ghettos.

[13] The proportions reported by the decennial censuses are: 1951, 7%; 1961, 31%; 1971, 31%; 1981, 43%.

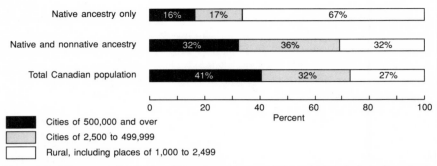

Figure 8.7. Urban–rural distribution of Canadian native population (which includes Indians, Inuits, and Métis): 1981. Source: 1981 Census of Canada, *Population*, Catalogue 92-911, Volume 1, Table 2.

Convergence is on its way at the end of the twentieth century. In 1981, 16% of those who reported having only Indian ancestry lived in cities containing 500,000 or more people (Figure 8.7). Among those reporting both native and nonnative ancestry, the "mixed," twice as many lived in these largest cities. The "mixed" begin to resemble the general Canadian population.

Detribalization or Conversion

"Through the residential school system, the government policy of assimilation continued unabated" (*Canadian Indian* 1986, p. 86) to about the time of World War II. Following this war, Canadian public opinion as well as the efforts of the Amerindians began to redress the Indians' grievances. The plight of the war veterans influenced this change. "Although considered good enough to fight, Indian veterans were nevertheless treated as government wards on their return home. This obvious injustice helped increase the [Canadian] public's awareness of Indian people's disadvantaged situation."

Our impression of the changes in Indian culture—changes abetted by changes in the mainstream environment—is of increased convergence of Indian and white cultures and lifestyles. These mainstream changes included changes in Canadian public attitudes and government policy, and the growth of private economic enterprises such as logging, building of dams for electricity, and the like. Apparently there is but little desire on the part of the Indians to return to their traditional lifestyles.[14] Instead, they desire elements of the Canadian culture, such as schooling and education, hospitals and other medical facilities, jobs, freedom for the individual, in short, "a better life." Following are two measures of convergence that indicate (or illustrate) these changes; other indica-

[14] See also Price 1979, pp. 213 ff.

tors are presented in subsequent chapters, including information on births and deaths, and intermarriage with non-Indians.

Religion

As in the United States, the onslaught of European-origin religion was too much for the Canadian Indians, and they succumbed. In 1900 only about 15% were still "pagans" (according to the Department of Indian Affairs); in 1954 only between 2 and 3% were reported as "professing Aboriginal Beliefs."[15] The 1981 census did not include a "pagan" or "aboriginal belief" category. Instead, and following the specific religious categories (almost all of which is one or another Christian church), is that of "no preference."

Among those natives who report having only native ethnicity, fewer than 1 in 10 claims "no preference." This is about the same as for the general Canadian population. Of those who reported having both native and nonnative ethnicity, about 1 in 6 claimed "no preference." These proportions tell us nothing about the depth or intensity of religious feeling. They only suggest that change or convergence has occurred; the "old-style religion" is no more. And these "mixed" have converged more than have the "nonmixed."

Language

An important indicator of cultural change and convergence is the discarding of traditional language and the adoption of the mainstream language. Canada has two official languages, English and French. In 1981 only 3 in 10 natives reported having a native language as *mother tongue,* 6 in 10 reported English, and 1 in 10 French or some other nonnative language (Figure 8.8).

Even fewer reported using the native language as the *language spoken most frequently at home.* About 2 in 10 so reported.

Those who reported having only native ancestors were more likely to have a native language as mother tongue, 4 in 10; this is especially so for those living on reserves. Among those of mixed ancestry, fewer claimed a native language as mother tongue (1981). Once intermixture occurs, the original and traditional language is likely to be discarded.

Of those with only native ancestors, 1 in 4 uses the native language at home. On the other hand, virtually all of those having mixed ancestry spoke English or French at home. Clearly, many whose mother tongue was a native language subsequently switched to English or French as the language spoken at

---

[15] Annual reports of the Indian Affairs Branch, Ottawa. 1981 Canadian census, Population, Catalogue 92-911, Vol. 1, Table 5.

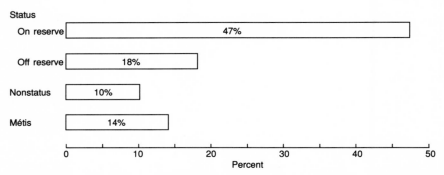

Figure 8.8. Percentage reporting native language as mother tongue: 1981. Source: *Canada's Native People,* Statistics Canada.

home. Of the first group, 3 in 10 switched to a mainstream language, and of the mixed population, almost all switched (Figure 8.9).

Leaving the reserves for city life is strongly related to forsaking native tongues. Among urban dwellers (in 1971), 3 in 10 reported a native mother tongue; among the rural dwellers (including the reserves population), 7 in 10 so reported.

Of the urban dwellers between 1 and 2 in 10 reported using a native language most often at home; among the ruralites between 5 and 6 in 10 so reported.

Further evidence that isolation on a reserve slows any convergence that may be going on is seen by comparing the reserve population (1981) with other natives. Half of the status Indians who live on reserves reported a native mother tongue. Among the status Indians who live off the reserve, the nonstatus, and the Métis, between 1 and 2 in 10 reported a native mother tongue.

When did the natives begin to change languages from native to European? Probably there have been a few natives with a European mother tongue for as long as anyone can remember or written history can testify. The only definite information we have is that as recently as the latter part of the nineteenth century and continuing until the time of World War I, close to three-quarters had native language mother tongues.[16] From about the time of World War I to

---

[16] We estimated these proportions from 1971 age data which can be converted to year of birth as follows:

Age	Period of birth	Comments
Under 20	1951 to 1971	Post-World War II
20 to 24	1947 to 1951	Shortly after World War II
25 to 29	1942 to 1946	During World War II
30 to 34	1937 to 1941	Interwar and beginning of World War II
35 to 44	1927 to 1936	Interwars
45 to 54	1917 to 1926	World War I and postwar
55 to 64	1907 to 1916	Shortly before World War I
65 to 84	1887 to 1906	Peacetime(?)
85 and older	Before 1886	Life on the reserve

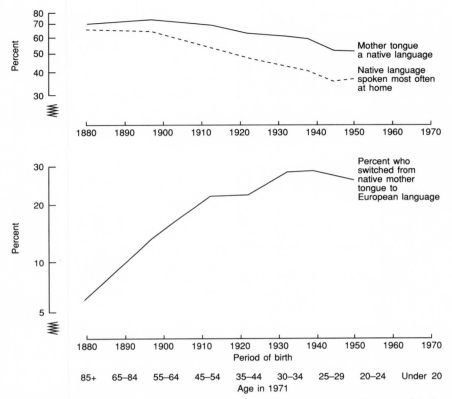

Figure 8.9. Percentage of native population (a) whose mother tongue is a native language; (b) who speak a native language most often at home; and (c) who switched use from a native to a European language, by year of birth or age: Canada, 1971. Source: 1971 Census of Canada, *Population,* Catalogue 92-733, Volume 1, Part 4, Table 10.

World War II there was a steady decline in the proportions having a native language mother tongue. During the time of the latter war there was a somewhat more precipitous decrease in native mother-tongue usage, and following, an apparent leveling off (Figure 8.9).[17]

---

[17] Language spoken by young people, say under 20 years of age, does not necessarily have any connection with the possibility of convergence of lifestyles. Even the most rebellious children speak the language they hear at home. However, after leaving the parental home, the language they choose to speak is more likely to reflect their degree of convergence to a different and non-parental culture. Hence, we show no information for those under age 20 in 1971. Unfortunately, we have no comparable information from the 1981 census.

About two-thirds spoke a native language at home during the last quarter of the nineteenth century. From around the beginning of the twentieth century to about the end of World War II, the proportion declined steadily.

Since more people reported having a native-language mother tongue than spoke a native language at home, some of the native mother-tongue people must have shifted to a nonnative language. This switching seems to have been increasing steadily from the latter nineteenth century to the time of World War II. At this time—the mid-twentieth century—the switching amounted to about 3 in 10 of all who reported having a native mother tongue.

We shall converge.

SUMMARY

A short synopsis of Amerindian life in the nineteenth century:

- In the beginning, the Indians were being segregated onto isolated reservation-ghettos.
- The reservation-ghettos retarded social and cultural change.
- At the end of the century, they were starting to leave the reserves and reservations, albeit slowly.
- During this century, many began to converge toward mainstream U.S. and Canadian life as they mixed with the non-Indian people.
- The trend toward convergence gathered speed as it continued well into the twentieth century.

We cannot specify cause and effect, what "causes" convergence. We only emphasize that all the elements we analyzed in this chapter—increasing urbanism, leaving the tribe or band, adopting the Christian religion, forsaking native languages or at least becoming bilingual—all together are both instigators of and indicators of cultural change and convergence to the white man's/woman's way of life. We have an interrelated matrix of elements.

In subsequent chapters we shall look into additional social and economic changes. One trend, or change, may be increasing tolerance of ethnic or minority groups during the twentieth century, on the part of the dominant, white, European-origin culture. Such increased tolerance permits change, but by itself does not explain why change occurred. Increased tolerance is a necessary but not sufficient condition to bring about cultural change.

Chapter 9

The Vital Numbers:
Births and Deaths

INTRODUCTION

The general rule applicable to all living creatures is simple. If more births than deaths occur, a population is increasing in numbers. If there are more deaths, the population decreases. Of course, for any particular area such as a city or state or province, the increase or decrease in the number of people may result from in- or outmigration. But here we are considering only the result of births and deaths upon population size. Hence, we shall examine the course of births and deaths among the Amerindians of Canada and the United States with particular emphasis on the twentieth century. (For detailed information about the basic information available and how we analyzed it, see Appendix 8.)

First let us present a very brief summary of the history of Amerindian vital numbers:

1. From ancient times to about the fifteenth or sixteenth century the numbers of births and deaths must have been very great in any one year; births generally outnumbered deaths slightly, and population growth was very slow.
2. From the time of the coming of the Europeans to about the middle or end of the nineteenth century, the numbers of deaths must have greatly outnumbered births. The large population decline (which we noted in Chapter 7) could have occurred only via an excess of deaths.
3. The birthrate, however measured, seems not to have changed much during the four centuries 1500 to 1900.

4. During the twentieth century, the rates at which Indians were born and died—the birth and death rates—declined, especially after World War II.
5. Question: How much did these rates decline?
6. Although the extent of decline is uncertain, there is no doubt that the vital rates are tending toward those of the general populations of Canada and the United States, as the Indians are leaving their reserve–reservation ghettos.

BIRTHRATES

Introduction

There are several measures of the birthrate, and each measures a different aspect of the rates at which women are giving birth. *There is no single, uniquely correct rate.* To the extent that women may be having fewer, or more, children at one time as compared with another is indicated the several measures. But precisely how many fewer, or more, children will vary in accordance with the specific measure used. In the following discussion we use two measures, or rates: the *Total Fertility Rate* (TFR), and the average number of *Children Ever Born per Woman* (CEB). Let us explain them briefly.

TFR is the number of births that 1,000 women (or 1 woman) would have in their (her) lifetime if, at each year of age, they (she) experienced the birthrates among all women occurring at that age in the specified year. TFR includes both male and female births (see Appendix 8).

CEB is just that. How many births does the average woman have? This may be the simplest measure to obtain. Simply ask a group of women how many children they gave birth to and divide the total births by the number of women queried. A commonly used CEB is that for women at the completion of the childbearing age, sometimes taken as 35 to 44 years, or 40 to 44, or 45 to 49.

United States

From Prehistoric Times to the Twentieth Century

Between the pre-European era and the latter part of the nineteenth or beginning of the twentieth century, there seems to have been but a slight decline in TFR. We estimated (Chapter 5) that the TFR for the pre-European agriculturalists may have been around 7. We estimate TFR at the beginning of the twentieth century to have been about 6 or perhaps over; at this date a large number of the Amerindians were agriculturalists.

Declining Rates in the Twentieth Century

The significant declines in the birthrate of the Indian people occurred during the twentieth century, especially in the latter half (Figure 9.1). Note the remarkable parallelism between TFR for the Amerindians and that for the total U.S. population. Once the Amerindians began to escape from their sequestered reservations and enter—or approach—the mainline culture, they came under the influences of forces that affected all segments of the U.S. people, schooling and literacy, a money economy, urbanism, and so forth.

The Total Fertility Rate. The Indian TFR has been higher than that of the nation's total population throughout the twentieth century. In 1900 the Indian rate probably was half again or more above that for the total country. Birthrates, both Indian and total country, declined during the Great Depression of the 1930s, and then, about the time of the end of World War II, rose. The Amerindians contributed to the famous "baby boom"—approximately 1945 to 1957. The following decline from around 1960 to 1980 was similar to that of the total U.S. population (Figure 9.1).

By 1980 the Indian TFR was only about one-quarter (20 to 25%) higher than the national TFR.

Prior to 1930 most of the Indians lived in rural areas, largely on reservations; there were almost no urban dwellers, and we have no TFR for the few urbanites. During these three decades, 1900 to 1930, the rural TFR was above 5 and the same as that for all Amerindians. From 1930 to 1980 both the urban and rural TFRs declined (Appendix 8, Table 8.1); that of the rural population declined to about half of its 1930 level. That of the urban population declined about one-third. In 1980 the urban Indian TFR was about 1.9 and that for the total U.S. population about 1.8. The two rates are identical for all practical purposes.

Children Ever Born. The CEB for Indian women aged 35 to 44 in 1910, around the beginning of the twentieth century, may have been 6 or more. This number is close to double that for all women in the United States in 1910.[1]

Between the beginning of this century and the post–World War II years, the Indian birthrate decreased as the TFR records. We expect the TFR and CEB to show much the same changes over time, and they do.

Why analyze both rates then, when both tell much the same story? Our

---

[1] The CEB in 1910 for all women in the nation aged 35 to 44 is recorded as 3.55 (PC80-1-C1, Table 84). However, the table carries the footnote: "Data shown for 1940 and 1910 include estimates of children for women with no report on children ever born." We suggest that the true rate in 1910 was between 3.8 and 4.0. Detailed information on how the number of children not reported was estimated by Census personnel is needed to ascertain a more nearly correct figure.

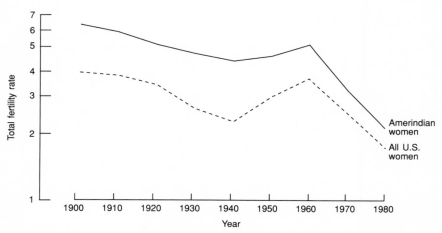

Figure 9.1. Total fertility rate for Amerindian and all U.S. women: 1900 to 1980. Source: Appendix 8 table.

answer is that the CEB measure provides one very important piece of information that the TFR does not, namely the ancestry of the Indian women. Those women who reported having only Indian ancestors consistently had higher birthrates as measured by CEB (Figure 9.2) than did those women who reported having both Indian and non-Indian ancestors—the mixed. The CEB rates for both groups are decreasing, but the mixed remain significantly lower.

By 1950 the Indian CEB rate had decreased to about 3.8 and that for total United States to 2.3. Both rates increased by 1960 as a result of the baby boom, and then both decreased to 1980. We expect the Indian CEB to approach the national CEB more closely within the next generation or so, by early or mid-twenty-first century. We base our thoughts on the observation that the Indian women who are of mixed ancestry had CEB rates (in 1980), as we discuss later, of about 2.6. This is close to the national rate for all women in 1980.

More and more Indian women are of mixed ancestry, are high-school or college graduates, live in larger cities, and are employed. These are the Indian women who are more likely to marry non-Indians. Remember that these women have the lowest birthrate of all Indian women. As their numbers increase, as we expect to happen, the TRF and CEB for all Indian women will tend toward that of the general population. These Indian women are and will be subject to the same influences as all women, and these influences will be reflected in their birthrate.

Add to the previous observation our observation that the CEB (or any other measure of the birthrate) of those who report only Indian ancestry also is declin-

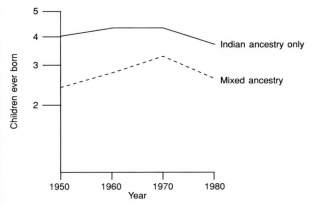

Figure 9.2. Children-ever-born rate for U.S. Indian women (age 35–44) by ancestry: 1950 to 1980. Source: Appendix 8 table.

ing. How far it may decline we cannot say. We are confident only that if the rates for both ancestry groups are decreasing, the total CEB also must decrease.

At the time of our writing we have information only for one generation of women who were exposed to post–World War II conditions. We should have the experiences of at least two generations prior to further discussion. We hope that some day such information will be available.

Influences on the Birthrate

Several demographic elements are well known to influence the birthrate. Married women have more children than do the unmarried, rural dwellers more than urban, those with less formal schooling more than those with more schooling,[2] those not employed more than the employed. All of these are well documented and require no proof here. In addition, there are many psychological and cultural elements that are connected to higher or lower fertility. For example, the Shakers, who insisted on celibacy, had a birthrate of zero, or close to it.

There are several demographic elements that we have not enumerated but which do influence Indian fertility. We suspect that they are indications of more basic influences and hence may act indirectly on the birthrate. We shall examine them in more detail after reviewing briefly the generally accepted elements for all women. Following is the story for the Indian women aged 35 to 44 (1980), at which age so many have completed their childbearing.

---

[2] Family income is so highly related to extent of schooling that little is served by showing income separately.

Marital status	Married women living with their husbands had a CEB of 3.6
	Never or formerly married or separated, 3.2
Urban–rural	Urban, 3.3
	Rural, 3.9
Schooling	Under 12 years, 4.2
	12 years or more, 2.9
Employment status	Employed, 3.2
	Not employed, 3.9

Three additional elements may be more pertinent for the Amerindians than for other people. One is the section of the country in which they live. One section we call the Historical Reservation Area, where so many of the Indians had been sequestered in the nineteenth century and where there still is in 1980 a large population living on or near reservations. The other area consists of all other states (excluding Alaska and Hawaii).

The average CEB unquestionably is higher in the Historical Reservation Area than elsewhere in the United States.

A second influence is the ancestry, or "degree of Indianism," of the woman. Those who said that they had only Indian ancestors had a greater CEB than did those who reported having both Indian and non-Indian ancestors—the mixed. Whether this difference in reported ancestry is truly biological is irrelevant. Perhaps it is mainly a social designation. Nevertheless, the difference in average CEB between the two types of ancestries can have significant implications. Ancestry distinctions, whether imagined or not, do affect the behavior of the people, births, marriages and other events.

A third influence on married women is the ethnicity of her spouse. If he reports to the census that he is Indian, CEB for the Indian woman (of Indian ancestry only) is highest. On the other hand, if the husband reports other than Indian race, average CEB is lowest. (See Figure 9.3 and Appendix Table 8.4 for further details.)

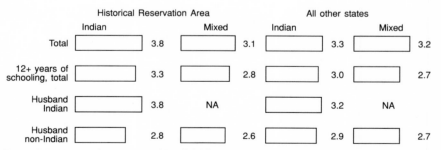

Figure 9.3. Estimated average number of children ever born to married Indian women, aged 35 to 44 and living in cities, by several characteristics: United States, 1980. NA = not available; too few cases to report. See Appendix Table 8.4 for further details.

The *largest average CEB, about 5.2 children,* is found among rural Indian women (of Indian ancestry only), married, living in the Historical Reservation Area, who had not completed high school (under 12 years of schooling), and whose husbands also reported Indian ethnicity. Not being employed added almost nothing to the average of 5.2.

The *smallest CEB, about 2.6,* is found among the married urban women of mixed ancestry, in whatever part of the country they live, who completed high school (12 or more years of schooling), and whose husbands were not Indians. Employment of the woman seems to have but little additional influence.

The same pattern of interrelated influences operated at all ages for married women. For women who were not married at the time of the 1980 census (or had no "significant other") all rates—average number of children ever born—were lower. But the pattern of influences was similar.

We noted the end product of several interrelated forces or influences, which together raise or lower the Indian birthrate in the latter part of the twentieth century. To attempt to measure the importance of each separate influence, we feel, is a useless endeavor. The basic census information varies in quality from one component to another; for example, the information on urban or rural residence is of better quality than that on ancestry. Perhaps one element appears to be stronger than another simply because the original census (or other) information was better, or worse. Who knows?

Furthermore, we must ask whether any one of these influences can exist by itself. For example, if a woman lives on a reservation, she is likely to meet fewer non-Indian men than if she lives in a city distant from the reservation and that has an abundance of non-Indian men. Are these two components, marriage to a non-Indian and urban residence, two separate influences? Or are they both indicators of more basic underlying forces at work?

We can conclude that the latter part of the twentieth century, and perhaps earlier, the conditions that influenced the birthrate of the total country also influenced that of the Indian people. Add to this the history that is unique to the natives, and we have explained as much as possible about why the birthrate decreased and what differences there are within the total "Indian population," however Indian is defined.

Canada

From Prehistoric Times to the Twentieth Century

We suggest that the birthrate as measured by TFR for the Canadian natives was close to, but perhaps a mite higher than that of their south-of-the-border cousins, in the centuries and millennia prior to the European invasion. No Ancestors and few natives who lived in the nineteenth century are present today to enlighten us, and they left no written records; therefore, there is no point in pursuing further this pre–twentieth century period.

Declining Rates in the Twentieth Century

There was a general decline in TFR, especially in the latter part (Figure 9.4). Further, the changes from one decade to the next were remarkably similar for the Canadian natives, the total Canadian population, and the U.S. Indians. Clearly, the same major and pervasive influences were operating in both countries and on all the inhabitants of each.

The TFR of the Canadian Indians may have declined but little or not at all, during the first third of the century. During the Depression years of the 1930s, it fell somewhat and rose in the post-World War II boom years to its previous pre-Depression level. The most pronounced decline (so far) occurred in the 1960s and 1970s.

Romaniuc (n.d.) analyzed the information about Indian women for the years 1961, 1971, and 1981, and found

> further evidence of the prevalence of a relatively uncontrolled marital fertility prior to the 1960s. The 1961 census series could actually be regarded as reflecting the regime of "natural" fertility, that is, one characterized by the absence of significant family limitation within marriage. (p. 8)

Romaniuc's remarks about the "prevalence of a relatively uncontrolled marital fertility prior to the 1960s" is suggested by the trends of TFR and CEB (Figures 9.4 and 9.5). There was no or little change in the TFR from 1931 to 1961,[3] after which there was a significant decrease. The CEB rates also show little or no change between the end of World War II and 1961, after which the rate begins to decline. Romaniuc provides no information for the earlier part of the twentieth century, and we were unable to estimate TFR prior to 1931. Nevertheless, we surmise from his analysis that earlier in the twentieth century, the TFR and probably CEB changed comparatively little until the time of World War II. TFR for the Canadian Native People most likely was of the order we estimated for their south-of-the-border kinfolk, about 6 or 7 children.

TFR and CEB for the Canadian natives are significantly higher than for the total Canadian population. We believe that as the forces that influence the birthrate continue to operate, the Amerindian birthrate will approach closer to that of the national rate. In 1981 the Amerindian TFR was about half again as high as the national, 2.8 as compared with 1.8. By the year 2001, we anticipate that the Indian TFR will be significantly closer to the national rate.

---

[3] See Romaniuc n.d., pp. 18–21, "Canada's Indians: Transition from Traditional High to Modern Low."

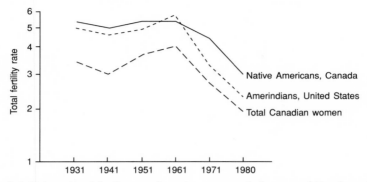

Figure 9.4. Estimated total fertility rates for native women and all women of Canada aged 35 to 44, 1931 to 1981, and U.S. Amerindians, 1930 to 1980. Source: See Appendix 8 table.

Trovato (1987, p. 481) arrived at much the same conclusion, a continuing narrowing of the gap, on the basis of his analysis. He wrote:

> This analysis suggests that while modernization generally implies long-term declines in Native Indian fertility, their above average reproductive levels in comparison with the rest of Canada are likely to persist for some time into the future. Native Indian subculture on the one hand, and the discontinuous nature of modernization on the other, serve to enhance reproductive performance among this minority group, therefore slowing their fertility decline.

The CEB measure, as the TFR (Figure 9.4 and 9.5), indicates that the decreases in the birthrate are a rather recent development. In 1961 the CEB for native women aged 35 to 44 was well over 6; in 1981 it had fallen to about 4.6. The future? Native CEB is still above that of the nonnative women, but for how much longer? Unfortunately, we have no information for native women of mixed Indian and non-Indian ancestry. If such information were available, we might be able to see the future more clearly.

Influences on the Birthrate

The same elements on both sides of the border affect the birthrate. Certainly, urbanism lowers the rate (TFR) for the status and nonstatus Indians, the Métis, and even the Inuit who live in the Arctic areas (Figure 9.6).

The Canadian Indian's birthrate, like that of her southern relatives, is also influenced by the heritage of the person. The status Indians have Indian ancestors and comparatively little non-Indian blood (see Chapter 10). This group is comparable to the U.S. Indians, both biologically and culturally, whom we characterized as "reporting only Indian ancestors." The nonstatus Indians are largely of mixed ancestry. Clearly, the status people have higher TFR than the nonstatus. The Métis, by definition, are people of mixed ancestry. The nonstatus

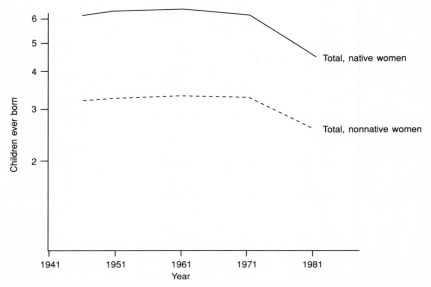

Figure 9.5. Children-ever-born rates for native women and all women of Canada (ever married women) aged 35 to 44: 1946 to 1981.

and the Métis together are the Canadian counterpart, both biologically and culturally, of the U.S. Indians whom we referred to as the "mixed," people having both Indian and non-Indian ancestry.

Rural Canadian status Amerindians, particularly those living on reserves, had a TFR of 3.4, whereas the rural nonstatus had a TFR of 2.7, short of one child fewer. On the other hand, there is no difference between the two groups in the birthrate in urban areas.

The Métis have virtually the same birthrate as the status Indians.

The Inuit have the highest birthrate of all. Dr. James Smith (personal correspondence) has attributed this to their geographic isolation and recent introduction to the amenities of the white man's/woman's culture.

Information on amount of schooling and the birthrate is available for status women. The CEB per woman (in 1981 for those aged 40 to 44) was:

Less than 9 grades	6.1 children
9 to 13 grades	4.4
Postsecondary	3.8

This pattern holds at every age level.

Increased schooling is associated with urbanism and probably type of ethnicity and ancestors. However, it is impossible for us to untangle these

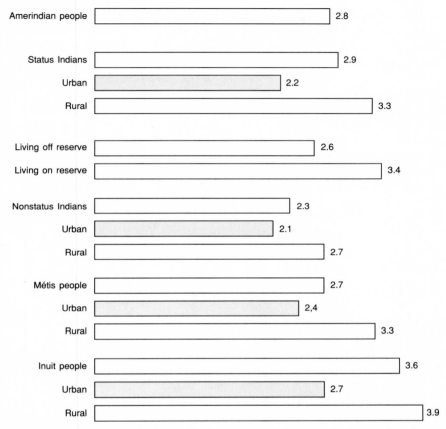

Figure 9.6. Estimated total fertility rate for the Native People by type and urban–rural residence: Canada, 1981. See Appendix Table 8.3.

various elements in Canada as we did for the U.S. Indian people; we do not have sufficient basic information.

DEATH RATES AND LENGTH OF LIFE

Introduction

There are several ways of measuring the death rate, and each measures a somewhat different aspect. There are death rates for each age, for each sex, crude death rates, and so forth. Each type of rate provides a different number. But all will generally show the same direction of movement or change. Is the movement for one group, for example, city people, different from another group, for example, rural people? Is the death rate increasing, decreasing, or remaining largely unchanged, for any group of people? We choose to use the life table as our measure of the death rate; more specifically, length of life, or life expectancy at birth, is the number of main interest for our purposes. (See Appendix 8 for technical details.)

Obviously, every *Homo sapiens sapiens,* as well as all other life forms, must die, but some live for a shorter time than do others; they die sooner. For example, if life expectancy at the time of birth is 30 years for one group and 40 years for another, we can say with confidence that the first group has a higher death rate, however you may care to measure it. In the following discussion, the term *life expectancy* or length of life (how many years are you likely to live?), if used without further specification, always refers to the number of years of life to which a newborn can look forward or expect. If any other age is discussed, we specify the age, for example, life expectancy at age 20, 40, 90, or whatever.

United States

From Prehistoric Times to the Twentieth Century

The number of Indian people decreased considerably between 1500 and the last quarter of the nineteenth century. The wars with the whites and the Great Father–Mother in Washington, together with intertribal warfare, disease, and hunger, all must have contributed to a large increase in the death rate (Chapter 7). Exactly how much the death rate increased and how much, if any, the birthrate may have fallen to produce the great decrease in population we shall never know.

Toward the end of the nineteenth century, wars and intertribal killings had largely stopped. The natives were ensconced on reservations and the Great Father–Mother was supplying some food and medical attention. The death rate must have fallen, and the people began to increase in numbers.[4] Whether an increase in the birthrate also contributed its mite to population growth we shall never know. Suffice it to say that toward the end of the nineteenth century, the death rate must have been lower than it was in prehistoric times; this is our best estimate.

Increase in Life Expectancy during the Twentieth Century

At the beginning of the twentieth century, the number of years of life expectancy at birth was in the mid-30s. This is about double what it was in the

---

[4] See also *Indian Land Tenure,* 1935, pp. 66–67.

pre-European era, as we saw in Chapter 4. By 1980 reported life expectancy had doubled again, and rose to an estimated 67 years for men and 75 years for women (Table 9.1). In the twentieth century women outlived men, the reverse of the pre-European experiences.

Clearly, the years of life expectancy for the Indian population are significantly lower than that of the total population, especially before World War II. In 1940 the gap was between 10 and 15 years. In 1980 the reported gap was less than 5 years. The sizes of these gaps are about the same for men and women (Figures 9.7 and 9.8).

We believe that the direction of the changes—that is, decreasing death rates and increasing life expectancy—are correct. Nevertheless, we must note some limitations to the reported life tables. The tables prepared by the Indian Health Service[5] generally refer only to the people served by the Indian Health Service and account for approximately half the number who reported themselves as Amerindians to the 1980 census. Those served by the IHS are the only ones for which it is responsible. Furthermore, most of those served by the IHS reside on or near reservations. Those people who live away from the reservation areas and are interspersed with the general population tend to be omitted, especially if they do not qualify for IHS medical attention. We think that those Indians not included probably have death rates and life expectancy rather similar to that of the general U.S. population.

Violent Deaths

The higher total death rates from all causes and lower life expectancy of the Indian people in contrast to non-Indians, has been attributed in part to their higher death rate from violence. The ratio of the Indian death rates (if the Indians had the same age distribution as the total U.S. population) to that of the total United States follows.[6] A ratio of 1.0 means that both sets of rates are the same; above 1.0 signifies a higher Indian death rate.

	Male	Female
Motor vehicle accidents	3.3	3.9
Other accidents	3.6	2.7
Homicide	1.9	2.7
Suicide	1.9	1.0
All causes of death	1.3	1.4

An analogous study of causes of death in the rural parts of the Mountain

[5] See Appendix 8.
[6] Indian Health Service, photocopies.

Table 9.1. Estimated Years of Life Expectancy at Birth by Sex:
United States, Indians and Total: 1910 to 1980

Years	Indians		Total United States	
	Men	Women	Men	Women
1910	34.0	37.7	50.2	53.6
1939–41	51.3	51.9	62.0	65.3
1949–51	53.1	62.2	65.5	71.0
1959–61[a]	NA	NA	66.8	73.3
1969–71	60.7	71.2	67.1	74.5
1979–81	67.1	75.1	70.0	77.5

Source: See Appendix 8.
[a]Information not available for Indians by sex. For both sexes combined, life
  expectancy was 61.7 years at birth.

states made by Greenberg *et al.* (1985) of white youth aged 15 to 24, revealed substantially the same pattern. (A very large proportion of deaths from violence occur in this age group.) Greenberg expressed the death rate as a percentage of the national rate as follows:

	Male	Female
Motor vehicle accidents	148%	165%
Other accidents	143	110
Homicide	129	150
Suicide	167	209
All causes of death	139	139

The authors ascribe the higher death rates from violence in these Mountain states to geographic and cultural origins. For example, auto accidents are related to more driving because of greater distances and greater geographic isolation; compare the rural Rocky Mountain region with any city.

Although Greenberg's numbers are not precisely comparable to those of *Indian Health Care* (1986), they tell much the same story. Hence, Greenberg's findings are significant for interpreting the Amerindian life tables and death rates. Recall that the available life tables favor the reservation population, the majority of whom live west of the Mississippi River. And under geographic conditions similar to those studied by Greenberg. We conclude that excessive mortality from violence is not necessarily a unique Indian characteristic. Probably all people who live under these "Wild West" conditions have more violent deaths.

The death rates from all other causes may be approximately the same for the Indian Health constituency and the total United States. We cannot determine this possibility from the information available to us.

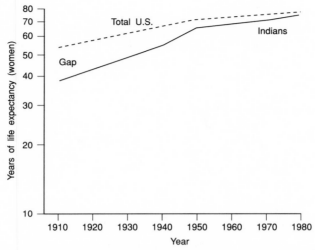

Figure 9.7. Estimated years of life expectancy for women at birth: U.S. Indians and total, 1910 to 1980.

Canada

The saga of the Canadian Indians is much the same as that of their southern cousins. The death rate must have increased between 1500 and the mid- or latter 1800s, then decreased somewhat. The major decrease occurred during the latter part of the twentieth century.

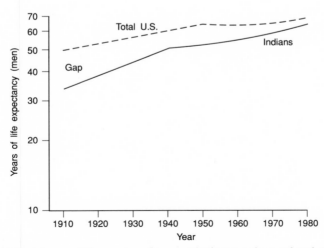

Figure 9.8. Estimated years of life expectancy for men at birth: U.S. Indians and total, 1910 to 1980.

Our major information on life expectancy for the Canadian native people begins with the period 1960–64. For the prior years the only information we located was the estimated crude death rates from 1900 on (these rates are the numbers of deaths per 1,000 population). The crude death rate and life expectancy generally show similar direction of change, although the precise amount of change may differ.

Latulippe-Sakamoto estimated crude death rates for the years 1900 to 1968, based on whatever fragments of data were available (we updated her series to 1980). Although these rates are only for the registered or status Indians, they reflect the general pattern of decreasing death rates for all Canadian Indians.

From the start of the twentieth century to the mid-1930s, the death rate declined slowly (Figure 9.9). During the years of World War II and until the mid-1960s, the rate plunged and reached a level some two-thirds below that at the beginning of the century. From the mid-1960s on, the rates continued to decline but slowly. By the 1980s, the crude death rate of the status Amerindians appears to be very close to that of the total national population.

Length of life (at birth) increased about 4 years for men (from 60 to 64 years), and perhaps 9 years for women (from 64 to 73 years), among the status Indians during the 1960s, 1970s, and 1980s (see Appendix Table 8.7). The status people comprise about two-thirds of all natives (excluding the Inuit). No life tables are available for the nonstatus and Métis.

Siggner explains (1979, pp. 7–9) why mortality among the status Indians is somewhat higher than that of the general Canadian population: "The first is

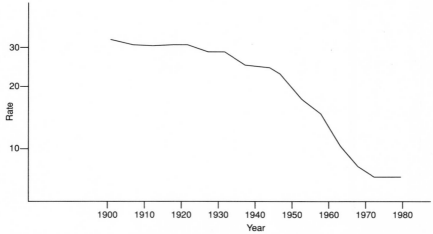

Figure 9.9. Estimated crude death rate for the registered (status) Indians of Canada: 1900 to 1979 (rate per 1,000 population). Source: Appendix Table 8.6.

that the Indian population still has much higher death rates among infants . . .
the relative isolation of Indian communities, the quality of housing, lack of
sewage disposal and potable water, and lack of access to medical facilities" (see
also Appendix Table 8.7).

VITAL EVENTS AND POPULATION GROWTH—A SUMMARY

We have seen how the birth and death rates of the Native Americans, both north
and south of the border, are converging toward that of the general populations
of the two countries. We now combine births and deaths to measure population
growth in the future, if not at the moment, using the *net reproduction rate* (NRR).
We explain this rate.

The NRR measures the rate at which a population is growing at present
(i.e., the date of the vital statistics) or may increase or decrease in the future if
the vital rates do *not* change. It is based on female births only and death rates
of women during the reproductive years, generally considered to be between 15
and 44 (or 49) years of age. It answers the question: How many female descendants would a group of women in the reproductive ages leave alive to replace the
mothers after all the mothers have died or passed the childbearing ages? A rate
of 1.0 means that the number of female births after taking the number of deaths
into consideration will just equal the number of original mothers. Hence, the
population is not changing in size. If the rate is *less than 1.0* the total population
would decline—if the birth and death rates at each age remain unchanged in
future years. If the rate is *more than 1.0,* the total population would increase
absent any changes in the birth and death rates.

The size of the NRR indicates how much the population is likely to increase
or decrease in each generation, about 30 years, if the vital rates do not change.
For example, an estimated NRR of 1.1 tells us that the population would
increase by 10% over the next generation. A rate of .9 (.9 minus 1.0 = −.1)
indicates a potential decline of 10% per generation.

The NRR of the Indian people decreased substantially since 1910 (Appendix
Table 8.1) in the United States. Our best estimate is about 1.6 for 1910, 1.4 for
1970, and still lower for 1980. Judging from the information for CEB, we estimate
that NRR may have decreased to between 1.0 and 1.2 in the United States in 1980.

In Canada the NRR decreased from an estimated 1.9 in 1931 to 1.4 in 1981
(Figure 9.10).

The TFR (total fertility rate) also declined substantially in both countries,
but much more than did the NRR. The very rapid decline in the death rate
during the twentieth century compensated in part for the decline in the birthrate. By the 1980s, however, the Indian death rate was rapidly approaching that
of the total population; hence, future changes in the Amerindian NRR will result

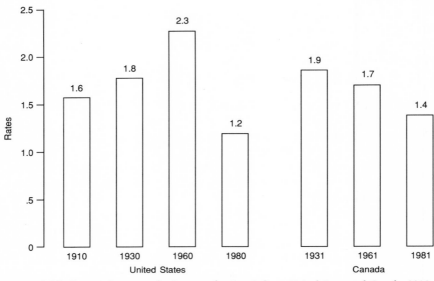

Figure 9.10. Estimated net reproduction rates for Amerindians, United States and Canada: 1910 to 1980. Source: Appendix Tables 8.1 and 8.3.

mostly from changes in the TFR. If and when the Indian TFR equals (or almost equals) that of the total U.S. and Canadian populations, the NRRs will be very similar to that countrywide.

In the meantime, we note that in 1980 and 1985 the NRR for the total U.S. population was about .95, and about the same or perhaps a little lower in Canada. This indicates a potential loss of population. Nevertheless, the populations in both countries continue to grow. Why? Both countries import people instead of producing all their own. Population production is considered in the same light as the manufacturing of steel or automobiles.[7] There are other reasons also, but this is not the place for a lengthy presentation on the dynamics of population growth.

Convergence of the Amerindian demographic characteristics with that of the Eastern Hemisphere-origin people who settled north of the Rio Grande is continuing. Will the two ever meet? Check this in about the middle of the twenty-first century.

[7] There is no or very little actual in or outmigration of American Indians between the United States and the rest of the world. However, change in reported ethnicity amounts to migration. One who reports to the Census as Indian in one census and as non-Indian in the following enumeration is equivalent to an emigrant. A shift from non-Indian to Indian is the equivalent of immigration.

Chapter 10

The Mixing of the Genes: Intermarriage

INTRODUCTION

Amerindian and Eastern Hemisphere genes have been mixing since at least the eleventh century. In that century Vikings under Leif Ericson reached northern Newfoundland and settled in what is now L'Anse aux Meadows (Morison 1971, Chapter 3). The Vikings referred to the natives whom they encountered, and of course fought, as Skraelings. It is uncertain whether these were the last of the Dorset Eskimo (the sagas describe them as attacking in skin boats) or the Beothuk Indians (Such 1978, p. 38). We cannot say for certain that Viking and native genes mixed, but we assume that they did. There are no Dorset Eskimo nor Beothuk alive today to give evidence.

Between the time of the Vikings and Columbus, very little gene mixing probably occurred. A few European fishermen reached the Grand Bank of Newfoundland, but when they landed in order to smoke their fish to preserve it, how much contact they may have had with the natives is unknown.

Once Columbus and his party arrived, gene mixture began in earnest.

Our central questions, hence, are:

1. How much gene mixing has occurred near the close of the twentieth century?
2. Is the rate of admixture more or less rapid in the latter part of the twentieth century than in earlier times?
3. What are the social and other influences that result in the mixing of the genes?

The answer to "how much?" is simply "very much." There are no statistics to tell us precisely what proportion of the present Amerindian population is full-blood.

The answer to the second question, we believe, is that the rate of mixing is more rapid since World War II than earlier, as we discuss subsequently.

The third question is answered, in part at least, in this and the following chapters.

Generalized answers to these questions were presented in the 1930 U.S. Census (1930, p. 70); we quote the relevant parts. We shall update these 1930 observations and amplify them using the new information and statistics for both Canada and the United States.

Classification by Admixture of Blood

The degree of admixture of white or Negro blood among the Indians, in relation both to geographic location and to tribal affiliation, is very important in any sociological study of the race. An admixture of the blood of other races is usually accompanied by a breakdown of tribal customs, and by adoption, in whole or in part, of the habits and manner of life of another race. An admixture of white blood began with the earliest white settlement in all parts of the United States. The marriage of Pocohontas to John Rolfe is only one instance of the admixture of races in Virginia. The French settlers in the North mingled freely with the Indians, as did the Spaniards of the South. With the introduction of Negro slaves into the South still another racial element was introduced. Fugitive slaves found refuge among the southern Indian tribes, and at a later date many Indians, particularly of the Choctaw, Creek, Cherokee, and Chickasaw tribes, themselves became slave owners and carried Negro slaves with them on their forced migrations west of the Mississippi. After emancipation, these Negroes continued to live with the tribe as freedmen, speaking the Indian language and observing many tribal customs. Such close relationship cannot long exist without admixture of blood.

UNITED STATES

Full versus Mixed Blood

In 1910, the earliest date for which we could find information, the census reported that at least one in three Indians was of mixed blood, and a little under two in three were "full" blood. It is likely that the proportion who were full blood was really smaller than that reported (Table 10.1).

Oklahoma was the final home of multitudes of eastern Indians who were driven from their homes and forcibly settled in Indian Territory, the original name of this state (Foreman 1982; Wright 1981). Presumably, by the time of their removal, there had been considerable intermixture with the European invaders. The Historical Reservation Area (see Appendix 6) originally was inhabited largely by Indians native to this part of the United States, probably since pre-European times. In the HRA, about one person in three reported being mixed. But many members of this mixed group lived in Oklahoma. The popu-

Table 10.1. Admixture Reported, Amerindians: U.S. 1910 and 1930

	1910[a]				1930[b]			
	Total	Full blood	Mixed blood	Not reported	Total	Full blood	Mixed blood	Not reported
U.S. total	100%	61	38	1	100%	46	42	11
Historical Reservation Areas	100%	64	34	2	100%	53	41	7
Oklahoma	100%	36	63	1	100%	28	66	6
Other states	100%	81	17	2	100%	69	24	7
All other states	100%	53	46	1	100%	31	47	22

[a]U.S. Census, 1910: pp. 31–42.
[b]U.S. Census, 1930: Chapter 3.

lation in the Historical Reservation Area, except in Oklahoma, reported fewer than one in five as being mixed (Table 10.1 and Figure 10.1).

In the remaining states—those outside the Historical Reservation Area—about one in two reported as being of mixed blood in 1910. These people were largely the remnants of the tribes east of the Mississippi River who had been in contact with the Eastern Hemisphere people since at least the time of Columbus.

We emphasize the difference between the HRA and other states mainly to indicate the social and cultural differences between them. These differences that we shall explore are related to our third question: What are the social conditions that result in the mixing of the genes?

By 1930 the picture seems not to have changed. The census again attempted to collect statistics on full and mixed blood. If any change had oc-

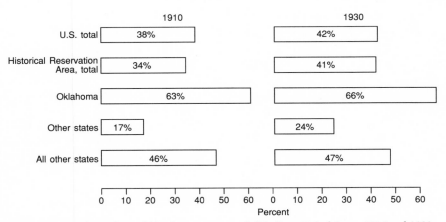

Figure 10.1. Indians of mixed blood as percentage of all Indians: United States, 1910 and 1930.
Source: U.S. Census 1910 and 1930.

curred since 1910 the census data are too imprecise to record it (Table 10.1 and Figure 10.1).

As far as we can determine there was comparatively little change in Amerindian society during these two decades, 1910 to 1930, and no change in geography of residence. About 7 in 10 lived in the HRA at both dates, and most lived on or near reservations.

Since 1930 the census has not attempted to obtain information regarding the extent of full versus mixed blood. We believe, nevertheless, that the number (and proportion) of Indians of mixed Indian and non-Indian ancestry has increased significantly since 1930. This is indicated by the increased volume of interracial marriages to be discussed next.

Marriage to Non-Indians

How Many?

By "marriage" we mean simply heterosexual unions, official or unofficial, which the census reports under the heading "married." (The census has enquired about civil condition since 1880, with no significant changes in definition of "married.") Unfortunately, for purposes of studies such as ours, there is no uniquely correct way of measuring and interpreting information on the amount or the rate of outmarriage, in our case marriages of Indians to non-Indians. Let us illustrate with this hypothetical example.

Suppose that we have two men and two women—Amerindians or members of any other ethnic group. All four are married or otherwise coupled as follows:

- Indian man married to an Indian woman
- Indian man married to a non-Indian woman
- Indian woman married to a non-Indian man

We have three couples, only one of which consists of both spouses being Indian. Shall we say that two out of three married non-Indians? Or shall we say that half of the Indian men and women married non-Indians?

As of 1980 we have (Figure 10.2):

- Of all couples involving Amerindians in only three in 10 were both spouses Indian. In seven in 10 one spouse was not an Indian—that is, outmarriage.
- Of all Indian women with spouse in 1980, about half were married to non-Indian men.
- Of all Indian men with spouse in 1980, about half were married to non-Indians.

These 1980 rates of outmarriage are significantly higher than those esti-

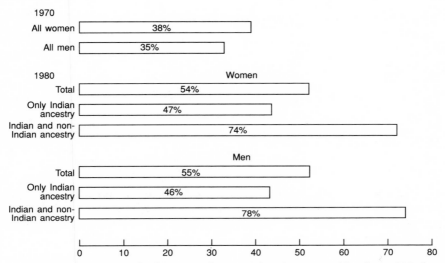

Figure 10.2. Percentage of Indians married to non-Indians by sex, ages 15 and over: United States, 1970 and 1980. Source: Tables 10.2 and 10.3.

mated for 1970 when only about 4 in 10 were reported as married to non-Indians. We believe, despite the inadequacies of the basic census data, that an increase in outmarriage and a decrease in marriage between Indians did occur (Tables 10.2 and 10.3).

The Rate of Outmarriages Has Increased

One indicator of outmarriage (or intermarriage) is the reported number of births by reported race of mother and father. Thanks to the Indian Health Service we have unpublished information for the years 1964–66, 1974–76, and 1985–86. Newborns are classified as both parents Indian, only mother Indian, and only father Indian. In the 1960s a little over one in three of the births was reported as having a non-Indian parent, in the 1970s a little over half, and in the 1980s about two in three of all births were so reported. Presumably, these numbers indicate that there was a significant increase in outmarriage during the last three decades, even if the numbers of births are only approximations. On the other hand, these numbers may have resulted from people changing their racial designation from non-Indian to Indian since World War II (as we discussed in Chapter 1). However, as we shall see, the information on outmarriage by age of the woman, lends credence to the conclusion that there was a true increase despite our inability to measure the change precisely.

Table 10.2. Percentage of Indian Women Married to Non-Indian Men: U.S. 1970

Age	U.S.	HRA[a]	Other states
All ages	38	29	49
16–19	40	32	47
20–24	41	32	48
25–34	39	29	49
35–44	38	27	51
45–64	37	27	48
65+	36	29	46

[a]HRA = Historical Reservation Area.

The type of marriage at each age reflects the extent of outmarriage at some past time.[1] For example, in 1980 married women aged 15 to 24 most probably married between 1975 and 1980. Women aged 25 to 34 probably married between 1965 and 1975. Most of the women aged 55 and over probably married around the time of World War II. Hence, by examining the extent of out-marriages at each age, we obtain a glimpse of the amount of outmarriage at the time that this age group first married.

Prior to World War II, we think that there were no appreciable long-time changes or trends in the extent of intermarriage (Table 10.3 and Figure 10.3). Some unions with non-Indians occurred in colonial times and all during the decades of confinement on reservations. The presence of so many of mixed blood in the early twentieth century attests to this. We suggest that augmented increases began around the time of World War II.

Much of the increase in outmarriages over the last several decades occurred outside the Historical Reservation Area. The proportion of Indian women whose husbands were not Indians was significantly higher in the younger age groups than in the older ones (Table 10.3), implying an increase in outmarriage since at least World War II. This pattern appears for both those reporting only Indian ancestry and those women reporting mixed ancestry.

Within the HRA, however, there is little difference among the age groups. Perhaps the amount of outmarriage was slightly higher in the youngest age group (15 to 24). Either there is less outmarriage in these states, or many of those who marry non-Indians leave. Or perhaps unmarried individuals leave the Historical Reservation Area for the El Dorados of California or the eastern states where they meet and marry non-Indians.

---

[1] This interpretation of marriage rates for converting an age distribution into a time series is developed in Chapter 8, footnote 16. It is based on the assumptions that (a) the intermarriage rates observed in 1980 or any other point in time are very similar to those at the time of marriage; and (b) different death rates and/or divorce or separation or remarriage rates among the several age groups have not distorted the age comparisons.

Table 10.3. Estimated Percentage of Indian Women Married to Non-Indian Men:
U.S. 1980

Age	U.S.	HRA[a] states	Other states	HRA states ancestry[b]		Other states ancestry[b]	
				Indian only	Mixed	Indian only	Mixed
All ages	54	40	65	33	74	60	74
15–24	60	44	72	36	77	67	82
25–34	55	40	67	33	74	62	75
35–44	53	39	64	33	73	59	71
45–54	51	40	62	34	70	55	72
55+	49	40	58	31	73	52	70

[a]HRA = Historical Reservation Area.
[b]See Appendix 2.

Influences Conducive to Outmarriage

The same demographic characteristics that influence the birthrate also are important influences on outmarriage of Indians. Indeed, the experiences of the Amerindians in North America may be but little different from those of other ethnic groups (see Appendix Table 10.3):

1. Indian women in *urban areas* are more likely to have non-Indian husbands than are those living in rural areas.
2. Those who *completed high school* are more likely to have non-Indian husbands than are those who did not complete high school.
3. Indian women who reported having *both Indian and non-Indian ancestors* are more likely to have non-Indian mates than are those women who reported having only Indian ancestors.
4. Residence *outside the Historical Reservation Area* is conducive to, or at least associated with, marriage to non-Indians.

The combination of demographic characteristics that lead to the least amount of outmarriage, only one in six, is found among women who reported only Indian ancestry, lived in rural parts of the HRA, and did not complete high school.

The most outmarriage, four in five women, occurred among those who reported mixed ancestry, non-Indian and Indian, lived outside of the HRA, and had completed high school.

Probably the single most important influence on inmarriage or outmarriage, marrying an Indian or non-Indian spouse, is residence in an area where there are large numbers of Indians and a strong community that can provide support and spouses to its members. The reservation supplies these functions. Because reservations are generally located in rural areas and mostly in the Historical Reservation Area, we find one factor contributes to the observed urban–rural difference.

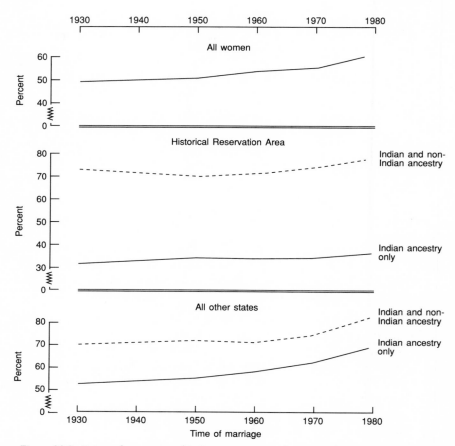

Figure 10.3. Estimated percentage of Indian women married to non-Indian men: United States, pre-World War II to 1980. Source: See Table 10.3 and text.

Urban residence is a recent condition. In 1910 only about 1 in 20 lived in cities; in 1940 some 1 in 10; in 1950 about 15%; and one generation later, in 1980, over half were urbanites. We expect that this vast increase since World War II resulted in a significant increase in intermarriage (Figure 10.4).

Urban growth reflects the lessening importance of the Historical Reservation Area. At the turn of the twentieth century, about 7 in 10 lived in these states. By the outbreak of World War II around 1940, 6 in 10, and by 1980 less than half. The Amerindians are leaving the ghettos.

The importance of higher schooling, graduation from high school or more, is also a result of reservation life, in part at least. The number of jobs requiring advanced education are limited on reservations, as is the case for everyone living

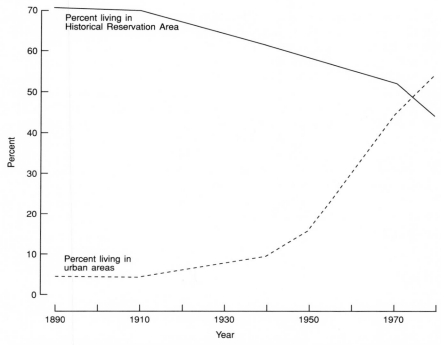

Figure 10.4. Percentage of Indians living in Historical Reservation Area and percentage living in urban areas: United States, 1890 to 1980. Source: See text.

in small towns and cities elsewhere. How many physicians, surgeons, lawyers, certified public accountants, museum curators, private secretaries, or other such positions are available in a population of even 5,000, and most reservations have fewer inhabitants. If the people living adjacent to reservations are included (as the Bureau of Indian Affairs counts) there may be an average of about 5,000 inhabitants per reservation and in adjacent areas. (We have been unable to obtain a definition of "adjacent.") As a result, most Indians who do obtain advanced schooling probably leave the reservations and head for the larger cities where they have greater job opportunities. Some reservations are bedroom suburbs of larger cities, and inhabitants of such places can find jobs requiring higher education without leaving the reservation. Some of the New Mexico pueblos, for example, are within commuting distance of Los Alamos, Albuquerque, and the state capital, Santa Fe. But the majority of the reservations are located in the boondocks, and the residents do not have access to better jobs. So why go as far as even high-school graduation unless one expects to leave the reservation?

Those of mixed ancestry had progenitors who had made their peace with the white man before the establishment of reservations, or who had left reservations some time in the past and whose attachment to any tribe was minimal. These ancestors most likely had more contacts with non-Indians, as attested to by those of mixed ancestry living in 1980. Whatever the sequel of historical events may have been, those of mixed ancestry in 1980 had more schooling, and many more were urban residents. They were sufficiently detribalized to marry non-Indians. Or they were living in areas where only non-Indian mates were available at the time they were seeking mates.

In short, leaving the reservation-ghettos and settling in cities led to more contacts with non-Indians. And as Ajax de Smyrna's first law says: "More outmarriages follow more contacts." Every ethnic group finds this to be true.

Why so many left the Historical Reservation Area, why so many went to the cities, and what the pull of the outside world may be, is a topic suitable for another study.

CANADA

Introduction

The story of the Native Peoples (so designated in the 1981 population census) in Canada is very similar to that of their brethren living in what is now the United States. Indeed, since the Vikings landed in Newfoundland in the eleventh century, we expect that admixture began then, perhaps four centuries before intermixture began south of the present border.

A major impetus to intermarriage (or outmarriage) originally was the fur trade.[2] In the sixteenth century and later, there was a great demand in Europe for furs, especially beaver pelts for hat making. The Canadian wilderness apparently held an unlimited supply of fur-bearing animals, and the French, English, and others took advantage of this furry gold. Between 1534 and 1541, Jacques Cartier explored the St. Lawrence River system and began laying the groundwork for extensive trading with the Indians. Samuel de Champlain explored and fought Indians from 1603 to 1615; he took time out in 1608 to found Quebec City. While in Canada he explored the northern areas and arranged for Indians to trade their furs to the French. In 1610, Henry Hudson explored the Hudson Bay area, and the British Hudson's Bay Company was chartered in 1670 to trade with the Indians for furs.

The European traders needed the Indian men to hunt and trap the animals

---

[2] This very brief historical summary is abstracted from Harison (1985), Waldman (1985), and the *Atlas of Canada* (1981).

and act as guides through the wilderness. Because these traders generally arrived with no families, they needed Indian women for family purposes, making clothes, cooking, and the like as well as sex, and to act as liaisons with the Indian tribes. A trader who married an Indian woman became a member of the tribe, in part at least, and had a permanent home in the Canadian wilderness.

The emphasis on the fur trade probably reflects the lack of much good farmland as well as the opportunity to "make a quick franc." If they had wanted to be farmers they could have gone south of the St. Lawrence River Valley and brought their European families with them.[3] As a result of entering the Canadian wilderness, intermarriage and gene mixture occurred early. The Métis (or "mixed") originated. Harison (1985), with tongue in cheek, wrote: "Some historians claim that the first Métis was born nine months after these European fur traders arrived" (p. 10).

Extent of Intermixture, Late Twentieth Century

Introduction

Four types of Native People are reported in the 1981 census of Canada: the Inuits (whom we omit from our analysis), status Indians, nonstatus Indians, and Métis. The 1981 census asked for self-identification, and these four categories were printed on the census schedule. (The difference between status and nonstatus is a legal one; only the former are entitled to certain government benefits.)

The Native People's categories contain significant proportions of persons of mixed ancestry.[4] The Métis by definition are of mixed ancestry. However, over the centuries members have been lost to this group as some rejoined their maternal ancestral tribes and became Indians again, and some blended into the nonnative population. According to Harison (p. 15), the Métis in the 1980s "see themselves as different and separate from both Indians and whites . . . . Many contemporary Métis see themselves as a distinct people," neither Indian nor white.

Some Métis are known to have migrated to the United States. As far as the United States census is concerned, these immigrants lost their Métis designation.

---

[3] The influence of farming opportunities upon the size of the Indian population and European settlement was discussed in Chapter 7. That there were almost as many European-origin women as men in seventeenth- and eighteenth-century U.S. and fewer women in Canada, is suggested by scattered data in (for example) Sutherland (1936), and Greene and Harrington (1932).

[4] For information about ancestry or ethnicity from the 1981 census, catalogue 92-911, see p. vi, "Definitions." The native respondent could enter as many ethnic categories as desired, one to indicate that he/she is a native, and any others. Those who checked only one ethnic origin to indicate Native People were tabulated as "single response." Those who checked more than one were tabulated as "multiple response," that is, multiple ancestry. We assume that the latter are similar, more or less, to the U.S. Amerindians whom we designate as "mixed."

In terms of the U.S. 1980 census, these people can be classified as Indians or not depending on how they reported themselves.

The status and nonstatus Indians also include a number of mixed ancestry, in part due to Canadian law (this law was changed in 1985). If a status (or registered) Indian man married a woman who was not a status Indian (white, Métis, nonstatus, or other race), she became a member of the tribe or band and a status Indian. Obviously, the children of such intermarriages must have been of mixed ancestry.

Further, if a status Indian woman married a man who was not a status Indian, she became a nonstatus Indian. The children of many of these women must have been of mixed ancestry.

The nonstatus population contains an unknown proportion of full-blood Indians as well as mixed-blood. If for whatever reason an Indian group failed to be recognized by the Canadian government, its members became nonstatus.

Some Numbers

Significantly more than one in three of the Native Peoples is of mixed ancestry. The Métis and nonstatus together comprise almost 4 in 10 of all Native People (excluding the Inuit). If the Métis are omitted, we still believe that at least 1 in 3 is of mixed ancestry. We claim no exactitude; the numbers simply indicate that, as in the United States, a large proportion have non-Indian ancestors (Table 10.4 and Figure 10.5).

The reported numbers in the 1981 census indicate that the number of mixed ancestry amounts to at least 152,000.[5] We believe that there are many more mixed who failed to report multiple ancestry. We suggest that if the census question had been asked differently, more of mixed ancestry would have been recorded. Hence, probably more than one in three is of mixed ancestry.

Indeed, according to the 1986 census (sample), there were close to 130,000 Métis (in comparison with the 98,000 reported in 1981) and about 240,000 Native People who reported multiple ancestral origins. The total number of status and nonstatus Indians in 1986—531,000—plus the 130,000 Métis (all of whom are of mixed ancestry by definition) provide an estimate of about 55% as being of mixed Indian and non-Indian ancestry. Before deciding whether one-third or one-half of the Native People are of mixed ancestry we must note apparent inconsistencies between the two censuses as described by Norris (1989) (see Appendix 5).

There are several estimates of the numbers of Métis and nonstatus from sources other than the census. Some estimates reach close to 1 million people for both groups combined. C. E. Taylor (1972), of Innis College, University of Toronto, assembled estimates from seven sources and commented upon them.

---

[5] This number includes the Métis. We set the number of Métis of multiple ancestry equal to the total number reported by the census, because by definition the Métis are of mixed ethnicity.

Table 10.4. Number of Native People by Classification: Canada 1981 and 1986[a]

	1981			1986		
	Total	Mixed (multiple responses)	Percentage mixed	Total	Mixed	Percentage mixed
Total	466,000	152,400	33	660,000	368,000	56
Métis	98,200	98,200	100	128,600	128,600	100
Other, total	367,800	54,200	15	531,400	239,400	45
Nonstatus	75,100	27,900	37	NA[b]	NA	NA
Status	292,700	26,300	9	NA	NA	NA

[a]See Appendix 5.
[b]NA = not available.

His first recommendation calls for more and better statistics and research. None of these reported estimates is included in our analysis.

Both Taylor and James Smith of the Museum of the American Indian emphasize that the distinction between Métis and nonstatus often is tenuous. Originally the term *Métis* was limited to the offspring of the European fur traders and Indian women. Over the years it began to be applied to many Indian–non-Indian mixed people, many of whom simply list themselves as nonstatus Indians. Classification is not simple.

How Do Canada and the United States Compare?

In Canada, 4 in 10 native women were married to nonnative men in 1981 (Figure 10.6). This is a lower outmarriage rate than in the United States, where between 5 and 6 in every 10 were reported as having non-Indian husbands.

Among the Canadian natives (single response) who are similar to those in the U.S. category "Indian ancestry only," close to 3 in 10 are married out. This compares with almost 5 in 10 south of the border.

Among those who are similar to the U.S. category "Mixed," between 6 and 7 are married out. This compares with almost 8 in 10 in the United States.

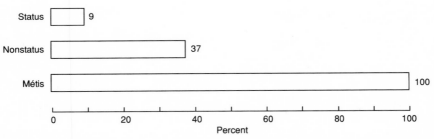

Figure 10.5. Percentage of Native People who are of mixed (i.e., multiple) ancestry by classification: Canada, 1981. See Table 10.4.

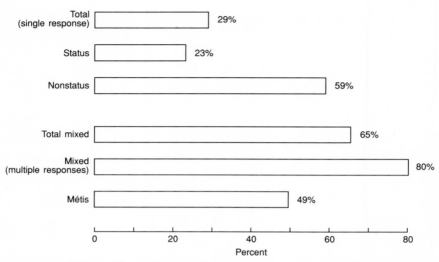

Figure 10.6. Percentage of native women married to nonnative men by classification: Canada, 1981. The "Total (single response)" category is approximately comparable to the U.S. category "Indian ancestors only." Source: See Appendix Table 10.4.

Note that among the nonstatus women about 6 in 10 are married to non-native men; this is virtually the same as the proportion of all Canadian mixed who have nonnative husbands (Figure 10.6). This resemblance strongly suggests that the nonstatus are largely of mixed ancestry; remember that in the United States, the mixed ancestry women married either mixed Indian or non-Indian men.

Note also that of the status women only one in four married out. We suggest that such a small proportion results in large measure from so many living in isolated reserves, far more than among the mixed Native People.

Among native men the amount of and patterns of outmarriage are rather similar to that for native women.

Outmarriage Has Increased

Intermarriage, or outmarriage, has increased in recent years, especially since World War II. We deduce this by comparing the percentage who reported having multiple ancestors among younger versus older people as of 1981. Consider:

Age in 1981	Years of birth	Percent multiple ancestry	Time of marriage of parents
Under 25 years	After 1957	17	Post-World War II
25 to 34 years	1947 to 1956	17	Around World War II or later
35 to 54 years	1927 to 1946	14	Pre-World War II
55 and over	Before 1927	11	Pre-World War II

Outmarriage in the parent generation apparently increased since World War II; compare the two younger age groups with the two older ones. There is also a suggestion that there was an increase between the two world wars; compare ages 35 to 54 with age 55 and over.

Outmarriage among the Status

Among the status, or registered, Indians, there is also an indication that outmarriage has increased in recent years. Marriage reports are compiled annually on the reserves.[6] Thus, we have current information on marriages; this is in contrast to the 1981 census information that reports the combined marriages for all years, many of which are of pre-World War II vintage. If outmarriage has increased significantly in recent years, then we expect to find a higher *current* outmarriage rate on the reserves than in the total status population at the time of the 1981 census.

This is what we find among the men. For women we find the reverse. The proportions on the reserves who married other than status (or registered) partners are as follows:

	Status women	Status men	Both sexes
1965 to 1969	34%	24%	30%
1970 to 1974	37	34	36
1975 to 1979	31	35	33
1980 to 1985	24	42	35

For both sexes combined, one in three of all who become married, marry out, and this proportion has increased since 1970. (We have no information before 1965.) According to the 1981 census, only about one in four had married out, as we noted previously.

The reader may be curious as to why the outmarriages for women decreased and those for men increased over these two decades. The reason lies (in part at least) in the shifting ratio of women to men. In the years 1965 to 1969 there were more status, or registered, Indian women than men who married. Therefore, some status women had to marry other than status men, which they did, or remain unmarried. By 1980 to 1985 there were significantly more men than women. More status women could now find status husbands, but more status men had to look elsewhere for brides. Why the numbers of men and women shifted in this manner we do not know.

---

[6] The reports from the reserves are mimeographed or photocopied sheets, available from Indian and Northern Affairs, Canada.

Urbanism as a Clue to Extent of Outmarriage

Does urbanism "cause" outmarriage, or does outmarriage "cause" urbanism? is an irrelevant question. Neither is a "cause" of the other. What we may say is that in Canada as well as the United States increases in extent of urbanism for an ethnic group most likely indicates increases in the rate of outmarriage.

The Native People of Canada, who are of multiple ancestry, that is, of mixed native and nonnative ancestry, are largely urbanites; one in three lived in a city of 500,000 population or over (1981). The single-ancestry people are largely rural and small-town dwellers. Among those reporting only native ancestors, only one in six lived in these very large cities (Figure 10.7).

We suggest the following sequence of events. Native persons of multiple ancestry are more likely to reside in urban areas *and* more likely to marry nonnatives. Trying to disentangle urbanism and ancestry as "causes" of outmarriage is futile. These two characteristics plus others—historical events, extent of schooling, and many others—interact. Each is simultaneously a "cause" and a "result." All that can be said is that as outmarriage increases, the percentage of all natives who live in urban areas also increases. Urban residence is an indication of outmarriage, and only under certain circumstances perhaps it facilitates outmarriage.

SOME CONCLUDING THOUGHTS ON OUTMARRIAGE OR ADMIXTURE

Intermixture of a male and a female from different tribes or groups probably began with the first hominids, who were biologically capable of such activ-

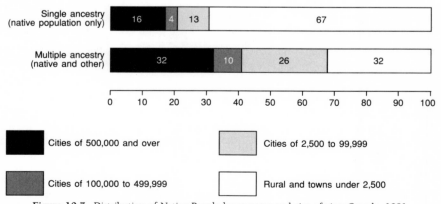

Figure 10.7. Distribution of Native People by ancestry and size of city: Canada, 1981.

ity and lived in tribes or bands. A million years ago? Who knows? The stories of Samson the Hebrew and Delilah the Philistine, of King Solomon and the Queen of Sheba, of Ahab the Israelite and Jezebel the Phoenician are well known. Perhaps their tragic results should be interpreted as a sign that the gods do not favor intermixture. Even if they do not favor it, admixture has gone on for many millennia.

Among the Amerindians, intermixture between members of different tribes has long occurred. Each tribe considers itself to be a separate nation, just as the Europeans consider their countries to be. Although these Amerindian intermixtures were cultural rather than genetic, they may have laid the basis for the subsequent intermixture of Indian and European. Was a European man thought to be any different from a man in another tribe?

In colonial times, and perhaps as late as the twentieth century, a large surplus of non-Indian men who were in geographic proximity to Indian women was conducive to outmarriage. European women also were involved in intermixture. In the event that an Indian war party overran a colonial settlement, sometimes women were abducted and adopted into the tribe.

As of 1900 if not later, in the United States there was an excess of non-Indian men in the states where most of the Indians lived. The excess of mostly white males amounted to about 1 million. Among the Indian population, the numbers of males and females were about equal. Since there were in all of the states, some one-quarter million Indians all told, an excess of 1 million non-Indian men resulted in the equivalent of the seventeenth and eighteenth centuries' "fur trader" situation. Some outmarriage was bound to occur. By 1940 there were about equal numbers of non-Indian men and women so that the "fur trader" situation had lost much of whatever relevancy it may have had in the nineteenth century and earlier.

In Canada as recently as 1921, there were about one-quarter million more nonnative men than women and only about 120,000 Amerindians. Presumably, this excess of nonnative men was conducive to some intermarriage. By 1951 there were about equal numbers of males and females, but by this time there must have been considerable intermarriage.

By the latter part of the twentieth century, the "fur trader" type of intermarriage based on an excess of European men is no longer an important reason for admixture. Instead, the dispersion of the Amerindians throughout the general society is very important. Very many have left their ghetto-type reservations and reserves and dispersed throughout the general U.S. and Canadian societies.

Increased schooling is probably important in leading to dispersion. If one has finished high school, as so many have (see Chapter 11), the El Dorados of outer space beckon. The local areas seem to hold no promises of good jobs unless the reservation is a suburb of a large city, as many are. Then the reservation becomes a bedroom suburb, and the central city furnishes the jobs.

Although outmarriage may not be as frequent in Canada as south of the border, the situations in the two countries do resemble each other. From this we deduce that the same social and cultural forces are influencing the natives and nonnatives of both countries.

Chapter 11

Schooling and the Hubris of the Settlers

INTRODUCTION

Some system for transmitting the knowledge of the elders to their children is required by all *Homo sapiens* and probably all hominids. Each successive generation cannot reinvent the wheel. Some forms of behavior may be passed on from parent to offspring by biological mechanisms. But in *Homo* most behavior and information must be passed on by what we call today schools. This is true of *Homo* in the remote past as well as today. Techniques for making fire, knapping stones to produce arrowheads and knives, stalking edible animals and finding edible plants—all forms of activity required for survival had to be learned by the young. All young went to school.

The pre-twentieth-century Amerindians were no different from all other people. The young must be inoculated with the knowledge of their elders. The Amerindians and their Asian predecessors had schools to do this. These schools differed from the whites' twentieth-century variety, but they were schools nevertheless.

We discuss only the twentieth-century school systems of Canada and the United States in this chapter—the white man's/woman's school system. We make no attempt to describe or assess the techniques for transmitting tribal knowledge that Amerindian elders may be using at the end of the twentieth century. In our study we are primarily interested in how the Indians adapt demographically to the white, economically developed Western world in which they find themselves. Hence, we are interested in the white, Western world school system.

The present (late-twentieth-century) level of formal schooling resulted in large measure from the hubris and subsequent expiation of the European settlers and their descendants. If the early Spaniards, French, English, and other-nationality settlers had been less egotistical, perhaps there would be no Indian Doctors of Philosophy and Doctors of Medicine in the latter part of the twentieth century. Permit us to explain.

The European-origin settlers of the sixteenth to nineteenth centuries faced a situation that confused them. The Amerindians were already in the Western Hemisphere when the Europeans arrived. The latter were sure of their own superiority, but were uncertain about how to subjugate the natives. Should the latter be annihilated as the English did to the original inhabitants of Tasmania or as the Spanish attempted in the Southwest? Both the Europeans and Indians could not occupy the same land, the former believed.

Or should the Indians be remade in the image of the Europeans, that is, as Christian farmers? It was unfortunate that the Indians could not be remade biologically; nevertheless, such was attempted by the Europeans.

As a compromise, at least two intermediate steps were advocated and practiced. One was to drive the Indians to lands not desired by the whites, in lieu of genocide. Another was to convert them to Christianity as the first step on the road to becoming Christian farmers. The first simply postponed the "final solution." The second, conversion to Christianity, launched the Amerindians on the road to higher university training and PhDs and MDs and the like.

The earliest schools for Indian children both in Canada and the United States were opened by missionaries of various churches and denominations. These missionaries intended to convert the "heathen" to Christianity, but to do so effectively the Indians had to be able to read the Bible, preferably in English, or in French in Quebec. As far as we can ascertain, the Spanish conquistadors were less interested in teaching reading and writing than were the English and French.

So schools had to be organized. It was thought that it was easier to educate children than adults, and even easier if the children were confined to live-in schools. Furthermore, when so confined they also could be taught the white man's agriculture and other "civilized" trades. The end result would be clones of the settlers in all respects except skin color.

In Canada, Jesuits had established schools as early as the seventeenth century. In the United States, such schools were attempted by the eighteenth century. Some Amerindians, of course, were interested in acquiring a white man's education, or at least the ability to read and write. Sequoyah, a Cherokee Indian who was born about the middle of the eighteenth century to a white settler and a Cherokee woman, devised an alphabet to be used for the Cherokee language. In 1821 his alphabet was accepted by the leading Cherokees, and soon almost the entire nation became literate (Lewis and Kneberg 1958, pp. 169 ff.).

UNITED STATES

The Early Years

By the end of the 1700s, the United Foreign Missionary Society and the American Board had begun to establish missions east of the Mississippi River. The Spanish were busy in the Southwest and Far West opening missions to "convert and educate the heathen"[1] almost from the time of Cortéz well into the eighteenth century.

By January 1817, the Brainerd school located east of Chattanooga was opened for Cherokee children (Viola 1974, pp. 32 ff.). It taught the children to read the Bible in English; the gospel must be brought to the heathen. In addition it taught agriculture to the boys and such household tasks as sewing, knitting, and spinning to the girls. We suspect that these advocates of schooling (reading, writing, and trades) had other, and to them more important, motives than simply teaching the white man's and woman's trades. Many tribes including the Cherokee had agriculture long before the colonists arrived. If they needed any training it was with respect to European crops and tools. The Cherokee, in addition, had their own alphabet devised by Sequoyah, and a national newspaper, the *Cherokee Phoenix*. This tribe met all the settlers' requirements for "civilization" except perhaps Christianity, toward which they were moving. Nevertheless, these evidences of "civilization" did not satisfy the whites. Literacy in a non-English language did not count. Agriculture would best be left in the hands of the whites. By 1835 the infamous treaty of New Echota was promulgated by the federal government. The Cherokee were forced to give up all of their lands east of the Mississippi River and to migrate west of the river.

Whatever may have been the original reasons for establishing Indian schools, they were established, and enrollment increased significantly after the Civil War. In 1877 average attendance at Indian schools amounted to about 4,000; total enrollment in all schools may have been a little higher. By 1900 enrollment in Indian schools rose to some 27,000 and in 1910 to about 38,000.[2] The large majority, six in every seven, attended schools supported by the federal government.

Of all students, about two-thirds were enrolled in boarding schools (in 1910) where, it was believed, they could be effectively controlled. That the conditions under which children were forced into schools and their treatment

---

[1] The interests of the Spanish in their missions may have differed somewhat from that of the English and French on the east coast. Perhaps the Spanish were more concerned with converting the Indians to Catholicism and less concerned with producing Spanish clones. We shall never know. Richman attempts to infer the Spaniards' intentions on the basis of available documents.

[2] U.S. Census, 1910, pp. 195 ff. These numbers were compiled by the Office of Indian Affairs.

therein were of a nature that today would be labeled *violations of human rights* are well documented by Polingaysi Qoyawayma (1984).[3] The author, a Hopi, was born in the 1890s and attended a boarding school beginning about the time of the 1910 census or shortly before. The federally mandated attendance disrupted her village. Some families wanted their children to adapt to the "new" lifestyle, whereas others insisted on retaining all traditional and cultural values and the old lifestyle. Qoyawayma described how the Feds abducted the unwilling village children whom they could find and incarcerated them in the school building. Indians from other tribes who spoke the Hopi language were recruited to do the actual kidnapping. The teachers then tried to eliminate the childrens' Hopi culture and substitute Washington–Federalese "culture." The children were forbidden to use their native language; diet, clothes, and all aspects of their tribal culture were obliterated insofar as the Feds could do so.

That the federal government either hoped to clone the Indians, or felt the need to make amends for its previous anti-human-rights treatment of them, or perhaps both reasons, is suggested by the following excerpt (1910 Census, p. 195):

> One of the most interesting social phenomena in American history is found in the development of the system of Indian schools upon the part of the Government, and in the development of an appreciation of schooling upon the part of the Indian. To secure a common language has been the first great object of the Indian school. Both races have profited through the mutual understanding which a common language and culture bring about. In their first report in 1869 the Board of Indian Commissioners discussed at some length the barriers in the way of sympathetic relations between the red and white races, and found them in differences of race, custom, and language. They went on to say that: "By educating the children of these tribes in the English language these differences would have disappeared and civilization would have followed at once. Nothing then would have been left but the antipathy of race, and that, too, is always softened in the beams of a higher civilization. In the difference of language to-day lies two-thirds of our troubles."

How important a part did, and is, the federal government playing in fostering schooling for the Amerindians? At the beginning of the nineteenth century, the private missionary schools were important. Before the Civil War and shortly afterwards, the federal government was spending very little, for example, $20,000 in 1877. By 1885, the Feds were spending $1 million per year on Indian education. By 1900, the amount had increased to about $2.9 million and by 1910 to $3.8 million. These increases appear to be genuine because the cost of living (as measured by the Federal Reserve Bank of New York and the Burgess, Douglas, and Riese indices) shows little or no change between 1885 and 1900, and only a small increase from 1900 to 1910.[4] Prior to World War I, of all young Indians aged 5 to 20 years who were reported as enrolled in school, the large

---

[3] Also known as Elizabeth Q. White.
[4] Cost-of-living indices from *Historical Statistics of the U.S., Colonial Times to 1957*, p. 127.

majority were in federal Indian schools. Evidently, the federal government was largely paying for Indian education at the beginning of the twentieth century.

By 1970, however, only about one in five was attending a federal Indian elementary or high school (*Statistical Abstract*, 1979, Table 244). Presumably, the major part of schooling costs and efforts in the latter twentieth century is borne by private organizations, Indian tribes, and state or local governments.

The Twentieth Century

School Enrollment

Enrollment increased significantly during the twentieth century (Table 11.1 and Figure 11.1). At the turn of the century, about 4 in 10 of all young Amerindians aged 5 to 20 attended school. In 1980 about 8 in 10 were enrolled. Throughout these decades the proportion of white children enrolled in schools was higher. The enrollment of Indian children nevertheless appears to be rapidly approaching that of all children.

The 1930 census commented on the "very definite increase in the proportion of Indians attending school since the beginning of the century" (p. 130). The writer considered this increase as indicating "cultural assimilation." The 1980 census, on the other hand, carries no comments.

Years of School Completed

The amount of schooling completed is a much better, but not perfect, indicator of the extent of schooling than is simply school attendance. Of the various possible measures of the amount of schooling, one of the most useful is completion of high school. It is almost a *sine qua non* for obtaining jobs, even those that illiterates can perform well. Military forces prefer recruits who have completed at least high school. Governments foster the completion of high school by

Table 11.1. Percentage of Persons Aged 5 to 20 Attending School, for Indians and Whites: U.S. 1900 to 1980

	Indians	*Whites*
1900	40	54
1910	51	63
1920	54	67
1930	60	72
1970	80	85
1980	82	85

Source: 1900 to 1930 data from Indian Population of the U.S. and Alaska, 1930, p. 131. 1970 and 1980 data from decennial censuses.

offering high-school-equivalency degrees, private employers often request that the applicant be a high-school graduate, and so forth.

Throughout the twentieth century, the proportion of those aged 25 and over who had completed high school increased steadily (Table 11.2; Figure 11.2). At the beginning of the century very few, perhaps only 1 in 20, were high-school graduates. In the 1960s and 1970s, about 3 in 4 who were of high-school age had completed 12 or more years of schooling. Nevertheless, the Indian people still lagged behind the total U.S. population.

The very small proportion estimated at the beginning of the twentieth century is corroborated by the extent of illiteracy.[5] Of those who had been of high-school age around 1900, we find the following proportions to be illiterate:

	Full blood	Mixed blood
Men	45%	9%
Women	55%	9%

Very few of the full-blood Indians had attended school around 1900, let alone finished high school. Those of mixed blood clearly had more schooling. If only 1 in 10 of the latter was illiterate, his or her schooling must have begun

---

[5] U.S. Census 1930, Chapter 7. Illiterates were defined as follows (p. 143):

> The Census Bureau defines as illiterate any person 10 years old or over who is not able to read and write, either in English or in some other language. The Census Bureau has never prescribed any specific test of ability to read or write. At the Census of 1930, the enumerator was instructed to write "yes" or "no" in response to the question on the schedule, "whether able to read and write." The enumerator was, however, specifically instructed not to write "yes" (which would classify the person as literate) simply because the person was able to write his or her name.

Full versus mixed bloods were defined this way (p. 70):

> *Enumeration by Blood in 1930 and 1910*
>
> In 1930, purity of blood was tabulated from the replies to one question as to whether the Indian enumerated was of full or mixed blood. In 1910 the inquiry as to blood was very elaborate. Indians reported as full blood were further classified as "full tribal," "mixed tribal," and "tribal blood unknown." The "mixed tribal" were again subdivided into those with admixture of "two tribes" and "three or more tribes." Mixed blood Indians were not only reported as "less than one-half White," "half White, Half Indian," "more than one-half white," and "unknown proportions," "less than one-half Negro," "half Negro," "half Indian," "more than one-half Negro," and "Negro, White, and Indian." Without attempting to pass judgment on the value of the 1910 classification, it is obviously impossible even for a trained investigator to obtain such detailed statistics without a considerable margin of error.

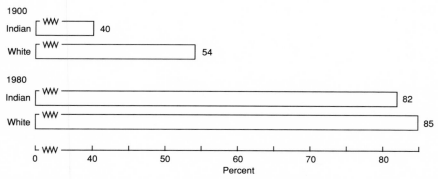

Figure 11.1. Percentage of persons aged 5 to 20 attending school, for Indians and whites: United States, 1900 and 1980. Source: See Table 11.1.

sometime well before 1900. The mixed, for example Sequoyah, most probably were the first Amerindians to be educated in the whites' schools.

One in 20 of those who reported having only Indian ancestors and 1 in 5 of the people of mixed ancestry—Indian and non-Indian—had completed high school at the beginning of the twentieth century. The mixed ancestry group had a headstart in the nineteenth century (the first Head Start Program) up the

Table 11.2. Estimated Proportion of Amerindian Women[a] by Ancestry Who Completed High School: U.S. 1900 to 1970

Age in 1980	Approximate years of high-school graduation	Percent completed high school for reported ancestry	
		Indian only	Indian and non-Indian
25 to 34	1965 to 1974	70	76
35 to 44	1955 to 1964	54	65
45 to 54	1945 to 1954: Soon after World War II	40	55
55 to 64	1935 to 1944: Just before and during World War II	36	52
65 to 74	1925 to 1934: Interwar years	25	44
75 to 84	1915 to 1924: Before and after World War I	18	37
85 to 94	1905 to 1914: Before World War I	8	28
95 and over	Before 1905: Beginning of twentieth century	4	18
65 and over	Before the Great Depression of the 1930s	20	32

[a]Women and men have virtually the same rates. Estimates to age class 65 and over from special tabulation of 1980 date; see Appendix 2. Estimates from age class 65 to 74 to 95 and over from published data in 1960 and 1970 censuses for "Indian-only ancestry." For those of both Indian and non-Indian ancestry, aged 65 and over, 10-year ages estimated by smoothing.

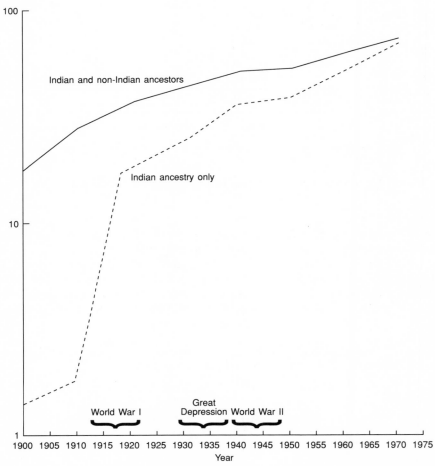

Figure 11.2. Estimated proportions of Amerindian women by ancestry who completed high school: United States, 1900 to 1970.

educational ladder. In the twentieth century those of Indian-only ancestry began attending school in large numbers. And by 1970 they had virtually caught up, at least as far as completing high school (Figure 11.2).

Those of mixed ancestry, we suspect, probably grew up in a social situation conducive to more formal education. As a result, whatever comparisons of the two groups we make (Figure 11.3), we see that more of those of mixed ancestry have completed high school. Even when we consider the influence of age, urban or rural residence, whether married or not, and other factors, it

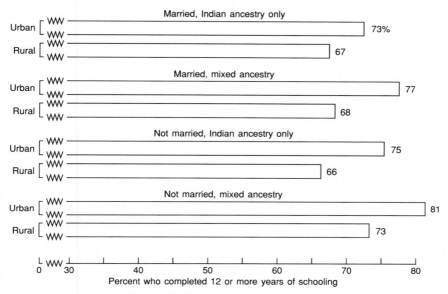

Figure 11.3. Percentage who completed 12 years or more of schooling for Amerindian women aged 25 to 34 by urban–rural residence, ancestry, and marital status: United States, 1980. See Appendix 5.

is apparent that ancestry is very important when trying to understand levels of schooling achieved. Through wars and depressions, schooling continued to increase.

To illustrate: In 1980, among married women living in urban areas who reported Indian-ancestry only, 73% had completed high school. Among their counterparts who reported both Indian and non-Indian ancestors, 77% had completed high school. This single comparison by itself does not prove our case, especially because the basic census data are not sufficiently precise (see Appendix 5). However, we have four comparisons for each 10-year age group, and four age groups (covering the range of 25 to 64 years) for a total of 16 comparisons. In 15 of these 16 comparisons more of the mixed ancestry have completed high school. Clearly we can say that type of ancestry indicates that there is a real difference between the two ancestry groups.

Urban, rather than rural, residence was and may still be very important in obtaining more schooling. Previously (Chapter 8), we suggested that leaving the reservation leads to demographic conversion with the general population. Since high schools were available only in cities, movement from the reservation to cities was needed if one was to obtain a high-school education. Also, having non-Indian as well as Indian ancestors indicates previous contact with the non-Indian population. By the 1980s, many more schools had been opened on reservations so that the difference in amount of precollege schooling between urban and rural areas may be decreasing.

Upward to Higher Education

The number who entered college and eventually earned degrees in higher education increased over the decades. As more Amerindians completed high school, such an educational progression is to be expected. The numbers enrolled in institutions of higher education increased from about 76,000 in 1976 to 84,000 in 1980 and to 90,000 in 1986. This growth amounted to 18% (Figure 11.4). Perhaps Indian enrollment grew a little more rapidly than did total enrollment of all races, about 15%. Because statistics in the field of education are notorious for being imprecise, we hesitate to place much credence on small differences.

Women accounted for all of the increase in Indian enrollment over the decade. Their enrollment grew from about 37,000 in 1976 to 50,000 in 1986. The enrollment of men, on the other hand, remained virtually constant, fluctuating only between 37,000 and 40,000. Indeed, in 1986, 55% of all Amerindian college students were women. This difference between the sexes parallels that found among all enrollees in the United States. Whereas the number of men remained unchanged over the decade, the number of women increased from a little over 5 million in 1976 to about 6½ million in 1986, when they constituted

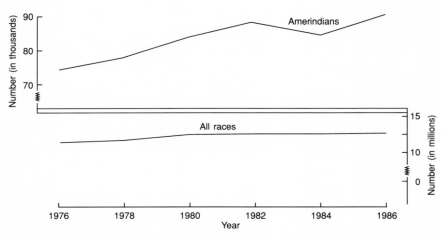

Figure 11.4. Enrollment in institutions of higher education, Native Americans and all races: United States, 1976 to 1986. Source: U.S. Department of Education, Center for Education Statistics, April 1988. Inuit and Aleuts are included with Indians.

over half of the student body. Where would the college professors be without women students?

Close to one in every four college-enrolled Indians was attending a California institution. Another one in four was enrolled in a college in Oklahoma, Arizona, New Mexico, or New York. All together, these five states accounted for half of all Amerindian enrollees. In contrast, only about one-quarter of students of all races were enrolled in these five states.

Tribal Colleges

In addition to conventional colleges, a small number attend tribal colleges, located on or near reservations (Boyer 1989). There were 24 such institutions in 1989; about half were community colleges. All together, they enrolled over 4,400 full-time equivalent students that year. The Navajo Community College, founded in 1968, is the first tribally controlled college and is the largest one at present. Twelve colleges are fully accredited, and eight others are candidates for accreditation.

These colleges were organized and supported in large part by tribes to help furnish the needs of the tribes and the reservation dwellers. Boyer lists four major purposes for organizing these institutions (pp. 3–5):

1. Tribal colleges establish a learning environment that encourages participation by and builds self-confidence in students who have come to view failure as the norm. Tribal colleges offer hope in a climate of despair.
2. Tribal colleges celebrate and help sustain the rich Native American traditions. Tribal languages are still spoken.
3. Tribal colleges provide essential services that enrich the communities surrounding them: adult education, high-school equivalency programs, vocational training, and so forth.
4. The colleges are often centers for research and scholarship; some have set up cooperative programs with state universities to conduct scientific research.

Another possible reason for starting the colleges (not mentioned in the literature) may be the wish to retain the people on the reservations. Whether this purpose is being achieved is uncertain.

Undergraduates in 1980

More Indian women than men were attending college in 1980, although about equal numbers had completed high school (Table 11.3). Of all who were reported as attending college, over half, 54%, were women. But more women

Table 11.3. The College and University Pipeline, Indians: U.S. around 1980

	Men	Women	
		Number	Percent
Completed high school	192,000	197,000	51
Attending college in 1980	30,800	36,600	54
Freshmen	10,100	13,600	57
Sophomores	7,700	9,400	55
Juniors	4,600	5,300	53
Seniors	3,800	4,100	52
Fifth and sixth years	2,900	3,000	50
Seven years or more	1,600	1,100	41
Doctor of Philosophy recipients			
1977 to 1981	251	115	31
1982 to 1986	244	180	42

Sources: Completed high school (12+ years): PC 80-1-D1-A, Table 262; attending college: U.S. Census, PC 80-1-D1-A, Table 260; Doctor of Philosophy recipients: Center for Education Statistics.

drop out than do men. Of 100 female freshmen, only about 30 become seniors. Of 100 male freshmen, close to 40 become seniors.[6]

More Indian men than women complete 4 years of college. Of all men aged 20 to 39 years, a little under 8% were college graduates, and of the women about 6%.

Graduate Study

Having completed 4 years of college, some go on to graduate study and eventually receive postbaccalaureate degrees. We were unable to ascertain the total number who receive such degrees, but the available information suggests that more and more are doing so. For example, the average number per year of Amerindian graduates of medical schools[7] increased as follows:

	Total	Women
1969–70 to 1974–75	11	NA
1976–77 to 1978–79	41	NA
1980–81 to 1982–83	44	NA
1983–84 to 1985–86	58	18

[6] The pipeline pattern is an approximation. Data are not available that would permit us to follow a cohort throughout their college experience; the best that we could do was to compare the numbers of freshmen and seniors as given in Table 260. Also, note that the numbers reported by the census as "enrolled in college" differ from the numbers reported by the Department of Education as "enrollment in institutions of higher education." Who knows why this difference exists?

[7] "Graduates in Medicine, Selected Years," *Professional Women and Minorities,* issued by the Commission of Professionals in Science and Technology, Washington, DC.

Law attracted many more than did medicine. The average number each year who attended law schools[8] increased as follows:

	Amerindians	All races
1971–72 to 1974–75	200	35,700
1975–76 to 1978–79	337	39,400
1979–80 to 1982–83	404	41,900
1983–84 to 1985–86	455	40,700

The number of Amerindians who received degrees as Doctors of Philosophy[9] also increased significantly during the decade 1977 to 1986. The reported numbers per year are:

	Indians		All races	
	Total	Women	Total	Women
1977 to 1981	73	31%	31,200	28%
1982 to 1986	85	42%	31,300	34%

Clearly, there are few Amerindian recipients of PhD degrees.

But also, the number is increasing more rapidly than that of the total population (all races), thanks to the Amerindian women. There was no increase in the number of men who received doctorates (Table 11.3) whereas the number of women recipients increased dramatically.

The Amerindian doctorate recipients (1981 to 1986) had chosen rather different fields of study as compared to all recipients. The distributions are:

	Amerindians	All recipients[10]
Total	100%	100%
Physical sciences	7	13
Engineering	4	6
Life sciences	16	18
Subtotal	27	37
Social sciences	17	20
Humanities	9	12
Education	42	25
Subtotal	68	57
Professional and other fields	5	6

[8] "Students Enrolled in J.D. Programs in Approved Law Schools," *A Review of Legal Education in the U.S., Fall 1986*, American Bar Association.

[9] *Center for Education Statistics*, U.S. Department of Education, annual.

[10] Includes all U.S. citizens and noncitizens who have permanent visas.

We assume that in future years the fields studied by the Amerindians will tend to resemble more closely those of all students. Often students tend to enter fields of study that they think will provide jobs upon graduation. Perhaps in the 1980s it was believed that the field of education was such a job-oriented subject, especially for women. We suspect that in future years other fields will provide more opportunities to women as well as men and the fields of the PhD candidates will change accordingly.

CANADA

The experiences of Canada's Native People were very similar to those of the U.S. Indians. What small differences there were—and are—resulted in part from differences in treatment by the Europeans and the religious and secular systems that they brought from Europe. We summarize very briefly: (a) only during the twentieth century and especially after World War II did schooling increase significantly among the natives; (b) nevertheless, the natives still (1981) lag behind the school levels of the general population; and (c) the natives of mixed Indian and non-Indian ancestry had more formal education than did those who reported only native ancestry.

The Early Years

In the beginning of the seventeenth century, Jesuit missionaries followed Champlain—Champlain sailed up the St. Lawrence River in 1603—to the New World. The Jesuits lived among many tribes and sought converts to Catholicism. (In addition, they recorded their observations of Indian life that they then sent to their superiors in France.) Besides seeking converts, they attempted to assimilate the Indians into French culture.

> Jesuits and Sulpicians [another religious order] also undertook the first attempts at full-scale assimilation of the Indian into French culture. The plan was to remove children from their home environment and educate them in live-in schools. . . . This scheme was not very successful, however, as all the students eventually returned to their people. (*The Canadian Indian,* 1986, pp. 50 ff.)

By the mid-1700s, the Jesuits had established Christian villages among Indian people. Some present-day reserves in Quebec are descendants of these villages.

During the seventeenth and eighteenth centuries, the Indians had been useful military allies of the British. After the War of 1812, however, the British no longer feared invasion from the United States, and the Canadian Indians were no longer useful military allies. What should be done with the Indians? The answer was: Assimilate them or somehow make them into Canadians. Various techniques to achieve assimilation were tried. One technique was that of settling the Indians on reserves and sending in teachers, government agents, and missionaries to "instruct" the natives (see Appendix 13). Other techniques involved converting the natives to farming.

In 1857, the Canadian government passed an act, the essence of which was "enfranchisement." An Indian man with the appropriate qualifications could enter into full citizenship. (Indians in the nineteenth century were not necessarily Canadian citizens.) Indian males over the age of 21 who were *literate in English or French, educated to an elementary level,* of good moral character, and free of debt could be "enfranchised" or "no longer deemed to be an Indian." (How many Canadian non-Indians could have met those qualifications?) Then in 1880, an amendment to the earlier act declared that *any Indian obtaining a university degree would be automatically enfranchised.*

Whether the Indians so wished or not, they were to be assimilated via the school system. That the government's educational efforts were virtually meaningless is evident from the fact that by the end of the nineteenth century very few Indians had received any significant amount of schooling.

The Twentieth Century

Natives Have Less Schooling Than Do Nonnative Canadians

Despite the very large increases in amount of schooling since the start of the twentieth century, the Native People in 1981 had less schooling than did the nonnative Canadians (Figure 11.5). About 2 in 5 natives had less than Grade 9

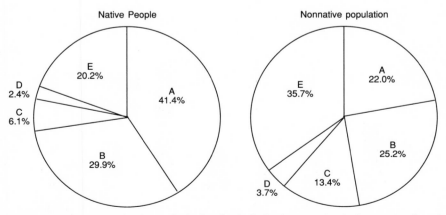

Figure 11.5. Percentage distribution by highest level of schooling completed of Native People and of the nonnative population (population 15 years and over not attending school full-time): Canada, 1981. Key: A = less than Grade 9; B = some high school; C = high school diploma; D = trades certificate; E = at least some postsecondary. Source: 1981 Census of Canada.

as compared with about 1 in 5 of the Canadian population. At the upper end of the school ladder, the most schooled, about 1 in 5 Native People had some postsecondary schooling; more of the nonnatives were in this upper bracket, over 1 in 3.

There are many reasons for the natives' lesser amount of schooling. The authors of *Perspective Canada III* (1980, p. 173) suggest the following:

> The problems of native education may be closely related to the differences between the values central to contemporary liberal, urban-oriented education and the cultural experiences, traditions, interests, and aspirations of native children. This factor, combined with the discontinuity of socialization and discrimination often associated with the education of native children, has resulted in diminished motivation, increased negativism, poor self-images, and low levels of aspiration, in addition to limited achievement for this group. The result is that many native children have been alienated from their own way of life, without having been prepared in any significant fashion for a different society.

We add that the isolation of the ghetto–reserve works against acquiring more white man's education than the minimum needed for carrying on life on the reserves. Only when the native lives in the nonnative world and attempts to cope with the problems there including competition for present-day jobs—book-keeper, trained nurse, tractor-trailer driver, and the like—is there a felt need for more than the minimum schooling. If the nonnative also is antagonistic to the reserve Indian, the latter has even less incentive to become a college graduate.

The nonstatus Indians have the most schooling (as of 1981). The status people who live off the reserve are in second place, followed very closely by the Métis. The status Indians who live on the reserves had significantly less schooling, and the Inuits the least (Figure 11.6) (*Canada's Native People*).

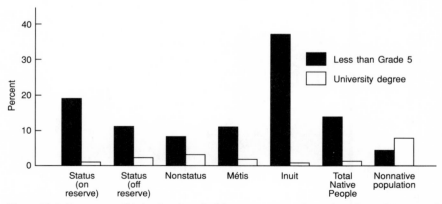

Figure 11.6. Percentage of Native People and of the nonnative population (population 15 years and over not attending school full-time) with less than Grade 5 and with university degrees: Canada, 1981. Source: 1981 Census of Canada.

All these five types had considerably less schooling than did the Canadian nonnative population. Indeed, of the latter twice as many had university degrees as had completed less than Grade 5. Among the nonstatus (who had the most schooling of the natives), the ratio was reversed; about twice as many had less than Grade 5 as had university degrees.

The Canadian status Indians, in particular those living on reserves, are most similar to the U.S. Indians who reported having only Indian ancestors (see Chapter 10). The status who live off the reserves, plus the nonstatus and Métis, are analogous to the south-of-the-border Amerindians who reported having both Indian and non-Indian ancestors. In both countries, many of those who are largely of Indian ancestry (i.e., claiming only Indian ancestors) tend to live on reserves or reservations in rural areas and away from the urbanized majority of the country's people. Those of mixed (or multiple) ancestry tend to live in or near urban areas where there are more school facilities.

Devereaux (who prepared *Canada's Native People,* 1984) wrote:

> Just 7% of the native people living in urban areas had less than Grade 5, compared with 20% in rural regions. About a quarter of urban natives had never attended high school, but among those in rural areas, the proportion rose to more than half. Over 3% of the natives living in cities had university degrees, compared with fewer than 1% of natives in rural areas.

Amount of Schooling Is Increasing

At the beginning of the twentieth century, we estimate that more than 9 in 10 of all the Native People achieved less than nine grades of schooling. Only 1 or 2 in 100 obtained "more" schooling that we define for present purposes as nonuniversity plus university[11] (Table 11.4, Figures 11.7 and 11.8).

Apparently, the proportion who had *less than 9 years of schooling* began to decrease about the time of World War I. During the 1920s and 1930s, more people received more schooling and the proportion having less than Grade 9 decreased noticeably. About the time of World War II, the decrease became precipitous and then began to slow down in the late 1950s and 1960s. This pattern was observed in all the types (Figure 11.7).

The proportion who had *more schooling* began to increase in the latter 1920s, then increased noticeably during the 1930s, and continued to increase following World War II (Figure 11.8).[12]

The diverse patterns of change in the lower and upper rungs of the school ladder appear reasonable. As school facilities and attendance increase, we begin

---

[11] The Canadian classification system as reported in the census differs from that reported by the U.S. census. See Appendix 5.

[12] The patterns of change for men and women are almost identical; see Table 11.3.

Table 11.4. Estimated Educational Level of Native Population by Type: Canada before World War I to 1981

		Status		Nonstatus		Métis	
Least schooling		M	F	M	F	M	F
Less than nine grades		Percentage reporting					
Age in 1981	Years of school completion[a]						
25–34	1966–1971	26	28	20	18	25	21
35–44	1956–1961	40	44	22	26	31	35
45–54	1946–1951	40	66	43	48	52	58
55–64	1936–1941	83	86	69	72	76	78
65–74	1926–1931	85	86	78	78	82	80
75–84	1916–1921	89	89	90	88	90	86
85+	Before World War I	90–95	90–95	90–95	90–95	90–95	90–95
Most schooling							
Nonuniversity plus university		Percentage reporting					
25–34	—	36	34	41	40	38	35
35–44	—	22	20	31	27	26	23
45–54	—	13	10	21	17	17	14
55–64	—	7	6	13	11	11	9
65–74	—	5	3	6	7	6	4
75–84	—	3	2	2	4	2	2
85+	—	1	1	1	1	1	1

[a]Years when age group (as of 1981) was between 15 and 20 years of age. Calculated from the mean age of the cohort (e.g., 30 is the mean of 25–34).

to see smaller proportions of those with little schooling. More young people remain in school longer and gradually fill the pipeline to the higher grades. And a few years later, more appear on the upper rungs, provided that postsecondary teaching facilities are available. Finally, at some time, the people have as much schooling as they wish, and there are no longer any changes in the proportions on the various rungs.

We cannot predict where this stopping point may be for the Indians. We can only suggest that these historic changes will continue for another decade, or two, or three, or more. As Devereaux wrote: "Young people have more education than their elders."

SUMMARY

The European missionaries in the seventeenth century started the process of schooling the Amerindians. In their eagerness to convert the natives to Christianity, they opened schools so that the "heathen" could learn to read the Bible. A very small number did become literate in European languages. Those of mixed

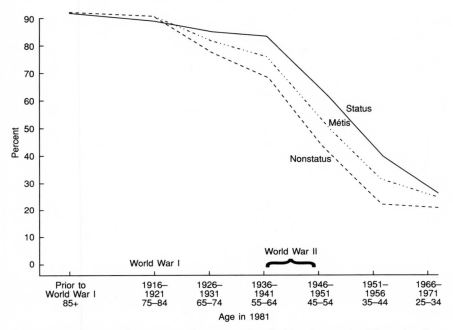

Figure 11.7. Estimated proportions of native men by ethnicity who completed fewer than 9 grades of school: Canada, prior to World War I to 1971.

parentage—of Indian and non-Indian ancestry—were the first to acquire learning. Those whose ancestry was only Indian began acquiring the white man's learning only in the late nineteenth century.

As long as the Indians were able to carry on their original way of life

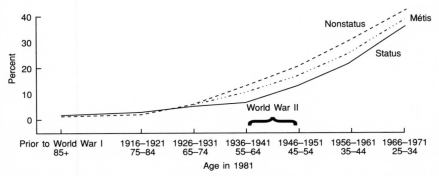

Figure 11.8. Estimated proportions of native men by ethnicity who had nonuniversity or university schooling: Canada, prior to World War I to 1971.

they had no need for the whites' schools. Even when sequestered onto reservations and reserves and forced to change at least part of their lifestyle, they had but little or no need for education as defined by the whites. Toward the end of the nineteenth century and into the mid-twentieth century, circumstances began to change. First (we must start someplace), they began leaving the reservations for the larger U.S. and Canadian society, in particular the cities. They are now mixing with the non-Indian world. And now the white man's schooling became necessary.

Second, there was considerable intermarriage with non-Indians. By 1980 or 1981, perhaps half or more of the Indians were married to non-Indians, if the census data are to be believed (Chapter 10).

Third, in the latter part of the twentieth century, there appears to be increased racial and ethnic tolerance on the part of the dominant whites. The various civil rights laws could not have been passed if the whites had been unalterably opposed to such tolerant behavior.[13] By contrast, in colonial times there appears to have been but very little tolerance of the Indians. In his description of the Virginia Tidewater, Wright (1981, p. 78) wrote: "The English tried to drive the natives out of . . . the Tidewater . . . assuming that the only lasting peace was that of the grave." Such an attitude is not common in the latter twentieth century. By condoning the mixing of Indians and non-Indians, increased schooling of the Indians is a by-product. Or perhaps we should say that increased tolerance and increased schooling accompany each other.

The events of World War I and especially World War II and their accompanying social and economic changes seem to have contributed to these changes in Indian life, or at least are associated with increased urbanism, increased marriage to non-Indians, and increased schooling. Precisely how much each event contributes we will leave to others to estimate.

Nevertheless, the Amerindian had less schooling in the 1980s than did the whites. But we predict that in future years schooling of Indians will increase further.

---

[13] See *Indian Tribes: A Continuing Quest for Survival*, U.S. Commission on Civil Rights, June 1981; see especially pp. 15–58. For Canada, see *The Canadian Indian*, pp. 86–98.

Chapter 12

What Is Your Occupation?

INTRODUCTION[1]

People who have jobs that society deems to be less desirable generally receive less pay for their work. Included as "undesirable" are unskilled work, farm laborers, and the like, jobs often associated in the public mind with illegal foreign entrants into a country. Hence, the occupation reported may be considered as an indicator of the economic position of the person or group relative to others, that is, better or worse off than others. In addition to the economic or money payoff, an occupation may have more or less status in the public eye; compare, for example, an engineer versus a laborer on a construction job. Hence, by observing the occupations that the Amerindians had and have now we obtain clues regarding their changing economic and status positions (if they are changing) in the United States and Canada.

(We have a practical reason for analyzing occupations instead of money. We may infer eighteenth-, nineteenth-, and twentieth-century economic changes via occupational composition. Information on money income, however, is available largely for post-World War II.)

It is well known that toward the end of the twentieth century a larger proportion of the Indians than of all workers have lower paying and less desirable jobs. But there is considerable economic variation among the Amerindians. Some are rich and some are very poor. Some are high-level profession-

---

[1] There is a vast literature on definition, classification, and numbers for occupation, industry, class of worker, labor force, gainfully occupied, working force, employment and unemployment, and so forth. For a quick review, see, for example, Jaffe and Stewart (1951), the several articles in the *International Encyclopedia of the Social Sciences,* the definitions and explanations in the Canadian and U.S. census volumes, and the annual volumes of the *Statistical Abstract of the United States;* for Canada, see Urquhart and Buckley (1965). For further information, see Appendix 5.

als—college professors, physicians, lawyers—and some are agricultural laborers. There is nothing new in these observations and belaboring the situation will serve no useful end. Hence, we shall examine only long-time changes in the occupational composition in order to determine: (a) the possible extent of occupational improvement—that is, climbing the occupational ladder—during the twentieth century; and (b) the extent to which the Amerindians may be approaching occupationally the total population. With this information, we may be able to peer into the future.

We must remind our readers that the historical information and statistics on occupations leave much to be desired, especially when trying to unravel and understand changes over time. The information for any two dates may or may not be comparable. One reason is that the census classification systems, both in Canada and the United States, were changed several times during the nineteenth and twentieth centuries. In theory, these diverse classifications can be made "comparable" over the last century, according to Solomon's wisdom. However, there is no guarantee that any "adjusted" numbers, if and when prepared, are more nearly indicative of the true historical events than are the unadjusted original numbers.

Further, we note that job contents have changed considerably over time so that even an identical title may refer to nonidentical job contents. For example, the job of a salesclerk in a supermarket of 1990 is not necessarily identical to that of a clerk in a rural general store in 1910, even though the census consistently may classify both as "salesclerks."

We attempt to get around this statistical problem by seeking major trends and differences rather than precise numbers. For example, when we note that the percentage of Indian men engaged in agriculture decreased from about 8 in 10 in 1910 to 1 in 20 in 1980, we have an unmistakable downward change; this change is correct whether or not the census classifications of "farmers" and "farm laborers" at these two dates are "precisely comparable." Or if we say that the proportion of Amerindian men engaged in agriculture in 1980 in the United States hardly differs, if at all, from the general U.S. male population, that statement is correct even though we cannot guarantee that the numbers are "precisely correct."

This is the spirit in which the following discussion should be read.

UNITED STATES

Pre-Twentieth Century

Pre-Columbus

Some of the tribes had well-developed agriculture by 1492; however, because they had no domestic animals, meat and fish were obtained by hunting and fishing, and some additional plant food by gathering. Other tribes depended entirely (or almost so) on hunting, fishing, and gathering. If these people had been classified according to the 1980 census occupational classification system, probably most could have been included under "farming, forestry, and fishing occupations." Conceivably also, an overzealous census enumerator could have included a few as "jewelers" ("precious stones and metal workers"). Others could have been classified under "miscellaneous hand-working occupations" to include the making of stone tools, pottery, baskets, textiles, and the like. Further, the chief of the tribe could have been enumerated as "chief executive, public administration."

Precisely what the people did to earn their livings varied considerably depending on the availability and quality of farmland, of animals to hunt and fish to fish, of wild, edible vegetation, and such other opportunities as nature may have provided. Such variation from tribe to tribe has been adequately covered by others such as the *Handbook of the North American Indians*. We shall say no more.

Sixteenth to Nineteenth Centuries

The Spanish invaders sought gold and silver, and as a result mining became an important occupation where there were precious metals to mine.[2] They also "enriched" the Indians' list of occupations by adding domestic servants, farm laborers, and other such specialities as were needed by the Spaniards to carry on their lifestyle.

The English settlers had their own idea—get rid of the natives, especially if they were on high-quality farmland. Hence, the Indians were gradually pushed westward into territories largely devoid of Europeans. Here they could continue, more or less, their accustomed economic and occupational lifestyles to the extent that the natural environment permitted.

The European fur traders may have contributed to an increase in "hunters and trappers" at the expense of "farmers," as they traded vast quantities of whiskey for even larger quantities of furs. One of the biggest operators in the United States in the beginning of the nineteenth century was John Jacob Astor, owner of the American Fur Company, a director of the Bank of the United States, and one of the richest men in the country; a large part of his wealth came from trading for furs with the Indians (Viola 1974, pp. 51 ff.). At the same time, there may have been a decrease in stone working and other traditional "manufacturing" as guns, metal pots, glass beads, and other European-made products were substituted for the traditional items.

Perhaps the single most important influence on the occupational composition was the policy advocated by McKenney and others who believed that

---

[2] Presumably, some of the pre-Columbian Indians who sought copper could have been classified as miners.

" . . . the salvation of the tribes could best be achieved through agriculture" (Viola 1974, p. 25).

For at least 200 years, and longer where the Spaniards ruled, the policy was to change "Red" into "White." A white occupational structure naturally would be included. Salvation at last. By the end of the nineteenth century, almost all Indians were engaged in subsistence agriculture on their isolated reservations west of the Mississippi River. They participated only minimally in the occupational and economic life of the general population, and there was little reason for them to adopt the "new whites' occupations," especially those involved in the new technologies emerging in the nineteenth and twentieth centuries. The Indians remained "farmers."

Twentieth Century

In the Beginning

The occupational structure and economic life in general seems to have resembled life as it may have been lived in the nineteenth century and perhaps earlier, except that the Indians could no longer roam about as they wished. Subsistence agriculture was the mainstay; hunting and fishing were often side operations. As the proportion who were engaged in agriculture subsequently decreased during the twentieth century, the climb up the white man's occupational ladder began in earnest.

The few men who were engaged in nonagricultural jobs in the early part of the century were mostly laborers (Appendix Table 12.5). Most of the Indian women engaged in nonagriculture were in "semiskilled" jobs in manufacturing at home (not in factories) or in the servant classes. They made objects for their own use or for sale to tourists as souvenirs. Occupationally, the Amerindians resembled the people in the grossly underdeveloped parts of the Third World in the 1980s.

Very few of all gainfully occupied men and women were reported as "professional persons" in 1910 and perhaps a few more in 1930. We have detailed occupational information for 1910. Of the total of 927 "professional" men, over 1 in 3 (360) were reported as in "semiprofessional and recreational pursuits," "actors and showmen," "musicians and teachers of music," and "artists and teachers of art." Another 205 were simply listed as "teachers." "Clergymen" numbered 127, plus a scattering of others. We have no information on the 239 reported as "all other professionals" (Table 12.1).

Among the 357 "professional women" 2 in every 3, or 245 women, were listed as "teachers," 4 were "trained nurses," and the remaining 108 were scattered in various semiprofessional occupations. Very few of these jobs were of a technologically advanced nature.

Table 12.1. Professional Occupations of Amerindians for Men and Women: United States, 1910 and 1930

	Men				Women			
	1910		1930		1910		1930	
	Number	Percent	Number	Percent	Number	Percent	Number	Percent
Total	927	100	1,531	100	357	100	824	100
Semiprofessional and recreational	156	17	451	29	19	5	39	5
Actors and showmen	146	16	136	9	26	7	26	3
Subtotal	302	33	587	38	45	13	65	8
Teachers	110	12	205	13	245	69	511	62
Musicians and teachers of music	45	5	95	6	28	8	44	5
Artists, sculptors, and teachers of art	13	1	16	1	4	1	5	1
Subtotal	168	18	316	21	277	78	560	68
Clergymen	127	14	229	15	—	—	4	*
Lawyers, judges, justices	87	9	86	6	—	—	1	*
Trained nurses	4	*	4	*	16	4	134	16
All other	239	26	309	20	19	5	60	7
Subtotal	457	49	628	41	35	9	199	24

Source: 1930 Census, Table 59.
*Less than one-half of 1%.

Among the 1,511 semiskilled men reported in 1910, 591 were "operatives not in factories." The census stated that this group "includes Indian blanket weavers, basket makers, pottery workers, etc." An additional 487 were servants, or "servant class." Of the 6,541 semiskilled women reported, almost all, 6,055, were weavers, potters, and the like. Another 2,978 women were reported as "personal service workers," or servant class.

The picture in 1930 was not very different (Appendix Table 10.5). Indian lifestyle may be labeled as that of a peasant society—only some 10% were urban dwellers—before World War II. Of the few nonagricultural workers, probably many lived in urban areas. In short, we see a society (or societies) on the fringes of the modern technological world that was unfolding in the United States. The Amerindians were barely participating in the emerging modern economy, and most probably did not live very differently from the ways of the pre-twentieth century. Only hunting game diminished in importance.

Fewer Farmers Now

The percentage of all workers who are engaged in agriculture may be the single most useful overall measure of occupational and socioeconomic levels and trends. In an underdeveloped economy—a Third World nation—a very large percentage are engaged in agriculture. As the economy advances technologically (if it does so), the level of living increases, and the proportion who do farmwork decreases. If there is any doubt, compare the United States and Mexico in 1980. The proportions of men engaged in agriculture in the two countries are as follows: United States 4%; Mexico 31%.

Among North American Indian men in 1910 (the earliest date for which we have reasonably complete census information), about 8 in 10 were reported as "farmers, owners, and tenants," or "agricultural laborers." In the entire United States, only about 1 in 3 of the gainfully occupied men were so reported (Figure 12.1), less than half that of the Indian men.

From 1910 to 1930, the proportion of men, Indian and non-Indian, who worked in agriculture decreased but slowly. Then came the Great Depression of the 1930s. The only men who left agriculture were those who lost their farms because of the Great Drought or the Great Depression, or those who could not find work as agricultural laborers.

The experiences of World War II and the availability of nonfarm jobs after the war attracted vast numbers into nonfarming occupations during the 1940s and well into the 1950s. Both Amerindian and all other men participated in this movement.

From 1950 to 1980, there was a precipitous decline in both the proportions and numbers of Indian and non-Indian men in farming. Temporary farm workers from Latin America and the Caribbean were recruited to augment the U.S. agricultural working force. In 1980, only about 1 man in 20 worked in agriculture. The proportion of Indian men so occupied was close to that of all men. By 1980, 2½ million men in the United States were producing more than did the 10 million in 1910.

The pattern of decrease was similar for Indian women, although many fewer reported as being engaged in agriculture throughout the twentieth century. In 1910, about 3 in 10 were so reported, and in 1980 but 1 in 100.

Converging, Occupationally Speaking

With increasing years of schooling and the urbanward movement away from the reservations, it is not surprising that the Indians began filling much the same (but not necessarily identical) occupations as other residents of the United States. The events of World War II and its aftermath hastened the process of occupational convergence.

It is to be expected that a person is most likely to obtain employment in any specific city or other area in accordance with the kinds of jobs and occupations available there and one's ability to do the work. Historically, reservation life offered jobs and occupations that were rather different from those offered in cities, especially large ones. Hence, as people left the reservations and their

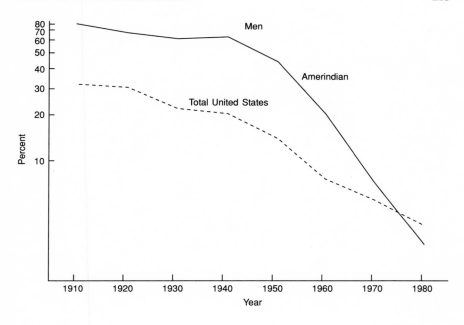

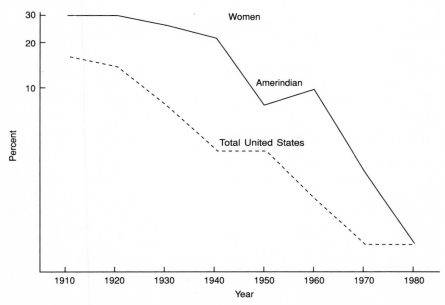

Figure 12.1. Proportion of workforce engaged in agriculture, Amerindians and total United States, for men and women: 1910 to 1980.

surrounding environments, the occupational structure also changed. *Now That the Buffalo's Gone,*[3] other aspects of life can be expected to change.

The occupational composition of the Amerindians, at least in broad outline, is converging during the twentieth century toward that of total United States (see Table 12.2, Figure 12.2, and Figure 12.3). But the nation is not homogeneous. The several states and other areas differ in the jobs that they provide at present and will continue to differ in the future. Hence, no segment of the U.S. population is identical to that of the total country. The Amerindians are no different; among those who live in New York City there are no sheep herders, and sheep country has no brain surgeons.

By 1980, in comparison with the 1910 situation, the Amerindian population had changed considerably and was now more nearly similar to that of the country's total working force. Nevertheless, relatively fewer Indian men and women were in the higher-paying white-collar jobs in 1980, more in the crafts or skilled—the intermediate-paying jobs—and relatively many more in the lower-paying jobs. Part of the lower level of the Indians' occupational structure is accounted for by differences in the amount of schooling. If the Indians had the same amount of schooling as the total population, more of the former would be in occupations higher up on the occupational ladder. We illustrate with men aged 35 to 44:

	Percentage reported in 1980 census	*Percentage if Indians had the same amount of schooling as all men*
Executives and administrators		
Indians	10	14
Total	17	17
Indian deficit	7	3
Laborers		
Indians	7	6
Total	3	3
Indian excess	4	3

The narrowing of the gap is evident for both sexes, all ages, and all occupations.

Living off the reservations (Table 12.3) is conducive to jobs higher up on the socioeconomic ladder and providing higher annual earnings (Table 12.3). We anticipate that as the younger people receive more schooling, and as more leave the reservations, there will be more movement into better-paying jobs. The precise size of the difference in 1980 between those living on and off reservations, and estimated projections into the future cannot be made because of uncertain basic information. One of the problems previously discussed is the impossibly large increase between 1970 and 1980 in the number of people

[3] Josephy (1982).

Table 12.2. Percentage Distribution by Socioeconomic Classification of Amerindians and Total U.S. Population for Men and Women: 1910 to 1980

	Men					Women				
	1910	1930	1940	1960	1980	1910	1930	1940	1960	1980
	Amerindians									
Total	100	100	100	100	100	100	100	100	100	100
Upper white collar[a]	4	3	3	8	16	3	6	6	11	20
Lower white collar[b]	1	2	2	5	10	1	5	5	18	35
Craft[c]	3	5	6	15	24	*	*	1	1	3
Other blue collar[d]	17	26	22	48	44	66	63	65	60	41
Total nonagriculture	25	36	33	76	94	70	74	77	90	99
Agriculture	75	64	67	24	6	30	26	23	10	1
	Total United States									
Total	100	100	100	100	100	100	100	100	100	100
Upper white collar	11	13	14	21	25	11	15	15	17	24
Lower white collar	9	13	13	13	16	13	29	29	39	43
Craft	14	16	15	20	21	1	1	1	1	2
Other blue collar	31	33	36	33	34	53	47	51	41	30
Total nonagriculture	65	75	78	87	96	78	92	96	98	99
Agriculture	35	25	22	13	4	22	8	4	2	1

[a]Upper white collar: professional and managerial, excluding agriculture.
[b]Lower white collar: sales and clerical (or administrative support).
[c]Craft: skilled workers.
[d]Other blue collar: semiskilled and unskilled (operatives, fabricators, and laborers), service, agriculture.
*Less than one-half of 1%.

reported as Indian. Our best estimate is that this influx contains many of mixed-Indian and non-Indian ancestry; these mixed-ancestry people are less likely to live on reservations and do have more schooling. Hence, the higher socioeconomic level of those living off the reservations probably reflects the presence of more mixed-ancestry people. How did these people (in 1980) report their race in 1970, and how will they report it in the year 2000? If we knew, we could better predict occupation in the future.

Further, some reservations are virtually bedroom suburbs of large cities. Hence, some Amerindians can live on reservations and still commute to non-reservation jobs and occupations. The census reports occupations according to where the person lives and not where he/she may work.

CANADA

Pre-World War II

The natives living in present-day Canada climbed the white man's occupational ladder as did the Amerindians south of the border. Occupationally the north-of-

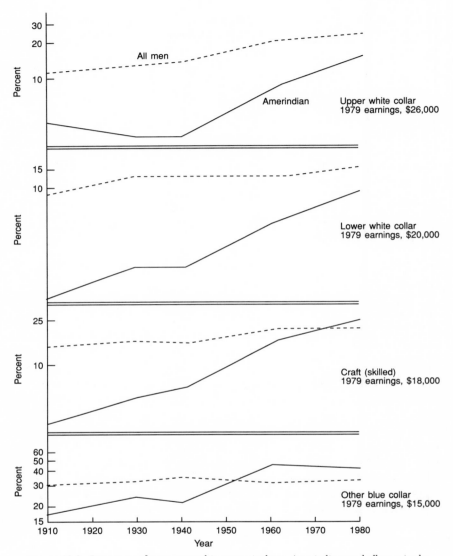

Figure 12.2. Percentage of men engaged in nonagriculture, Amerindians and all men in the United States: 1910 to 1980.

the-border natives in 1500 must have resembled their south-of-the-border relatives. Then, as the fur trade expanded in the sixteenth to nineteenth centuries, probably many who had practiced agriculture became hunters and trappers.

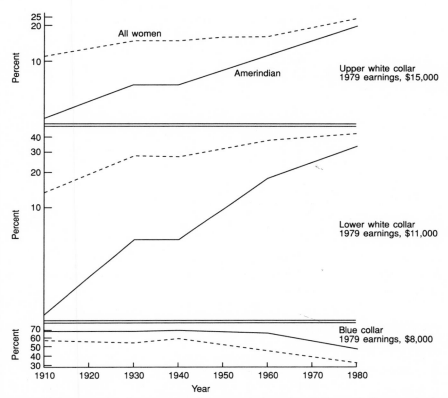

Figure 12.3. Percentage of women engaged in nonagriculture, Amerindians and all women in the United States: 1910 to 1980. "1979 earnings" represent estimated average earnings of all full-time workers in 1979 (PC 80-2-8 B, Table 2). Source: Table 12.2.

Once the reserves had been organized, many of those relegated to areas not suitable for agriculture had to continue to hunt, fish, and trap for saleable furs.

By the end of the nineteenth century, government furnished some financial assistance, but "welfare recipient" is not an officially recognized occupation. By this time, too, a few had modern, or European-introduced, occupations; workers at trading posts, military or police or other protective-service jobs, occupations in transport, and the like.[4] We suspect, however, that very few (as in the United States) had these "new" jobs; unfortunately, we could find no definitive information bearing on their occupations around the turn of the century. (The earliest

---

[4] For descriptive information about how some natives, the Métis, for example, earned their living, see Harison (1985). For some time buffalo hunting was a lucrative occupation. As the herds diminished, some Métis took on the white man's occupations.

Table 12.3. Occupational Classification of Indians On
versus Off Reservations: United States, 1980

	Reservation[a]	
	On[b]	Off[b]
Total	100	100
Upper white collar	13	17
Lower white collar	22	25
Precision production, craft and repair	12	15
Operators, semiskilled	16[c]	17
Handlers, unskilled	9	6
Service	21	17
Agriculture	7	3

[a]Including Historic Areas of Oklahoma.
[b]We do not have separate information for men and women.
[c]Includes "traditional" occupations such as pottery, weaving, and so forth.

date for which we have census information is 1951.) Any who lived in cities, of course, must have worked in occupations that are generally found in urban areas rather than in rural reserves.

Post-World War II, 1951 to 1971

The Canadian census changed its labor force definition and concept and its occupational classification system since World War II. The information on occupations that we report next do not take these changes into consideration because the census has not adjusted them and we are unable to do so. Hence, the comparisons shown are approximations only. However, insofar as the statistics show large changes in one direction or another, we may accept that these directional changes did occur.

As late as 1951, about 6 in every 10 men were in the traditional rural occupations, namely, agriculture, hunting, fishing, trapping, logging, and mining. These traditional occupations are the "fossils" of the occupations followed by all natives in the sixteenth century and earlier. Also, they reflect the more rural habitat of the 1950s natives in contrast to the total Canadian population.

Another 3 in 10 had blue-collar occupations ranging from highly skilled to unskilled. One in 10 had a white-collar or service job (Figure 12.4). Only 70 Amerindian men in all of Canada were reported as engaged in professional jobs, and 92 men worked in proprietary and managerial occupations.

Among women in 1951, about 6 in 10 were reported in service jobs, and 1 in 4 in blue-collar jobs. About 1 in 10 was in a traditional occupation (mostly in agriculture), and 1 in 10 in a white-collar occupation.

Clearly, in 1951 the occupational composition of the Canadian Indians

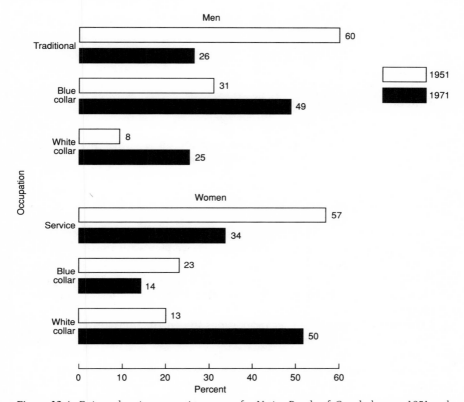

Figure 12.4. Estimated major occupation groups for Native People of Canada by sex: 1951 and 1971. "White collar" includes managerial, professional, and white-collar jobs in communication, finance, and commerce, as well as service jobs. Source: 1951 Census data for Indians and Eskimos combined (the data are not available separately) by detailed occupation and sex; 1951 Census, Volume IV, Table 12. 1971 Census data for native Indians by detailed occupation and sex; 1971 Census, Bulletin 94-734, Table 4.

resembled that of many Third World underdeveloped economies in the latter part of the twentieth century.

By 1971, half of the men were engaged in blue-collar work and another one-quarter (1 in 4) were in the traditional rural jobs. One in 4 had a white-collar or service job. The 1971 census reported over 2,000 men as being in professional occupations and 700 in proprietary and managerial jobs.

By 1971, almost half of the women were engaged in white-collar occupations, and 1 in 3 in service.

Obviously, there was considerable movement up the occupational ladder during these two decades for both men and women. Perhaps 1961 to 1971 was the decade of maximum change. During these two decades following World War II, people were leaving the reserves for cities, and more younger people were attending school. The native population was preparing itself for higher-paying and higher-status jobs.

The Incomplete Picture in 1981

The 1981 census did not publish occupational information for the total of Native People. We found detailed data only for those who reported having only Indian ancestors. We found no information for those of mixed parentage or multiple ancestry.

Natives of Single Origin

By the latter part of the twentieth century, the occupations of the people who reported having only native ancestors[5] were converging with those of the total Canadian population (Table 12.4). In comparison with all Canadian men, the native men have smaller proportions in upper white collar (managerial, professional, technical), lower white collar (clerical and sales), farming, and manufacturing (processing, machining, product fabricating, and assembly).

The native men have higher proportions in construction, lower-blue-collar occupations (transport, material handling, other crafts, equipment operating), and the miscellaneous category simply designated as "other."

Native women are found almost exclusively in white-collar and service occupations. In the white-collar occupations, the native women lag behind all Canadian women. In the service occupations, the natives greatly exceed. Very few women, native and nonnative, have blue-collar or other occupations.

Those of Mixed or Multiple Origin

We believe that information for these people, if available, would show that the multiple-ancestry natives had converged occupationally more than had those whom we have just reviewed. We arrive at this conclusion on the basis of the following information:

1. The proportions who lived in urban areas in 1981 were: status, 32%; nonstatus, 67%; and Métis, 59%.
2. Educational level (see Chapter 11) was lowest for the status Indians living on reserves, higher for the status Indians living off the reserves and for the Métis, and highest for the nonstatus people.

---

[5] These are the people listed in the 1981 census (Catalogue 92-918, Table 1) as "Native People of Single Origin." Most of these people, we believe, are status Indians, probably living on reserves.

Table 12.4. Occupational Distribution by Socioeconomic Groups and by Sex for Natives and Nonnatives: Canada, 1981 (Single Ancestry)

	Men		Women	
Occupation	Native	Nonnative	Native	Nonnative
Total	100	100	100	100
White collar	22	39	57	71
Managerial, professional, technical	14	24	23	25
Clerical	5	7	27	37
Sales	3	8	7	9
Service	10	9	27	16
Traditional	15	7	2	2
Farming	4	5	1	2
Fishing, hunting to mining	11	2	1	0
Blue collar	48	43	8	7
Processing to assembling	17	20	8	7
Construction	18	12	0	0
Transport, etc.	13	11	0	0
All other	5	2	5	4

3. Finally, we note that average income in 1980 was lowest for the status groups on reserves, \$7,100[6]; higher for the status living off the reserves, \$8,800; and still higher for the Métis, \$9,500, and the nonstatus groups, \$9,900.

These three criteria unquestionably indicate that those of mixed ancestry are higher on the occupational ladder than are those of single ethnic origin. The better occupations tend to be held by more schooled urbanites, and in turn, these jobs provide larger earnings. How much higher on the ladder, how much closer they may have converged to total Canada, we do not know.

World War II and the Changing Scene

When did occupational convergence start to gain momentum? A few natives had held white man's occupations well before the twentieth century. However, it was not until the mid-twentieth century, about the time of World War II, that occupational convergence began to embrace the masses.

Such convergence is associated with changes in lifestyle, including the increase in the proportion living in urban areas—7% in 1951 increased to 42% in 1981. Presumably many of the new urbanites are former reserve residents. It is also associated with the large increases in schooling (see Chapter 11, Figure 11.7 and 11.8) since World War II. In addition, there appears to be greater

[6] Canadian dollars. See *Canada's Native People*.

tolerance of the Native People by the whites, judging from the Parliament
Joint Committee Hearings of 1946–48, the 1951 Indian Act, the 1969 White
Paper, and other actions taken by the federal government (*The Canadian Indian,*
pp. 86 ff.). Exactly how much more tolerance there may be in the 1980s as
compared with, say, pre-World War I, we cannot say.

The Professional Specialist Occupations, 1981

Fewer native men (of single origin) were in professional, semiprofessional, or
technical occupations as compared with all Canadian men—about 1 in 12 as
compared with 1 in 8. Among women, both native and nonnative, about 1 in 5
was in such an occupation. The women were largely in technical or semiprofessional jobs, for example, occupations in welfare and community services; technicians in libraries, museums, and archival services; nursing attendants and
medical laboratory technologists and technicians; and so forth.

Within this professional group the natives tend to be, less frequently than
all Canadian workers, in what may be called the more "difficult" occupations
(Figure 12.5). This group (as we have defined it) includes natural sciences,
engineering, and mathematics; and selected occupations in social science.[7] These
are the subjects sometimes referred to as "hard" in college circles.

The natives, both men and women, tended to be engaged in the less
"difficult" occupations, more often than the general Canadian population.[8] These
are the "softer" subjects in college. If information were available for those of
multiple origin, we suspect that there would be more in the "harder" and fewer
in the "softer"; perhaps someday we shall know for certain.

This dichotomy between "hard" and "soft" resembles that noted about
the subjects of recipients of Doctor of Philosophy degrees from U.S. universities (Chapter 11). Relatively fewer Amerindians earned PhDs in physics, as-
tronomy, and the other "hard" subjects; more earned degrees in education and
other "soft" subjects.

SUMMARY

As the entire lifestyle of the Amerindians changes, so do their occupations.
Insofar as they live among the general population, as very large numbers do
in the latter part of the twentieth century, so do they engage in more or
less similar occupations.

---

[7] Canadian classification Major Group 21 plus group 231.

[8] Major Groups 233 to 239 inclusive, 251, 273, and 33. The category "medicine and health," 31,
was omitted because it appears to be too varied.

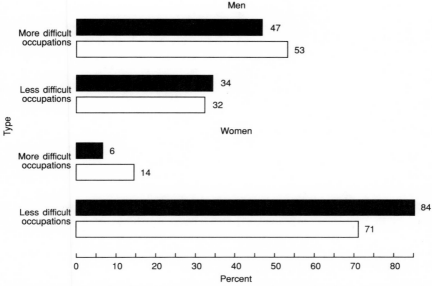

Figure 12.5. Types of professional occupations for men and women, single-origin natives and total Canada: 1981. Source: See footnotes 7 and 8.

Occupational conversion begins by taking jobs on the lower rungs of the occupational ladder and gradually climbing upward. On the ladder of professional jobs, this sequence also tends to be followed. The easier subjects to master eventually lead to the higher-rung professional jobs. Such ladder climbing may extend over two or more generations.

Many of the Indians still hold lower-paying and otherwise less desirable occupations. But the process of convergence with the white majority is still proceeding.

Chapter *13*

Summary and Reflections

SUMMARY

The Prehistorics

Natural forces dominated the lives of the Amerindians as these same forces led the First Immigrants from Asia eastward. Sometime in the past—no one knows how long ago—people, *Homo sapiens,* journeyed from northeastern Asia to the northwest corner of the Western Hemisphere. Some may have come from present-day Siberia, some from the Pacific coastal areas stretching from Japan northward. Some may have reached present-day Alaska; others perhaps reached present-day British Columbia.

When and how they came depended on the actions of the glaciers that covered most of Canada and the northern United States from time to time. When the glaciers were piled high and deep, they locked up much water and the seas between northeastern Asia and Alaska were lowered and land—Beringia or the Bering Land Bridge of sea bottom—was exposed. People and animals were able to walk from one continent to the other. Enough water remained in the seas so that crossing by watercraft was also possible. Presumably, some walked and some came by nascent Mayflowers.

We suggest that this migration consisted of many uncoordinated small bands who gradually worked their way eastward to the Western Hemisphere. They followed a large variety of trails, both by land and water; their movements depended on when they felt compelled to move. The ever-changing climatic conditions determined the specific trails (if that term may be used) to follow. Certainly there was no clearly defined path with arrows pointing to Alaska.

All during these remote millennia, glaciers piled high and then melted, and the seas fell and rose. This seesaw was repeated over and over. Precisely when any Ancestor arrived is unknown. 10,000 years ago? 30,000 years? 50,000? Even earlier?

From the northwest corner of the Western Hemisphere, they gradually worked their way across the entire hemisphere. They moved south and east when climatic conditions were right, when the food trails beckoned, and when the geography permitted. We think that more than 10 millennia elapsed after the time of first arrival before every nook, cranny, mountaintop, jungle, and island had been peopled. We ask: Because people and animals are dependent upon vegetation, how rapidly can vegetation migrate in response to changing climate? One possible answer may lie in the answer to the question: "How fast can trees migrate?" As the glaciers advanced southward so did the vegetation. Davis and Zabinski (see Roberts 1989) suggest that 25 to 50 miles in a century is a good clip, or 250 to 500 miles in 1,000 years. From Alaska to San Francisco is some 3,000 miles. Did it take 6,000 years, more or less, just to reach San Francisco?

Initially, the immigrants were hunters and fishers and gatherers of wild vegetation. But how much meat and fish did they eat and how much vegetation? No one knows. The mighty hunter can be dramatized and made into a mighty movie star. But how can you make a hero of someone collecting berries or digging for roots, especially if that person is a woman or child? This way of earning a living began with the first hominid. The early Asian immigrants brought hunting, fishing, and gathering with them and continued using these methods for obtaining their food as they trekked about.

Cultural change, at least technological change, continued over these millennia—improved stone implements, pottery, straw or basket weaving, and the like. What social changes accompanied these technological changes?

Eventually, perhaps some 10,000 years ago, the first glimmerings of agriculture appeared, possibly south of the Rio Grande. Agriculture may have begun here almost as early as in the Eastern Hemisphere. Maize, beans, chiles, squash, cotton, sunflower, cattail, and so forth were cultivated, some south and some north of the Rio Grande. Maize was introduced into what is now the Southwest United States from south of the border, possibly 3,000 to 4,000 years ago; by about A.D. 1000, more or less, it became the most popular food crop for North American Indians who lived where maize could be grown.

The spread of agriculture in North America, we expect, was accompanied by vast changes in many aspects of American life: Irrigation works and dams, the rise of sedentary societies, the rise of chieftainships, possibly class societies, and who knows what other social and cultural changes accompanied agriculture.

Population probably increased more rapidly with the spread of agriculture. We infer this from our observation that length of life was greater among those who had agriculture than among the hunters and gatherers.

How long did the average person live? Life was very short in those prehistoric days, as compared with the end of the twentieth century. Among the newborns, we find the average number of years of life expected to be about:

	Nonagriculture	Agriculture
Males	16 to 17 years	18 to 19 years
Females	14 to 15 years	17 to 18 years

Fewer than half of these newborns survived to the ages of 15 to 19 years. For those who did survive, future life expectancy was about the same as at birth. Let us illustrate. The comparative few newborn males among the hunters and gatherers who survived to the age of 15 to 19 could look forward to another 15 to 20 years of life. This is the time span in which the next generation can be produced.

Of course, a very few lived to "Social Security age" (65 years) and beyond, but not many, less than 1 in 100. (See Appendix 3 for further details.)

Short length of life means that the death rate was very high by modern standards. One result—family life was influenced by the high death rates. The nuclear family, if and when it existed, did not long remain intact. One partner died within a few years of the start of the union. Couples broken by death of a member were then reformed with new partners, and then shortly thereafter broken again by death, and so on. Divorce was not needed to end an unhappy union.

Another result of such high mortality is that the group had to have arrangements for caring for infants whose mothers died. We suppose that the extended family, perhaps the entire band or group, was of major importance in the family life of the prehistoric Amerindians. If the group as a cohesive unit had been dependent for its well-being and survival on the nuclear family alone, the band would have long since disappeared.

The very high death rates were accompanied by very high birthrates, probably close to the physiological maximum. A woman may have had (on the average) as many as nine births if she lived through the reproductive years. Another result of the high birth and death rates was the youthfulness of the tribe or band. The average age (median) probably was between 15 and 17 years. Close to half of the people were under 15 years of age, and perhaps 1 in 20 was 40 years or older.

From Columbus to the End of the Nineteenth Century

When Columbus first arrived, there may have been about 1¼ million Amerindians in the United States and Canada. The majority lived in what is now the United States.

From 1492 to almost the end of the nineteenth century, DAWG—Disease (especially smallpox), Alcohol, Warfare, Guns—depleted their numbers. We estimate that in 1890 there were about 400,000. The numbers increased slowly thereafter.

From time to time, efforts were made by governments and missionaries to "civilize" the Amerindians, that is, become literate in English or French, be devout Christians, and otherwise emulate the settlers. Eventually, then, the Indians would be assimilated into European society. This approach was opposed by other officials and settlers who wanted to get rid of the Indians in any way possible. The Indians, we suppose, were not eager for social change of either variety.

By the latter part of the nineteenth century, the displacement was completed. The Original People had been forced out of their homelands and resettled on lands that were not desired by the European settlers. They were settled on reserves and reservations located in the boondocks where they had little contact with the general population. Perhaps the major change that they were forced to undergo was to become farmers if they had been hunters and gatherers previously. Many lost the right to travel as they may have desired. They were confined to the reservation territory.

Such enforced immobilization, in turn, may have led to a decrease in intertribal warfare. Further, insofar as several tribes may have been assigned to one reservation or reserve, some social change may have come about from the intertribal contacts. Otherwise, social change was probably minimized.

There was little demographic change (as far as can be ascertained) except for the decrease in numbers and the relocation of many tribes from the sixteenth century to about the time of the Civil War in the United States. The birthrate, age, and sex distribution were largely the same; they were still rural dwellers; they were still not citizens of the United States and Canada; they were on the scrapheaps of Canadian and U.S. life. Only the death rate had fallen significantly, probably in the latter part of the nineteenth century, since intertribal warfare had been stopped, plagues had been brought under some control, and the governments stopped killing them.

We summarize these four centuries, sixteenth to nineteenth inclusive, as a period of demographic and cultural disintegration at worst, or as a period of demographic immobility at best.

The Twentieth Century

Some, but not much, population change occurred until about the time of World War II. Leaving the reservations and moving to cities was getting underway during the four decades preceding the war, the amount of schooling gradually increased, the birth and death rates began to decline, population growth increased, the Amerindians became national citizens and served in World Wars I and II, and marriage to non-Indians increased. By the middle of the twentieth century, the censuses counted a little over one-half million.

Three decades later, at the beginning of the 1980s, the two censuses counted about 2 million. This vast increase in 30 years from one-half to 2 million is too large to be acceptable. About 1 million of the 1½ million increase occurred between 1970 (or 1971) and 1980 (or 1981). What happened, especially during the decade of the 1970s?

During this 30-year period, 1950 to 1980, there was apparently more convergence of the Indian population characteristics with those of the dominant society than in preceding decades. There were vast increases in the numbers living in cities, many more of the younger people received more schooling, almost reaching the level of the general population, intermarriage with non-Indians may have increased considerably, and the birth and death rates fell almost to the national levels. Some of those living in the United States and who had been dispossessed from their lands east of the Mississippi River in the eighteenth and nineteenth centuries were returning to the east. In Canada, "the return of the natives" is not as clearly evident, although British Columbia was partially repopulated. How and why did this demographic renaissance come about?

To begin, possible improvements in the information obtained in the 1980 and 1981 censuses over those of the previous decade may have resulted in a greater reported increase in the amount of population change than actually occurred.

Probably of more importance was World War II and its accompanying changes in both military and civilian life. These changes helped to increase levels of tolerance and acceptance of minority ethnic groups. The U.S. military always had tried to keep the blacks and whites separated, although some integration had occurred prior to World War II. During this and the following wars (Korea and Vietnam), however, it was administratively too difficult to operate with two separate armies, a white one and a black one. Hence, the military was significantly more integrated by 1980 than it was at the start of World War II.

The civilian workforce had difficultly in obtaining enough workers, especially during the periods of actual fighting. Refusal to hire because of race or color or ethnicity made no sense. So the biases that previously had kept out ethnic minorities and women from jobs were partially lifted. These changes, we suggest, led to greater tolerance and acceptance in other aspects including intermarriage.

The increased acceptance of minority people may have benefited the Amerindians more than other groups. So many of the natives are of mixed Indian and white ancestry that many can report themselves of either race to the census, depending on circumstances. We suspect that many who had declared themselves as white in the U.S. censuses of 1960 and 1970, and in the Canadian censuses of 1961 and 1971, declared themselves to be Indians in 1980 or 1981. Now being an Indian is more acceptable. This factor, we believe, accounts for much of the very large increase in reported Amerindian population in this last decade.

To summarize the summary: (1) After being an endangered species from the time of first contact with the Europeans to the end of the nineteenth century, the Amerindians are recovering their numbers. (2) Their population characteristics are converging to those of the general populations of Canada and the United States. (3) So many of them in the twentieth century are of mixed Indian and non-Indian blood that many can claim either identification and can switch at will.

What Do the Amerindians Say?

We inferred what we could from the available statistics regarding demographic and social change and the possible changes in Indian–white relations over the half millennium past, A.D. 1500 to 2000. These statistics, however, reveal but one side of the picture. How today's descendants of the Ancients feel about these changes and how they view themselves is another part of the picture. Unfortunately for us, careful analysis of this part is too much for us to undertake. Instead, we read papers published by Indian organizations, other writings of Indian authors, whatever other material we could find, and we even looked through Volume IV of the *Handbook of North American Indians,* "History of Indian–White Relations." Some of the publications are: *Daybreak* (Maryland), *Eagle Wing Press* (Connecticut), *Akwesasne Notes* (New York), and *Native Self Sufficiency* (California). W. P. Kinsella provided in his short stories some insights into life on a Canadian reserve. From these readings and discussions with some natives, we formulated the brief summary at the end of this section.

In Appendix 13, we reproduce the only unpublished documents we found, documents that suggest the responses of the reserve Indians of Canada to the white government. Jim Smith, who had spent considerable time living on reserves, presumably prepared "Indian Band Dog Guidelines" (Circular W-17, July 30, 1975). This document caught the feelings of the reserve Indians as they were subjected to orders from the Canadian government and mocks the official circulars.

Circular W-7 (July 23, 1975) illustrates the Canadian government's attempts to control every aspect of Indian life. We suspect that there are some similarities with the situation in the United States. We are uncertain whether Circular W-7 is also a Jim Smith product or one of the Canadian government's "Ten Commandments."

The dates of these two documents raise questions about the sincerity of the government efforts as described in *The Canadian Indian,* "The Age of Resurgence" (pp. 86 ff.). Beginning in the late 1940s, efforts reportedly were made "to help

Indian people achieve equality." Apparently, 30 years later, in the mid-1970s, equality had not yet been achieved.

We summarize our impressions of "what the Native People say" as follows:

1. There must be great variation in the feelings of the Indians regarding the dominant whites and toward demographic and social change.
2. Many Native People do not show quite the feeling of tolerance and "brotherly love" toward the dominant whites, as some whites may like to believe.

SOME REFLECTIONS

Why?

Our analysis of the North American Indians documented the many measurable social and demographic changes over the half millennium since the first arrival of the Europeans. The Amerindian characteristics (those that we were able to study) in the latter part of the twentieth century differ considerably from those of pre-European times. Further, the present characteristics resemble those of the dominant whites much more than their Ancestors resembled the Europeans in the sixteenth century. This approaching similarity is what we referred to as "merging." For the Indians these changes are part of the process of sociocultural demographic change.

The entire concept of social change has two parts: (a) changes induced by the clash of cultures and in which the militarily stronger people impose change upon the subjugated weaker people; and (b) the internal forces generated within a society and that produce observable changes as, for example, increased urbanism or a lowered birthrate. We deal with part (b) very briefly in Appendix 12 and shall say no more here.

The experiences of the Indians fit the first part; the social and demographic changes that they underwent were imposed by the Europeans.

One important change for the Amerindians—largely a post-World War II change—seems to be increased tolerance on the part of the dominant whites. This is suggested by the apparent increase in intermarriage with non-Indians, as well as by other sociodemographic changes that we noted. Of course, tolerance by the dominant white society by itself does not make for social change among the Indians. Increased tolerance by white society is a necessary but not by itself sufficient condition for bringing about social change among the Indians or any other previously denigrated and numerically smaller ethnic group.

We tried to explain each change observed. However, we feel that each explanation offered is only a surface explanation; it applies to that particular characteristic at that time. For example, the rural-to-urban movement of the

Amerindians began slowly about the time of World War I and gained speed following World War II. Why this movement and why this timing? We suggested several possible "causes"—increased schooling, jobs in urban areas, increased tolerance and legal rights, and so forth.

But why are they more schooled now? Why do the Indians and other ethnic minorities have more legal rights in the latter twentieth century? Why the apparent increased tolerance on the part of white society—some of the whites if not all? Is the movement of Indians to urban areas (taking the time lag into consideration) related to the earlier urbanization of whites and blacks? In the United States in 1900, 4 in 10 whites were living in urban areas, 1 in 4 blacks, and 1 in 20 Indians. By the end of World War I (1920), half of the whites and 1 in 3 of the blacks were urbanites, but as yet only 1 in 20 Indians. It was only by about 1980 that half of the Indians were residing in urban areas.

One can continue to ask why and find an apparent explanation for each change. But that is unsatisfactory. Are there any models that will offer explanations as to why and when social changes occur? Were the observed social and demographic changes in the United States and Canada purely chance affairs? Or are they trying to tell us something?

Social Change and "Cultural Tectonic Plates"

We suggest that the sociodemographic changes that occurred and are occurring in the latter twentieth century are the observable effects of more generalized forces that may be called "cultural tectonic plates." Geological tectonic plates move continents. Perhaps there are "cultural tectonic plates" that contribute to the formation of various aspects of social change. For example, the forces that are changing the treatment of the Amerindians also may have led to increased emphasis on human rights throughout much of the world; these may (or may not) be very different from those forces which produced such profound political and economic changes in Eastern Europe in the last part of the twentieth century.

Perhaps history is the single most important element in these suggested "cultural tectonic plates"—historical events long since passed. For example, the signing of the Magna Carta in 1215 in Runnymede, we suggest, led to the U.S. Declaration of Independence, adopted in 1776, and the French Declaration of the Rights of Man in 1789, and perhaps similar measures elsewhere. Every event involving *Homo,* excluding glaciers and other natural events, has its antecedents. There are antecedents to the Magna Carta. And these antecedents, perhaps, compose the "cultural tectonic plate."

Study of such "plates" is a lifetime project. We can only repeat what Justice Holmes of the United States Supreme Court, age 94, reportedly said to Justice Brandeis, age 72, as they walked about in Washington, DC and passed a lovely lass: "Ah, to be 72 again."

Change and the Indians

Social change and outmarriage do not necessarily mean that a group will disappear. We expect that Amerindians will be living in North America for many generations into the future, at least 7 times 7. There are many examples of cultural groups that have survived many millennia. For example, the Parsi in India today are the descendants of the Persian Zoroastrians of three millennia ago. Some Chaldeans live in the United States in the twentieth century as well as in Iraq, their homeland over three millennia ago. Some Samaritans whose roots go back some 3,000 years or more still live in Israel. Ethnic groups may diminish in numbers, they may change names, but many continue and continue and continue.

Afterword

About 500 years ago, Christopher Columbus and associates linked the Old and New Worlds, launching events that dramatically changed the course of history in the Americas as well as in Europe. Since that time, academia has struggled toward understanding the complex history of the American Indian in the context of world history. Information on that history is not readily available. It must be scrupulously gleaned from the accounts of early European explorers, archaeology, language analysis, human remains, and the oral history of contemporary American Indians.

Because of the limitations of these sources, our knowledge of the history of the American Indian is far from complete. We do know that the American Indian population originated in Eastern Asia and migrated to the Americas in several waves beginning sometime prior to 10,000 years ago. By the time of the Columbus voyage in 1492, variation in their physical appearance was minimal in comparison with their tremendous variations in language, lifestyle, and other aspects of culture. To some extent, this variation reflects diversity in their Asian origins but mostly represents successful adaptation to the diverse environments within the Americas. Their numbers in North America, including Eskimo or Inuit and Aleut, in 1492 had likely grown to 2 million or more.

Estimates of population size of the American Indian population in North America by 1492 vary enormously, depending upon the data consulted and the perspective of the estimator. Jaffe offers a figure for North America of 1.25 million, excluding Eskimos and Aleuts, at about 1600. Historically, other estimates for all native peoples in North America at about 1492 have ranged from 900,000 by Kroeber to as many as 18,000,000 by Dobyns.

Prior to 1492, the Americas were hardly disease-free. Analysis of carefully dated human remains documents that morbidity in the Americas was on the increase, largely as a result of growing population size and density and a dietary shift in many areas to less variable agricultural products. The infant mortality rate was high, and tuberculosis and probably syphilis were among a variety of diseases limiting life expectancy. In spite of these problems, American Indian population size was, overall, on the increase.

The new culture contact initiated by Columbus not only brought profound cultural change to the Americas but introduced a variety of Old World diseases as well. Preexisting disease and morbidity did little to protect the American Indian population from smallpox, measles, mumps, typhoid, typhus, cholera, malaria, and other diseases of European origin. Tragically, their numbers were greatly reduced by about 1900.

After reaching a demographic low in the late nineteenth or early twentieth century, the American Indian population has once again demonstrated resilience and adaptability. By some counts, the American Indian population in North America may be approaching their number in 1492. Advances in health care and economic conditions have paid off demographically as indicators of morbidity, life expectancy, and the like march slowly but steadily toward the national averages of Canada and the United States.

The history of the aboriginal population of the Americas is unique. Slowly, through research, we learn more detail and complexity. The types of historical information remain mostly unchanged, but our research techniques and capabilities are improving rapidly. Ethnohistorians continue to accumulate a more sophisticated perspective to interpret the original sources and occasionally stumble onto new documents and information. Archaeologists and physical anthropologists reap the scholarly rewards of vast new technological advances that allow them to trace the geographic origins of lithic materials, thus documenting ancient trade patterns, and to chemically analyze bone fragments, clarifying diet, disease experience, and perhaps even population relationships.

In this volume, Jaffe largely defers to others discussions of estimating ancient population numbers and assessing disease experience from old bones. His major contribution for the pre-European period consists of the life tables that he developed separately for the hunters and gatherers and for those who had agriculture or horticulture. From these data he infers possible effects upon the family and tribal size, and some possible intertribal relations. In addition, he offers fresh perspectives on such other key demographic issues as the problems of the role of the natural and social environments in shaping American Indian demography, variability in the definitions of contemporary American Indians, and the direction of demographic change in the American Indian community. Indeed, the second half of his study is devoted mainly to developments in the late nineteenth century and the twentieth century, especially those developments and changes following World War II. Such information frequently falls between the interdisciplinary cracks of scholarship in history, anthropology, demography, and related fields yet offers the key to understanding the dynamics of demographic change.

The Jaffe book is a case in point on the need for a holistic approach to demographic interpretations and the value of interdisciplinary research. Anthropologists, archaeologists, and demographers have much to learn from one another. Life tables and related statistics gleaned from skeletal analysis offer unique demographic, social, and medical information but are minefields of academic interpretation for the nonspecialist. As Jaffe shows, geographers and geologists, historians, statisticians, demographers, and ethnologists all provide key pieces to the interpretive puzzle, but no one discipline by itself can put all the pieces together. This book does not provide all the answers, but it clearly amasses a great deal of relevant information and points the way for additional needed research. Hopefully, such research will allow us to more fully understand the unique and complex history of the American Indian, Eskimo, and Aleut peoples and how they continue to adapt to a changing world.

DOUGLAS H. UBELAKER

Smithsonian Institution
Washington, DC

Appendixes

Appendix 1

Who Is an American Indian?

There are several definitions of an American Indian. And each one produces different statistics about the people who are so called. This variety complicates the problem of analyzing Indian social change that we undertook. One begins with statistics obtained on the basis of one definition, and then, in the middle of the analysis, switches to statistics derived from a somewhat different definition. This is analogous to changing the rules a bit in the middle of the ballgame. The transition can be made, if done carefully.

Ed Deming, a well-known statistician, reportedly phrased the problem as follows: "Whatever number you get depends on how you count, and if you change the way you count, the number will change" (*Smithsonian,* August 1990, p. 82).

Why are there several definitions of an American Indian? James B. Waldran (*1885 and After,* 1986, p. 279) suggests that there are two basic origins for Indian identity. One is *cultural affiliation.* The other is a *legally imposed* definition. We suggest that these two origins can be combined in several ways, leading to at least three working definitions of American Indian.

1. Self-designation: A person is whatever he/she designates. This is used sometimes in national censuses, particularly that of the U.S. 1980 and Canada 1981. In the event that the person cannot self-classify, for example, little children, the census may assign race or ethnicity on the basis of the parents' or other members of the household.

2. Community definition: What the person is considered to be by the community residents. Originally, Indians were so defined by census enumerators (consciously or not) for decennial census purposes, and hence may be considered as reflecting the white community's definition. A problem is that the definition assigned by the white community was likely to be accepted by the Indian community, which had no option to do otherwise. Hence, if the whites

said that so-and-so was an Indian, the Indian community so defined the person, at least to the government agent. Upon being so defined, so-and-so regards him/herself as an Indian. If this definition resembles a corkscrew, so be it. As far as we know, almost the only use made of this definition at the time of our writing is in connection with civil-rights legislation including Affirmative Action and Equal Employment opportunities in the United States and similar-type legislation in Canada.

We illustrate. In the latter twentieth century, tribes officially recognized by the U.S. Bureau of Indian Affairs may use this community-recognition definition to decide who has legal tribal rights. To obtain health services from the Indian Health Service or benefits from other agencies, the person must be on the tribal rolls; this indicates recognition by the tribe or community. If he/she is not on the rolls, no benefits need be forthcoming. Thus this definition is closely tied to the legal definitions that follow.

3. Legal definition: The Bureau of Indian Affairs defines as Indians the people it will assist, as do the other agencies. The several agencies have different legal definitions of whom they will "assist," or count differently the number of people who qualify for services. We cannot explore all the details. That the various agencies have different counts on the numbers of Indians we show in Appendix 7.

In Canada, the situation may be simpler, or perhaps more complex, than in the United States. The people deemed to be "true" Indians were classified as *status,* or *registered,* Indians in the First Indian Act of 1876. Anyone claiming to be an Indian but not officially so classified is *nonstatus* and not entitled to any government "benefits." Subsequently, the Métis, those of mixed Indian and non-Indian ancestry, were recognized as Métis, but as far as we know they receive no "benefits." The Inuit (Eskimo) were regarded as a subdivision of the Indians and classified in the same manner. The 1981 Canadian census listed all four groups as components of the major category "Native Population." In short, there are the "legitimate" Indians who are entitled to "benefits" (from the agency Indians and Northern Affairs Canada) and any others who may call themselves Indians but are not entitled to any "benefits" or services.

So: Who is an Amerindian?

In our present study, any findings based on the U.S. census of 1980 and the Canadian 1981 census are derived from data collected according to the first definition—self-identification.

In other cases, the definitions used for collecting the statistics may be vague. For example, the 1890 United States census instructed the enumerators as follows (Wright 1981):

SPECIAL ENUMERATION OF INDIANS (pp. 181–182)

The law provides that the Superintendent of Census may employ special agents or other means to make an enumeration of all Indians living within the jurisdiction of the United States, with such information as to their condition as may be obtainable, classifying them as to Indians taxed and Indians not taxed.

By the phrase "Indians not taxed" is meant Indians living on reservations under the care of Government agents or roaming individually or in bands over unsettled tracts of country.

Indians not in tribal relations, whether full-bloods or half-breeds, who are found mingled with the white population, residing in white families, engaged as servants or laborers, or living in huts or wigwams on the outskirts of towns or settlements, are to be regarded as a part of the ordinary population of the country, and are to be embraced in the enumeration.

The enumeration of Indians living on reservations will be made by special agents appointed directly from this office, and supervisors and enumerators will have no responsibility in this connection.

Many Indians, however, have voluntarily abandoned their tribal relations or have quit their reservations and now sustain themselves. When enumerators find Indians off of or living away from reservations, and in no ways dependent upon the agency or Government, such Indians, in addition to their enumeration on the population and supplemental schedules, in the same manner as for the population generally should be noted on a special schedule [7-917] by name, tribe, sex, age, occupation, and whether taxed or not taxed.

The object of this is to obtain an accurate census of all Indians living within the jurisdiction of the United States and to prevent double enumeration of certain Indians.

Where Indians are temporarily absent from their reservations the census enumerators need not note them, as the special enumerator for the Indian reservation will get their names.

COLOR, SEX, AND AGE (p. 187)

4. Whether white, black, mulatto, quadroon, octoroon, Chinese, Japanese, or Indian. Write white, black, mulatto, quadroon, octoroon, Chinese, Japanese, or Indian, according to the color or race of the person enumerated.

We must remember that all definitions are imprecise and that people and events are viewed and defined differently at different times. When all people who could be called Indians (or any other designation) lived on reservations or reserves, such place or residence was sufficient identification of ethnicity for all practical purposes. Once they leave the reservations and live among the general population, different definitions are used to identify people from ostensibly the same ethnic group.

People of mixed ancestry complicate the problem of definition in both countries, at least for purposes of analysis. If self-identification is used, the person must decide once and for all whether to be or not to be Indian. If he/she switches identification at will, analyses (except that attempting to estimate the amount of shift) are of little significance. We illustrate the problem with the number of births in the United States in the years 1974 to 1976 (Chapter 9). Births to parents both of whom reported being Indian numbered 12,380. There were 15,510 births where only one parent reported being Indian. Government agencies in their infinite wisdom define all such births as Indian, even though

56% were to parents only one of whom was a self-identified Indian. In the years 1985 and 1986, 67% of the births were to parents only one of whom was reported as Indian. How do we interpret the change from 56% to 67%? It is all in the definition as promulgated by the powers that be. Designate these births to mixed Indian–non-Indian parents as non-Indian, and the Indian birthrate, however measured, will plummet.

Appendix **2**

The Estimated Numbers
in the Seventeenth
to Nineteenth Centuries

Our estimates for these three centuries were derived from: (a) Mooney's estimates of the Indian population at about the time of first contact with the Europeans, (b) Clark's remarkable 1877 compilation for the United States, and (c) the U.S. censuses beginning with that of 1850 and the Canadian censuses beginning with 1881.

UNITED STATES

Mooney's Estimates

Mooney (1928) compiled estimates provided by early explorers and settlers, as to the probable population of each tribe when it was first contacted by the Europeans. He reviewed these writings and selected out what in his opinion were probably the most nearly accurate numbers. He arranged the tribes into 10 regional groups in the United States, plus 3 in Canada, 1 in Alaska, and 1 in Greenland. The dates of initial contact varied from about 1600 to 1845. At no time did Mooney ever claim that his data referred to the population at the time that Columbus landed, that is, the end of the fifteenth century. In both countries the average date of initial contact was around 1700 (Appendix Table 2.1).

    Mooney's estimate for each region we then reverse-projected to 1600, assuming a rate of decrease since 1600 of one-tenth of 1% per year. Other rates

Appendix Table 2.1. Mooney's Estimates of Amerindian Population by Region and Date: United States and Canada, Early Colonial Times

	Mooney's estimates		Our estimates
	Date	Population	Rounded
Total excluding Alaska and Hawaii	—	874,900	1,000,000
North Atlantic states	1600	55,600	60,000
South Atlantic states	1600	52,200	60,000
Gulf states	1650	114,400	120,000
Central states	1650	75,300	80,000
The Plains			
Northern	1780	100,800	120,000
Southern	1690	41,000	50,000
Columbia Region	1780	88,800	100,000
California	1769	260,000	310,000
Central Mountain Region	1845	19,300	20,000
New Mexico and Arizona	1680	72,000	80,000
Total Canada	—	165,000	210,000
Eastern	1600	50,600	70,000
Central	1670	28,650	20,000
British Columbia	1780	85,800	120,000

of decrease could have been assumed, but because we cannot ever know the correct population in 1600, it makes little practical difference what rate is assumed. Our reason for selecting one-tenth of one percent is: On the basis of our readings, the pronounced losses of population occurred after about 1700. For the eighteenth and nineteenth centuries, when it appears that the major losses occurred, we have several estimates and census counts.

Clark's Compilation and Remarks

Clark (1877) begins by stating: "It is entirely impractical to present any trust-worthy statement of the number of Indians in the whole territory comprised within the present limits of the United States in 1790, or in any subsequent period down to about the year 1850. . . . It is almost invariably true that estimates of the numbers of an Indian tribe exceed the real numbers . . . " (Indian Commissioner's Report, 1877).

The numbers issued by government officials that he then reports: 1789—76,000, 1791—less than 60,000, 1820–21—471,000, 1825—129,366, 1829—312,930, 1836—253,464, 1837—302,498, 1850—388,229, 1855—314,622, 1860—254,300, 1870—383,712, 1875—305,068, and 1876—291,882. Obviously, fluctuations of such magnitude do not occur in real life. A population may decrease rapidly, for example, 1855 to 1860, but it is impossible to increase as rapidly as the 1860 to 1870 figures, for example, suggest.

To begin, we discard the estimates for 1789, 1791, 1825, and probably 1836 and 1860. They appear to be too volatile, or out of line with preceding and following estimates. Note the decrease from 1829 to 1836 that is possible and then the increase to 1837 that is impossible. Similarly, the period 1855 to 1860 to 1870 suggests that 1860 is the oddball.

The estimate for 1850 with adjustments appears to be usable. Clark refers to an estimate of 388,000 plus "25,000 to 35,000 Indians within the area of the unexplored territories of the United States. This raises the total to about 420,000. The 1850 census reported 400,764 [note the unreliable precision] unrepresented and untaxed Indians" (*Compendium of the 7th Census,* p. 41). We increased this number to 450,000 to allow for possible underestimates and for some who were taxed, that is, living among the general population.

The 1870 census appears to be the first one in which the census made a significant attempt to count the Indians. Also, by 1870 the situation was more propitious for an enumeration because so many Indians were living on or near reservations. Hence, the federal agents could make a more nearly correct estimate. Clark commented as follows:

ENUMERATION OF 1870

The first attempt to embrace a general enumeration of the Indian population in the United States census was made by Gen. F. A. Walker, superintendent of the ninth census. On page xvi of the volume on Population and Social Statistics will be found the excellent reasons given by General Walker for making this attempt. In the same place he says:

With a view, therefore, to reaching the true population of the country as nearly as is practicable in the absence of distinct authority for the appointment of assistant marshals to enumerate the several tribes and bands of Indians, inquiries were conducted extensively through the agents of the Indian Office during the year 1870, the result of which, it is believed, has been to secure a closer approximation to the true numbers of this class of the population than has ever before been effected.

A detailed statement of the result, by States and Territories, including Alaska, will be found on page xvii of the volume before quoted. In brief, it is as follows:

Sustaining tribal relations (enumerated)	96,366
Sustaining tribal relations (estimated)	26,875
Sustaining tribal relations nomadic (estimated)	234,740
Out of tribal relations (enumerated)	25,731
Total	383,712

It will be seen at once that, notwithstanding all the efforts made, these results are far from being satisfactory, and that they must be accepted with the greatest caution.

Of these numbers 261,615, or more than 68 per cent, are based on "estimates," with all their imperfections and uncertainties. Included in the estimated population are 70,000* Alaska Indians, occupying a territory never thoroughly explored. Deducting this number, which is in the nature of the case only conjectural, we have 313,712 as the total Indian population (exclusive of Alaska Indians) in 1870.

The report of Indian affairs for the same year gives the total number of Indians, excluding the Indians of Alaska, at 287,640. Adding to this 25,721 Indians "out of tribal relations," reported in the census, we have 313,371; a substantial agreement with the returns of the United States census.

The count (or estimate) for coterminous United States (excluding Alaska and Hawaii) hence is 330,000. This estimate is in line with the 1875 report of the Commissioner of Indian Affairs, about 305,000. We now have four fixed estimates and can pass a line through them: 1600, 1700, 1850, and 1870.

After 1870

Beginning with the census of 1890, the number of Indians was reported every 10 years. (There is a rumor that the census of 1880 counted the Indians also, but we have never been able to uncover the truth.) The numbers move erratically from one census count to another (see Appendix 5). We simply plotted the unadjusted census counts and passed a smooth line through them, connecting to the 1870 information (Chapter 7, Figure 7.2).

Census of 1980

Trouble again. As discussed previously (Chapter 10), the very large increase in numbers from 1970 to 1980 appears to be impossible. It may be due in large measure to persons of mixed ancestry who reported themselves as non-Indian in 1970, reporting as Indian in 1980. We tested as follows.

The 1980 Public Use Microdata census sample provides the responses of each person to each question for 5% of the population. We sorted out those who had reported themselves as Amerindian and then classified them on the basis of reported ancestry. Those who reported both Indian and non-Indian ancestry were classified as "mixed." All others were classified as of "Indian ancestry only." The characteristics of these two groups are very different (as we noted previously); demographically the mixed tend to resemble the general population. Hence, switching to Indian in 1980 from non-Indian in 1970 appears to be plausible.

CANADA

1601 and 1701

These numbers were derived from Mooney's calculations in the same manner as for the United States. In Canada, the average date of Mooney's estimates is also about 1700. We found no estimates for any year between 1601 and 1701.

1881 to 1981

Beginning in 1881 the decennial censuses reported the numbers (see Chapter 7, Figure 7.2 and Table 7.1). These census counts seem to be reasonably comparable over time. When possible, we omitted the Inuit if reported separately, and do not know where the Métis are included in each census.

Censuses were taken annually of the status (registered) Indians by the Indian Affairs Branch, now named Indian and Inuit Affairs. These numbers correspond more or less with the numbers reported by Statistics Canada in the decennial censuses. For example, the 1981 census reported that there were 293,000 status Indians, and Indian and Inuit Affairs reported 320,000 registered Indians. There are sufficient differences in definition—who is to be counted and methods of collection—so that the two series cannot be completely comparable.

1981 and 1986

We believe that there was a changing racial identity in Canada just as in the United States between these two dates, and possibly since the census of 1971. Based on the information regarding rates of growth between 1981 and 1986, we are of the opinion that perhaps about 100,000 people shifted to Indian by 1986 or were missed in the 1981 census. If the 466,000 Indians plus Métis enumerated in 1981 had increased 3% per year there would have been about 540,000 in 1986, or 100,000 or so fewer than the number reported in 1986 (see also Appendix 5).

The Prehistoric Life Table

INTRODUCTION

Life tables customarily are constructed from reports of deaths classified by age and sex (and sometimes by other categories, e.g., race) and the numbers of people similarly classified in the total population as counted in a census. Such data are not available for the prehistoric Indians. Instead, we must estimate a life table from the skeletal remains uncovered by archaeologists.

Necessary Preconditions

An approximate life table can be constructed under the conditions described in the following:

1. The total population for whom a life table is being constructed must not change in size, or if it changes it must do so very slowly for several centuries, or preferably millennia (see also Cowgill 1975). In Figure 3.3 we indicated how a premodern population probably changes in size over long periods of time. The pattern is cyclical. In prosperous times, for example, retreating glaciers, plenty of food and the like, the population increases. At other times, for example, warfare, changing climate, insufficient food, the population decreases.

This cyclical pattern is found in various subdivisions of the total population, for example, the southeastern United States or British Columbia. But the several subdivisions need not necessarily follow parallel cycles. While population may be increasing in one area it may be decreasing in another.

2. The total population should be a virtually closed universe, that is, little or no immigration or emigration.

These two conditions are met in North America if a long enough time period is covered and information is obtained from a large number of sites. Life tables for single sites for short periods of time are useless.

The life tables can be constructed if the population is changing in size, if the rate of change is known. But among the prehistorics the rate of change is not known, nor is the initial size of the population being studied. See Chapter 8 in Frazier (1986) for a description of the impossibility of measuring the size of a pre-European population or the rate at which it may be changing.

The time covered for our life tables is over 5,000 years. Some sites are of Archaic Amerindians and others are from the fourteenth and fifteenth centuries. Altogether we found about 8,000 usable cases of skeletal remains judged to be of people aged 15 and over. About 5,400 are of agriculturalists and 2,600 of nonagriculturalists. About equal numbers of male and female skeletal remains were found, close to 4,000 of each.

We think that well over 100 sites are included in the reports that we used. The exact number depends on how a site is defined. Some of the reports we saw were compilations from several places. One report, for example, was the result of analyzing skeletons found in several museums and for which provenience was recorded. How many sites? In some cases several findings are reported, all from what seem to be the same area and time, but each is the work of a separate investigation. How many sites?

These are all the usable sites and cases we found. Many more were published, but we discarded them because the data were not presented by sex crossed by age. Also, we omitted insofar as possible studies made before World War II for the reason given next. Apparently, some thousands of skeletal remains were found at Pecos and Indian Knoll, but aging and sexing techniques were primitive. As far as we could determine, neither site was aged and sexed such that the skeletal remains could be used for life table construction.

Skeletal Remains as a Sample of Deaths

Millions of Amerindians must have died since the first people stepped onto Alaskan soil. We doubt that as many as 100,000 remains have been found by archaeologists in the United States and Canada. Museums and professors reportedly have quantities of remains that have never been reported in the literature. Hence, we have no way of determining how representative a sample we found of persons aged 15 and over.

We have but a handful of Paleo-Indians, the most ancient, very few infants or very young babies, and too few older children under 15 years of age. This lack of youngsters results from (a) the bones of youngsters deteriorate more rapidly than do those of adults and (b) in some cultures little children are not necessarily buried in cemeteries. This deficit of youngsters accounts for some of the methodology that we discuss subsequently.

Nevertheless, if physical anthropologists believe that it is worthwhile to find, analyze, and publish information about Indian skeletal remains, the least we can do is try to utilize their reports.

Estimating Age and Sex of Skeletal Remains

The procedures for such estimations are being improved constantly. (We cannot delve into the complexities of these techniques but simply refer the interested reader to D. H. Ubelaker [1978].) Prior to about World War II physical anthropologists generally reported age, if at all, in very broad categories, too broad for the construction of a life table. As techniques improved, age estimation became more nearly precise. These techniques have been checked against modern deaths of persons of known and recorded age and sex (Ubelaker 1978). This is our primary reason for excluding, insofar as possible, reports issued in the early part of the twentieth century.

Age is estimated from the bones and teeth. But different parts of the skeleton provide different ages. In the past, investigators often did not provide sufficient information as to what criteria they used for estimating age. By combining the reports of large numbers of physical anthropologists we hope that any differences in the capabilities and techniques of these people have been averaged out (see also Ubelaker 1978).

Willey and Mann suggest another problem with aging—that the remains of elderly people are sometimes overlooked, and if found, judged to be younger than their actual age. If enough such cases exist, then life expectancy is longer than that calculated by the investigator (Willey and Mann 1986).

Regarding the sex of the skeletal remains, Clabeaux thinks that the limited data that she had "suggest the existence of a sex difference in skeletal sexing. (Women physical anthropologists find more female remains than male investigators.) Bias in sexing, if it is indeed significant, may best be explained by cultural determined differences" (Clabeaux 1977).

We cannot evaluate either suggestion.

One problem with a life table for an individual site is precisely this: It represents one person's opinion as to the age and sex composition of the deaths found at that site. Very rarely are reports issued in which two or more investigators independently report on the same skeletal remains.

Distinguishing between Agriculturalists and Nonagriculturalists

This distinction was made as follows. In some cases the authors of site reports specifically designated their sites as agricultural or nonagricultural. In some cases the cultural designation was the clue; Paleo-Indian or Archaic clearly implies non-agriculture whereas Mississippian, for example, indicates agriculture. Also, we consulted with about a half dozen archaeologists and anthropologists and sought their information and knowledge on how to distinguish the two populations.

All agricultural populations must have engaged in hunting and fishing also, because they had no domestic animals except the dog and, in some places, turkey. Because there is no way of specifying precisely what proportion of all food eaten was obtained by hunting and gathering wild vegetation, versus agriculture, no strict statistical criterion could be applied; for example, 50% or more of all food derived from all agriculture signifies an agricultural population. In short, we relied on the best-informed judgment available to us.

Combining the Site Reports

The first step is smoothing the published data into 5-year age groups. Age distributions as published are variable; some show 5-year age groups, some 10-year, and some odd classes, for example, 18 to 22 or 25 to 39. Some stopped at age 40 and over, some 50 and over, and so forth. We smoothed these data generally with Sprague multipliers. Individual reports can now be combined for life table construction. (For further information on smoothing, see Jaffe [1969] and Shryock and Siegel [1971].)

Because we desired separate life tables for men and women, we created "units" that contained about 100 cases aged 15 and over for each sex. Some sites contained sufficient cases to constitute units. If the sites were small, several were combined to reach around 100. For each unit we calculated the percentage distribution by age and then averaged the percentage distributions. The reason for creating these units was to avoid giving undue weight to the small number of relatively large sites.

The final consolidated age and sex distributions are shown in Appendix Table 3.1.

Basic Methodology

The basic methodology for constructing a life table for a closed stationary population, from the distribution of deaths by age, can be traced back to Halley (1693). The most recent refinement is that of Acsadi and Nemerski (1970). With this methodology we can derive the life table values q_x, l_x, L_x, and e_x for the population aged 15 and over. (Halley's table is presented in Dublin and Lotka [1936].) The procedures are shown in Appendix Table 3.2.

Filling the Gap from Birth to Age 15

Reported deaths under age 15 are not usable for several reasons. Children were not always buried in cemeteries, and their bones are softer than those of adults

Appendix Table 3.1. Percentage Distribution of Consolidated
Skeletal Remains, Smoothed, by Age and Sex[a]

| Age | Agriculture | | Nonagriculture | |
	Men	Women	Men	Women
Total	100.0	100.0	100.0	100.0
15–19	8.7	12.3	11.5	17.4
20–24	13.2	16.4	17.0	22.8
25–29	13.3	14.9	16.5	16.8
30–34	13.7	13.5	12.6	11.4
35–39	12.2	10.0	12.4	10.5
40–44	11.7	9.1	10.6	8.0
45–49	10.5	9.4	8.7	6.3
50–54	7.5	6.5	5.7	3.7
55–59	4.7	4.0	2.4	1.6
60–64	2.4	2.6	1.8	0.9
65–69	1.4	1.1	0.7	0.4
70–74	0.5	0.2	0.1	0.2
75–79	0.1	0.0	0.0	0.0

[a]The distributions upon which the life tables shown in Appendix Tables 3.4
and 3.5 were based were carried out to one more place, to ease construction
of the life tables.

so that they decompose more quickly. Assigning age is difficult; sometimes the
jaws and teeth may be the only clues to age. Most important from the viewpoint
of constructing a life table for preteenage children is that sex is difficult, and
often impossible, to ascertain from the skeleton. Most reports that contain
information on the sex of adults do not classify children by sex. Yet we need this
information from birth on for the tables.

(Over age 50 so few deaths are reported that it makes almost no difference
in the final life table what the true ages may have been.)

We go about this task by asking whether life expectancy at birth can
be estimated from life expectancy at age 20, the age at which we have considerably more confidence in the basic age and sex data. The available model
life tables are of no help in estimating the possible life expectancy at birth
because none of them have a sufficiently short expectation at age 20. The
United Nations' *Model Life Tables,* for example, begin at age 35. In theory it is
possible to reverse extrapolate to an expectancy of under 20 years. But such a
procedure has no demographic merit. Weiss (1963) published a combined table
with e_{20} at 14.2 years and e_0 at 10.7 years. But such a low e_0 is impossible for
the reasons given later.

Accordingly, we searched the literature for the shortest e_x tables and calculated
e_0 (life expectancy at birth) divided by e_{20} (expectancy at age 20). (Most of these
life tables were found in the annual *United Nations Demographic Year Book.*) These
ratios are shown in Appendix Table 3.3 and Appendix Figures 3.1 and 3.2.

Appendix Table 3.2. Illustrative Procedures for Calculating an Abridged Life Table from Skeletal Remains

Age	Skeletal remains Number	Percent	l_x	L_x	T_x	e_x
15–19	25	.250	1,000	4,375	16,600	16.6
20–24	19	.190	750	3,275	12,225	16.3
25–29	11	.110	560	2,525	8,950	16.0
30–34	10	.100	450	2,000	6,425	14.3
35–39	11	.110	350	1,475	4,425	12.6
40–44	4	.040	240	1,100	2,950	12.3
45–49	6	.060	200	850	1,850	9.3
50–54	7	.070	140	525	1,000	7.1
55–59	3	.030	70	275	425	6.8
60–64	2	.020	40	150	200	5.0
65–69	2	.020	20	50	50	2.5
70+	0	0	0	0	0	—
Total	100	1.000	—	16,600		

Column explanations:
l_x: 1,000 − 250 = 750, etc.
L_x: [(1,000 + 750) ÷ 2](5) = (1,750)(2.5) = 4,375.
T_x: Sum of L_x column.
e_x: T_x ÷ l_x, 16,600 ÷ 1,000 = 16.6 = life expectancy at birth.

Clearly, when e_{20} is less than about 35 years, it is very close to e_0. The ratio of e_0 to e_{20} decreases with decreases in e_{20} and then around age 35 levels out at close to unity. Hence, we assume that if we estimate e_{20} for the prehistorics we have a close approximation to e_0. This relationship had to be determined because all the information available indicates that life expectancy at birth was under 20 years.

In Appendix Figures 3.1 and 3.2, we plotted e_0 divided by e_{20} for various values of e_{20}. Obviously a straight line appears to fit well over the observed e_{20} values. This is the case both for the ratios derived from published life tables (many of which an actuary would not like) and the United Nations Model Life Tables (the general pattern) that supposedly, are the height of perfection. Hence, we fitted a straight line to the ratio of males (as compiled from the published life tables) in order to predict e_0 when e_{20} is known. The equation is: $Y = .443 + (.071) (e_{20})$ where $Y = e_0$ divided by e_{20}. Then we estimate e_0 for several values of e_{20} as follows:

e_0	e_{20}	$1/e_0(1000)$
10.5	15	95
13.5	18	74
15.7	20	64
21.7	25	46
27.1	29	37

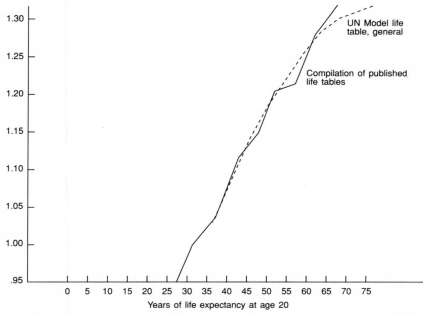

Appendix Figure 3.1. Comparison of life expectancies for men at birth and at age 20, published country tables vs. UN Model life table (general).

The last column is an estimate of the birthrate (assuming a closed universe) at a given e_0. The birthrates expected when e_0 is under about 15 years are far too high to be acceptable. Rates higher than 60 to 65 births per 1,000 population per year have never been documented. Therefore, we conclude that the projected ratio (or line) must turn and become horizontal at some point where e_{20} is under 30 years. We suspect that this may be around an e_{20} of 20 years.

From the computed life tables we have all the columns, including L_x, for ages 15 and over. By assuming that e_0 is close to e_{20}, we can fill in the remaining columns for ages under 15.

The completed life tables are shown in Appendix Tables 3.4 and 3.5.

Reconstructing a Prehistoric Census

The L_x column is the age distribution that a census, if one had been conducted in a stationary population, would have found. Hence, it can be used to calculate various population characteristics such as average age.

However, the L_x columns for men and women must be adjusted to obtain a "real-life" age by sex distribution for the total population. We assume that females are .485 of all births and adjust accordingly, as shown in Appendix Table 3.6.

Appendix Table 3.3a. Comparison of Life Expectancies at Birth and Age 20 (Based on Published Country Tables)

Age class of life tables	N	Male Average e_0	Male Average e_{20}	Male Average $\frac{e_0}{e_{20}}$	N	Female Average e_0	Female Average e_{20}	Female Average $\frac{e_0}{e_{20}}$
25–29	8	27.4	29.3	.935	4	26.9	30.9	.871
30–34	9	32.4	32.3	1.003	7	31.8	31.8	1.000
35–39	9	36.3	35.8	1.028	10	37.0	35.7	1.036
40–44	8	43.1	38.8	1.111	9	42.2	39.5	1.068
45–49	14	48.3	42.2	1.145	11	48.1	42.6	1.129
50–54	9	52.1	43.5	1.198	15	53.1	45.8	1.159
55–59	15	57.0	46.9	1.215	9	58.7	49.4	1.138
60–64	16	62.1	45.6	1.278	11	62.2	50.0	1.244
65+	7	67.8	51.2	1.324	19	69.5	53.9	1.289
Total	95	—	—	—	95	—	—	—

N = Number of countries.

The numbers shown in this table are not intended to refer to any particular tribe or Amerindian population. They are useful for obtaining information about the demographic characteristics of the entire Amerindian population. For exam-

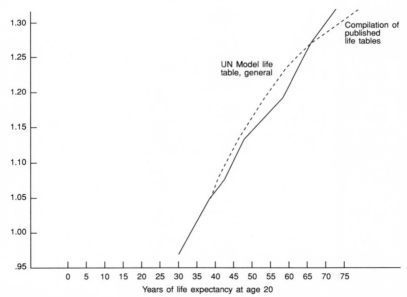

Appendix Figure 3.2. Comparison of life expectancies for women at birth and at age 20, published country tables vs. UN Model life table (general).

Appendix Table 3.3b. Comparison of Life Expectancies at Birth and Age 20 (Derived from United Nations Model Life Tables)

Male			Female		
e_0	e_{20}	$\frac{e_0}{e_{20}}$	e_0	e_{20}	$\frac{e_0}{e_{20}}$
—	—	—	—	—	
—	—	—	—	—	
37	36.0	1.028	37	35.8	1.034
43	38.9	1.125	42	38.7	1.085
48	41.4	1.159	48	42.0	1.143
52	43.4	1.198	53	44.8	1.183
57	46.0	1.239	59	48.2	1.224
62	48.7	1.273	62	49.9	1.242
65	52.3	1.800	70	54.7	1.280
—	—	—	—	—	—

ple, note that the average age (median) is about 15 years for the agriculturalists and somewhat less for the nonagriculturalists.

Neither are they meant to be accurate to the last place. The inadequacies in the basic raw data themselves prevent complete accuracy. We carried the calculations to four or more places only because this simplifies calculations and checking.

Appendix Table 3.4. Estimated Prehistoric Life Table for Nonagriculturalists: Amerindian Population of United States and Canada

Age	Men						Women					
	$q_x{}^a$	l_x	d_x	L_x	T_x	e_x	$q_x{}^a$	l_x	d_x	L_x	T_x	e_x
0–4	.4173	10,000	4,173	39,568	164,445	16.4	.4615	10,000	4,615	38,462	147,005	14.7
5–9	.2291	5,827	1,335	25,797	124,877	21.4	.2233	5,385	1,202	23,920	108,543	20.2
10–14	.0906	4,492	407	21,443	99,000	22.0	.0900	4,183	376	19,975	84,623	20.2
15–19	.1048	4,085	428	19,355	77,637	19.0	.1150	3,807	438	17,940	64,648	17.0
20–24	.1854	3,657	678	16,590	58,282	15.9	.2397	3,369	808	14,825	46,708	13.9
25–29	.2248	2,979	670	13,220	41,692	14.0	.2841	2,561	728	10,985	31,883	12.4
30–34	.2477	2,309	572	10,115	28,472	12.3	.2913	1,833	534	7,830	20,898	11.4
35–39	.2902	1,737	504	7,425	18,357	10.6	.3236	1,299	420	5,445	13,068	10.1
40–44	.3608	1,233	445	5,052	10,932	8.9	.3828	879	336	3,555	7,623	8.7
45–49	.4462	788	352	3,060	5,880	7.5	.4500	543	244	2,105	4,068	7.5
50–54	.5146	436	225	1,618	2,820	6.5	.5070	299	151	1,118	1,963	6.6
55–59	.5400	211	114	770	1,202	5.7	.5500	148	81	542	845	5.7
60–64	.6087	97	59	337	432	4.5	.6500	69	43	238	303	4.4
65–69	1.0000	38	38	95	95	2.5	1.0000	26	26	65	65	2.5
70 and over		0						0				

[a]We show to four places only to simplify subsequent calculations.

Appendix Table 3.5. Estimated Prehistoric Life Table for Agriculturalists: Amerindian Population of United States and Canada

	Men						Women					
Age	$q_x{}^a$	l_x	d_x	L_x	T_x	e_x	$q_x{}^a$	l_x	d_x	L_x	T_x	e_x
0–4	.3924	10,000	3,924	40,190	184,685	18.5	.3800	10,000	3,800	40,500	177,965	17.8
5–9	.2216	6,076	1,346	27,015	144,496	23.8	.2240	6,200	1,388	27,527	137,465	22.2
10–14	.0772	4,730	365	22,738	117,481	24.8	.1000	4,811	481	22,853	109,938	22.9
15–19	.1000	4,365	437	20,732	94,743	21.7	.1100	4,330	476	20,460	87,085	20.1
20–24	.1392	3,928	547	18,273	74,011	18.8	.1800	3,854	694	17,535	66,625	17.3
25–29	.1746	3,381	590	15,430	55,738	16.5	.2139	3,160	676	14,110	49,090	15.5
30–34	.2022	2,791	564	12,545	40,308	14.4	.2306	2,484	573	10,988	34,980	14.1
35–39	.2397	2,227	534	9,800	27,763	12.5	.2412	1,911	461	8,403	23,992	12.6
40–44	.2946	1,693	499	7,217	17,963	10.6	.2778	1,450	403	6,242	15,589	10.8
45–49	.3626	1,194	433	4,888	10,746	9.0	.3504	1,047	367	4,317	9,347	8.9
50–54	.4253	761	324	2,995	5,858	7.7	.4276	680	291	2,673	5,030	7.4
55–59	.4900	437	214	1,650	2,863	6.6	.5100	389	198	1,450	2,357	6.1
60–64	.5687	223	127	798	1,213	5.4	.6400	191	122	650	907	4.7
65–69	6364	96	61	328	415	4.3	.7500	69	52	215	257	3.7
70–74	1.0000	35	35	87	87	2.5	1.0000	17	17	42	42	2.5
75 and over		0						0				

^{a}We show to four places only to simplify subsequent calculations.

Notes on the Estimation of e_0

Might life expectancy at birth—e_0—be lower than e_{20}? We saw previously that e_0 of under 15 years is very unlikely. Hence, if e_{20} is 15 years, e_0 cannot be lower. If e_{20} is between 15 and 20 years as in the tables we present, e_0 may differ from e_{20} slightly, either larger or smaller. When e_{20} reaches the latter 20s or early 30s, e_0 is likely to be larger than e_{20}, as shown in Appendix Figures 3.1 and 3.2.

Might life expectancy at birth be higher than at age 20? This appears unlikely because all modern life tables indicate that expectancy at birth is higher than at age 20 only when expectancy at age 20 is about 35 years or older. Because we are concerned with populations in which expectancy at age 20 is under 20 years we have no basis for thinking that it might be higher at birth than at age 20.

Regarding the difference we noted between agriculturalists and nonagriculturalists, we can check our findings by asking whether the former had a larger proportion of older persons. If the agriculturalists truly had lived a little longer, there should be a larger proportion of older people among the skeletal remains. We can calculate the percentage aged 40 and over among all those skeletal remains estimated to be aged 15 and over, for each unit (see the section *Combining the site reports*). Of the total units about half consist of single sites, and the others are combinations of small sites.

The agricultural units had a significantly higher proportion aged 40+ than

Appendix Table 3.6. Reconstructed "Censuses" of the Prehistoric Indian Population of United States and Canada

	Nonagriculturalists					Agriculturalists				
		Women		Total			Women		Total	
Age	Number of men[a]	Number[b]	Ratio[c]	Number[d]	Percent women[e]	Number of men[a]	Number[b]	Ratio[c]	Number[d]	Percent women[e]
Total	164,445	144,276	—	308,721	46.7	184,685	169,175	—	353,860	47.8
0–4	39,568	37,748	.9540	77,316	48.8	40,190	38,500	.9580	78,690	48.9
5–9	25,797	23,479	.6220	49,276	47.6	27,015	26,168	.6797	53,183	49.2
10–14	21,443	19,603	.5193	41,046	47.7	22,738	21,725	.5643	44,463	48.9
15–19	19,355	17,606	.4664	36,961	47.6	20,732	19,450	.5052	40,182	48.4
20–24	16,590	14,548	.3854	31,138	46.7	18,273	16,670	.4330	34,943	47.7
25–29	13,220	10,781	.2856	24,001	44.9	15,430	13,413	.3484	28,843	46.5
30–34	10,115	7,685	.2036	17,800	43.2	12,545	10,445	.2713	22,990	45.4
35–39	7,425	5,345	.1416	12,770	41.9	9,800	7,989	.2075	17,789	44.9
40–44	5,052	3,488	.0924	8,540	40.8	7,217	5,933	.1541	13,150	45.1
45–49	3,060	2,065	.0547	5,125	40.3	4,888	4,104	.1066	8,992	45.6
50–54	1,618	1,098	.0291	2,716	40.4	2,995	2,541	.0660	5,536	45.9
55–59	770	532	.0141	1,302	40.9	1,650	1,378	.0358	3,028	45.5
60–64	337	234	.0062	571	41.0	798	616	.0160	1,414	43.6
65–69	95	64	.0017	159	40.3	328	204	.0053	532	38.8
70 and over	0	0	—	0		87	39	.0010	126	31.0
0–24	122,753	112,984	—	235,737	47.9	128,948	122,513	—	251,461	48.7
25–49	38,872	29,364	—	68,236	43.0	49,880	41,884	—	91,764	45.6
50–69	2,820	1,928	—	4,748	40.6	5,858	4,778	—	10,636	44.9

[a] L_x column from Appendix Tables 3.4 and 3.5.
[b] Product of estimated number of males aged 0 to 4 and ratios for higher ages. For age 0 to 4, the ratio is set at about the percentage of births that are female. A ratio of 485 female births per 1,000 total gives a ratio of about .95. Example: (39,568 males)(.9540) = 3,748 females.
[c] Ratios obtained by expressing L_x at each age as a proportion of L_{0-4} in Appendix Tables 3.3 and 3.4. Example: (37,748)(.622) = 23,478.
[d] Sum of columns a and b.
[e] Column b divided by column d.

did the nonagricultural units. The respective means are .395 and .287 for a combined total of .356. The respective medians are .405 and .311 for a combined median of .358. Because the means and medians are almost identical, both distributions are normal for all practical purposes. Can we use sampling theory to test for significance of the differences between the means or medians? We do not know whether the sites reported are a proper random distribution of all sites, and we do not know whether the skeletons located in each site are proper samples of all deaths that occurred at these sites, and never shall we know. Nevertheless, we can reason as follows:

The combined median is .358. Among the agricultural units, 8 out of 21 or 38% fell below the median; among the nonagricultural units, 9 out of 12 or 75% fell below the median. The difference between the two percentages is 37, and the error of the difference is about 18%. Hence, the difference is significant at the approximate 95% level.

In making these calculations, we have not processed the data as we do in forming life tables and have analyzed individual sites and units rather than simply the totality of nonagriculturalists versus agriculturalists. Notwithstanding, a significant difference between the two groups appears; the agriculturalists lived a bit longer. Exactly how much longer is debatable and will only be settled, if at all, by obtaining far more site reports, and improved aging and sexing.

The Major Sources

Following is a listing of the 23 reports that supplied 60% of the cases we used. The remaining 40% came from 67 published and unpublished reports.

Agriculture References

Benfer, R. A. (1968). *Casas grandes, Chihuahua, Mexico* (doctoral dissertation). University of Texas at Austin.

Bennett, K. A. (1973). *The Indians of Point of Pines, Arizona.* University of Arizona Press.

Birkby, W. H. *Grasshopper, Arizona.* Arizona State Museum (personal correspondence).

Birkby, W. H. *Skeletons.* Arizona State Museum (personal communication).

Blakely, R. L. (1977). Sociocultural implications of demographic data from Etowah, Georgia. In R. L. Blakely (Ed.), *Biocultural adaptation in prehistoric America* (pp. 45–66). University of Georgia Press.

Buikstra, J. E. (1976). Hopewell in the Lower Illinois Valley. *Scientific Paper, 2.* Northwestern University Archaeological Program.

Cybulski, J.S. (1967). *The demography of the Orchid Site Ossuary (Fort Erie, Ontario)* (doctoral dissertation). State University of New York at Buffalo.

Goldstein, L. G. (1980). Mississippian mortuary practices. *Scientific Paper, 4.* Northwestern University Archaeology Program.

Goldstein, M. S. (1953). Some vital statistics based on skeletal material. *Human Biology, 25,* pp. 3 ff.

Lallo, J. W. (1973). *The skeletal biology of three prehistoric American Indian societies from Dickson Mounds, Illinois* (doctoral dissertation). University of Massachusetts. ("Late Woodland" is included with nonagriculture; "Mississippi Acculturated" and Middle Mississippi included with agriculture.)

Ubelaker, D. H. (1974). Reconstruction of demographic profiles from ossuary skeletal samples. *Smithsonian Contributions to Archaeology, 18.*

Wiley, P. *Crow Creek, South Dakota.* University of Tennessee (personal communication).

Nonagriculture References

Cybulski, J. *Prince Ruppert, British Columbia* (personal communication).

Larsen, C. S. (1980). *Prehistoric human biological adaptation: A case study from the Georgia coast* (doctoral dissertation). University of Mississippi.

McWilliams, D. (1970). Physical anthropology of Wann and Sam, two Fourche Meline focus archaic sites in eastern Oklahoma. *Bulletin of the Oklahoma Anthropological Society, 19,* pp. 101 ff.

Moratto, M. J. (1972). *A study of prehistory in the southern Sierra Nevada Foothills* (doctoral dissertation). University of Oregon.

Moriarty, J. R., III. *La Jolla* University of San Diego (personal correspondence).

Pfeiffer, S. (1977). The skeletal biology of archaic populations of the Great Lakes region. *Archaeological Survey of Canada, 64*. National Museums of Canada.

So, J. K., & Wade, W. D. (March 1975). Preliminary paleodemographic analysis of the Gray site population, Swift Current, Saskatchewan. *Anthropology Paper, 13*.

Tuck, J. A. *Ancient peoples of Port Au Choix, Newfoundland: Skeletons aged and sexed by J. Cybulski* (personal communication).

Webb, W. S. (1950). The Carlson Annis Mound. *Reports in Anthropology, 7:4*, pp. 267–354.

Webb, W. S., & De Janette, D. L. (1948). The Perry site. *Museum Paper, 25*. Alabama Museum of National History.

Webb, W. S., & Snow, C. E. (September 1945). The Adena people. *Reports in Anthropology and Archaeology, 6*. University of Kentucky.

Appendix 4

Prehistoric Total Fertility Rates

Population growth over the millennia was very slow, as we discussed in Chapter 3. Hence, it is obvious that the birth and death rates must have been close to equal. The L_x column of the life table provides estimates of the number of births and the number of women in the reproductive ages. Note that the L_x column provides an age distribution comparable to a census count, in a population that increases very slowly as was the case with the Ancients.

In order to obtain an estimate of the TFR we also need reasonable estimates of the age-specific birthrates. (Then, using indirect standardization, we obtain the TFR.) We sought published sets of rates that might be applicable.

The very slow rate of population growth among the Ancients can be illustrated with Anna C. Roosevelt's study of Parmana, where there was considerable agriculture (in the southeastern part of the state of Guarico in Venezuela on the left bank of the Orinoco River). She concluded: "Thus for the first 1600 years of known occupation . . . (about 1200 B.C. to about A.D. 400), human population remained essentially stationary."

See Chapter 3 for a more extensive discussion of possible speeds of population growth. Thus, assuming a very slow rate of population growth, we can continue with making estimates of the possible TFR.

For the *nonagriculturalists* we found that the age-specific birthrates for rural Benin (U.N. *Demographic Year Book,* 1977, Table 11) when multiplied by the number of women in the L_x column, and the total compared with the estimated number of births as derived from the age class 0 to 4, provides a total fertility rate of about 7. Similar calculations using rates for Tunisia (U.N.D.Y.B., 1969, Table 15) provides an estimate of about 11. Interpolating the age-specific rates we get about 9 TFR; this matches the estimated number of births.

For the *agriculturalists* we applied the rural Benin age-specific birthrates to the L_x column of the agriculturalists. This produced an estimated rate of popu-

Appendix Table 4.1. Possible Age-Specific Birthrates per Woman in 5 Years: Pre-European North American Indians

	Births per woman	
Age of mother	Nonagricultural	Agricultural
15–19	1.1	1.0
20–24	2.4	2.0
25–29	2.6	1.7
30–34	1.6	1.4
35–39	1.0	0.9
40–44	0.0	0.5
Total	9.3	7.5
TFR, estimated	9	7 or 8

lation growth a little below stationary. Hence, we increased these rates so as to produce a rate of population growth essentially stationary as Roosevelt described, or slightly higher. The TFR thus works out to be 7 or 8.

These estimated age-specific rates are shown in Appendix Table 4.1.

Appendix 5

Some Notes on the
Quality of Census Data

MASTER: Statistics are created by *Homo sapiens s.*—not by Mother Nature. People are
   not perfect. Therefore statistics are not perfect.
DISCIPLES: What shall we do, Master? How do we deal with imperfect information?
MASTER: Cautiously.

Analects of Peng Shun Lu, No. 72

INTRODUCTION

Because so much of the basic information that we analyzed was obtained
from the censuses of Canada and the United States, some observations on
the quality of these data, in addition to those that appear in the text, are in
order. We present only a few examples of imperfections and how to detect
them. Any demographer, statistician, or actuary can evaluate any census statistics, as can the reader. Complicated formulae and powerful computers are
not essential.

Although census data are of human origin and contain all the frailties of
*Homo*kind, nevertheless they can be used for answering many questions. Indeed,
for analyzing many problems, there is no alternative to the information collected
in government censuses.

Use them judiciously. Remember! Only seek patterns such as differences
among people of different ages (or different ethnicities or whatever) in amount
of schooling. Or the differences in characteristics of women who have high
fertility versus those with low fertility.

267

NEVER EXPECT TO OBTAIN UNIQUELY CORRECT ANSWERS

Illustration: In the United States in 1970, among Amerindian women aged 35 to 44, 35% reported having completed high school. Among women aged 55 to 64, only 25% reported having finished high school. We are confident that the younger women have more schooling. But precisely what proportions graduated from high school, that is, completed 12 years or more of schooling—the uniquely correct proportions—we do not know.

SOME DETAILS

Definitions

Without precise definitions of the items of information that the census hopes to collect, one is never sure of what it is that is being analyzed. Example, does the category "married" include only legal marriages or does it also include the "significant-other" combination? The Canadian and U.S. censuses provide lengthy definitions. Read them.

Census Notes

Both censuses commented about the collection, definition, and limitations of their data. Following are the salient remarks about race for the United States in 1980, and ethnic origin for Canada in 1981. (See also Urquhart and Buckley 1965.)

> *Race.* The concept of race as used by the Census Bureau reflects self-identification by respondents; it does not denote any clear-cut scientific definition of biological stock. Since the 1980 census obtained information on race through self-identification, the data represent self-classification by people according to the race with which they identify . . . .
>
> For persons who could not provide a single response to the race question, the race of the person's mother was used; however, if a single response could not be provided for the person's mother, the first race reported by the person was used. This is a modification of the 1970 census procedure in which the race of the person's father was used. . . . .
>
> In 1980, persons who did not classify themselves in one of the specific race categories but marked "Other" and wrote in entries such as Cuban, Puerto Rican, Mexican, or Dominican were included in the "Other " race category; in the 1970 census, most of these persons were included in the "White" category . . . .
>
> The categories "American Indian," "Eskimo," and "Aleut" include persons who classified themselves as such in one of the specific race categories. In addition, persons who did not report themselves in one of the specific race categories but entered the name of an Indian tribe or reported such entries as Canadian Indian, French-American Indian, or Spanish-American Indian were classified as American Indian. (U.S. Census, 1980, PC 8-1-C1, pp. B3 and B4)

Ethnic Origin. Refers to the ethnic or cultural group to which the respondent or the respondent's ancestors belonged on first coming to this continent.

It should be noted that in earlier censuses, only the respondent's paternal ancestry was to be reported, theoretically resulting in one ethnic origin per respondent. For 1981, this restriction has been removed and a person may now report more than one ethnic origin. The distinction between single and multiple responses is maintained in these data, but not all available multiple ethnic origins have been published. . . .

The following factors should be noted in the analysis of the ethnic origin data:

(1) Previous censuses usually traced ethnic origin through the paternal ancestry. The 1981 Census is the first that does not restrict the tracing of ethnic origin to one side of the family.

(2) The 1981 Census is the first to allow more than one ethnic origin response per individual.

(3) Previous censuses reduced all multiple ethnic origin responses down to a single response. For the 1971 Census, if more than one origin was indicated on the questionnaire, one was arbitrarily selected.

(4) As 1971 Census processing reduced all multiple responses to a single response, it is not possible to compare 1971 data to 1981 for single responses. This comparison could underestimate the real change.

Similarly, a comparison of 1971 data to single plus multiple responses in 1981 could overestimate the real change. (Canadian Census, 1981 [Catalogue 92-911, pp. xii, xiii])

From these excerpts, it is clear that many changes are made in the census procedures from one time to the next. To what extent these changes affect the resulting statistics often can only be guessed. This is one reason why we place but little importance on "correct" census numbers.

Importance of Editing

The census form is reviewed and given a preliminary editing shortly after the form has been completed. Subsequently, if there appear to be any problems with any particular topics, these topics are given a second editing. Such was the case with the American Indians in the United States 1980 census. A second editing was given; as a result, the Amerindian population was increased by 114,490, or 8%. This increase came from those who failed to designate their preferred race.

This increase may appear to be small, but remember that the United States went to war against Granada, a country that has only about 90,000 people. Further, this increase is larger than the reported population in such headline news countries as Tonga, 93,000; and not much smaller than Belize, 147,000; and Western Samoa, 155,000.

In PC 80-1-C1, Table 74 (issued December 1983), the number of Amerindians is given as 1,478,523. In PC 80-1-B1, Table 47 (issued May 1983 before the second editing results were available), the number is given as 1,364,033.

The Canadians also had to double-check their Amerindian reports because some East Indians reported themselves as Amerindians.

Too Many People Fail to Answer All the Questions

In fairness to the census offices and the users of statistics, we must point out that far too many responses are nonexistent or deficient. In 1980 about half the United States population failed to answer completely all the census questions (PC80-1-C1, Table C1, "Percent of Allocation"). The person who wants to use such unprocessed data will find it difficult. What do you do with all the "no answers" or incomplete answers? Reinterviewing the respondents is far too expensive and almost an impossible task for a variety of reasons.

So, in order to make the raw data usable, they must be edited, and the unanswered questions "answered" or "allocated."

Comparison of Successive Censuses

In the U.S. 1970 census (PC (2)-1F, pp. x–xi) is the comment, "The unusual fluctuations in the count between censuses are largely a result of differing procedures used from census to census for classifying persons as Indians." The counts and fluctuations are as follows:

Year	Number in thousands	Percentage change	Year	Number in thousands	Percentage change
1980	1,478	86	1930	343	41
1970	793	51	1920	244	−12
1960	524	47	1910	277	17
1950	357	4	1900	237	—
1940	345	1			

Let us turn now to years of schooling completed. What proportion of U.S. Amerindian women completed 12 years or more of schooling, that is, are high-school graduates? Let us trace ostensibly the same group of women through three censuses:

> 1960, age 25 to 34, 25% reported 12 years or more
> 1970, age 35 to 44, 35% so reported
> 1980, age 45 to 54, 46% so reported

Presumably most of the women aged 45 to 54 in 1980 are the same as, or the survivors of the group, aged 25 to 34 in 1960. How can the large increase in high-school graduates be explained? Did women immigrants who were high-school and college graduates flood the United States during these 20 years? It is very unlikely that many of the women who had but little schooling returned to school in order to complete 12 years. It is possible, but highly unlikely that whatever deaths occurred between 1960 and 1980 were of women who had not completed 12 years, thus raising the percentage of completion among the survivors in 1980. It is more likely that at each successive census additional women were located who were of mixed origin and in 1960 were not recorded as Indian. This is suggested by the observation that of those women who reported (in 1980) having only Indian ancestors, 40% of those aged 45 to 54 had finished high school, whereas among those of mixed-Indian and non-Indian ancestry, 55% reported being high-school graduates.

Most likely is the simple observation that the Amerindians as all U.S. residents inflate their years of schooling from one census to the next. Note that of all U.S. women aged 25 to 29 in 1970, 54% reported completion of high school; in 1980 of these women now aged 35 to 39, 78% reported high school graduation. This upgrading appears in all segments of the population.

It is possible that some part of the increase between 1970 and 1980 stemmed from changes in census procedures:

> The 1980 instruction for persons who received a high school diploma by virtue of passing an equivalency test was not included in past census questionnaires. Persons who took equivalency tests may or may not have been reported as high school graduates in earlier censuses; however, completing high school by such means was not as common in earlier decades as it was in the decade prior to the 1980 census. (PC 80-1-C1, p. B6)

How much of the reported increase in high-school graduation between 1970 and 1980 can be attributed to this change in instructions?

Counting

Another example of data problems is the not-so-simple count of the numbers. In 1970 in the United States the number of Amerindians aged 10 to 49 is given as 453,000. In 1980 the survivors are now aged 20 to 59, and 734,000 are reported. Apparently, no one died during these 10 years.

Years of Schooling, Canada and the United States

We were unable to make years of schooling completed in the two countries comparable; the school systems are too different. Hence, we settled for high-school graduation in the United States, and in Canada "less" and "more" schooling as shown in Chapter 11.

Canada

This census has its problems also, many similar to the U.S. census. For example, in 1961 about 90,000 male Amerindians and Inuits aged from birth to 39 years were reported. In 1971 the same number were reported as aged 10 to 49 years.

No one died between 1961 and 1971: The 1981 census reported a decrease of about 10,000 from 90,000 to 80,000 men aged 20 to 59. Such a decrease is possible but seems unlikely unless there was a heavy emigration to other countries. Mortality alone is unlikely to account for such a size decrease in light of the known death rates.

In Canada, the count of all Indians (or are they sometimes mixed with Métis and Inuits?) except for 1981 seems to be more consistent from census to census than in the United States (Appendix Table 5.1). However, the data for the Métis are unsatisfactory. The number for 1941 appears to be an estimate; the 1941 census does not list Métis separately. No Métis are listed in the published censuses of 1951, 1961, and 1971. Where are they counted?

Moral: Draw general conclusions, never supposedly highly specific statistical answers.

The "New" Canadian Amerindians

These "new" Amerindians, we believe, are mostly people of multiple ethnic origins, that is, of mixed ancestry. This is indicated by the unusually large increase in their numbers between 1981 and 1986:

	1981	1986	Percent change
Status plus nonstatus	367,800	526,200	+43
Single origin	313,600	286,200	−9
Multiple origin	54,200	240,000	+343
All Indians and Métis	466,000	660,000	+42

The total aboriginal population (excluding the Inuit) increased by about 42% during the 5 years, 1981 to 1986. This is impossible. Norris (1989) reports that the rate of natural increase (excess of births over deaths) may have been around 3% in 1981. However, average annual increase as calculated

Appendix Table 5.1. Census Counts of Aboriginal Populations: Canada, 1941 to 1986 (Numbers in Thousands)

	Indians		Métis	
Census year	Number	Percent change[a]	Number	Percent change
1941	118	—	35[b]	—
1951	155	2.8	NA	—
1961	208	2.9	NA	—
1971	295	3.6	NA	—
1981	368	2.2	98	—
1986	531	7.6	129	5.6

Source: Norris 1989, Table 1.
[a]Average annual.
[b]See text.

from the census figures was 7.3%. The 3% figure is possible. The 7.3% figure is impossible. Are the counts in error, or are other factors operating to exaggerate the rate of growth?

Between 1981 and 1986 the number of single-origin Indians reported in the censuses decreased by about 9%, whereas the number of multiple-origin people increased over four times. The number of Métis reported increased about one-third. Such a pattern of change is not to be believed. We can only infer that any of mixed origin reconverted to their Indian ancestry when reporting ethnicity to the census; this is suggested by Norris.

Clearly, the Canadian experience in counting Indians duplicates that of counting the Amerindians in the United States.

Appendix 6

The Historical Reservation Area

The HRA, as we define it for our purposes, includes most of the states west of the Mississippi River: the census Mountain states, Texas, Oklahoma, Washington, Oregon, Minnesota, North and South Dakota, and Michigan.

Why did we set up the HRA? From our readings of the events prior to the twentieth century, we knew that many of the eastern Indians, when driven out of their homes by the rapacious, land-devouring whites, ended someplace west of the river, on land not desired by whites at that time; hence, the reservations were located on this "worthless" land. We hypothesized that such experiences must have had long-lasting demographic and cultural effects upon the Indians (see Chapters 7 and 8).

To begin, we compared the numbers of Indians as reported in the 1980 census and the number that the Federal Bureau of Indian Affairs reported for 1980,[1] state by state. We found substantial agreement. For the entire HRA, 4 out of every 5 Indians recorded by the census were also included in the BIA statistics, with some variation from one state to another.

In the remaining states (excluding Alaska and Hawaii), 2 of every 5 in the census count were also included in the BIA count. Furthermore, 9 in 10 in the BIA count lived in these HRA states.

These figures strongly suggested to us that there are differences between those living in the HRA and those living elsewhere in the United States. Our thought was that the HRA is populated by more traditionally inclined Indians, that is, people who are closer to or more involved with tribal culture than are those who live elsewhere. So we built this factor—residence in or out of the HRA—into our 1980 sample census tape and in our analysis.

---

[1] In addition to the BIA reservations there are a few reservations that states established.

As we saw in Chapters 9 to 12, the demographic characteristics of the two groups of Amerindians differed. We do not hold that place of residence "causes" these differences; rather, that place of residence is an index to some underlying differences. Those living outside of the HRA are largely descendants of the few eastern Indians who escaped deportation to the western ghettos in the nineteenth century. Or they are people who voluntarily moved out of the western reservations; these people tend to be self-selected and differ from those remaining on the reservations, as we discussed in Chapter 8.

When Mooney (1928) made his population estimates (as of the early eighteenth century), between 35 and 40% lived in what is now the HRA. By 1870 about 80% lived on reservations in this area. The proportion remained virtually unchanged through the 1950 census count. By 1960, it had fallen to 66%, 64% in 1970, and 57% in 1980.

Residency is related to ancestry and "blood," but the strength of the relationship is indeterminate. In 1980, two in three of all Amerindians who replied to the census that they had only Indian ancestors lived in the HRA. Of those who replied that they had Indian and non-Indian ancestors, only about one in three lived in the HRA. All that we can say is that at least since 1910, the HRA contained a larger proportion of "full" bloods and the other states a larger proportion of "mixed"-blood ancestry.

Our intuitive feelings that area of residence is worth including in the analysis, is correct.

Appendix 7

How Many Amerindians Were There in the 1980s?

As Ajax de Smyrna has said, "Give me a definition and I'll give you a number." The answer to "How many?" depends on the definition of Amerindian.

UNITED STATES

The largest number is obtained by self-identification, 1,478,000 in the 1980 census (PC 8-1-C1, Table 74).

Estimated tribal membership amounts to about 810,000; this is the number ostensibly on the tribal rolls, but the date of the estimate is uncertain. The Indian Health Service population, persons eligible for medical service from the Indian Health Service, number about 830,000 (*Indian Health Care* 1986, p. 272).

The Bureau of Indian Affairs reports having about 735,000 clients who live on or adjacent to reservations. (The population information is released annually in a photocopied document.)

The census made a special tabulation of Amerindians in 1980 who were living on identified reservations and in the historic areas of Oklahoma. The count amounted to about 336,000. Of this number, only 292,000 reported being enrolled in a tribe (PC 80-2-1D, Part 1, Tables 1 and 4).

IDENTIFIED HISTORIC AREAS OF OKLAHOMA
(Excluding Urbanized Areas)

The historic areas of Oklahoma (excluding urbanized areas) consist of the former reservations which had legally established boundaries during the period '1900–1907. These reservations were dissolved during the two-to-three year period preceding the statehood of Oklahoma in 1907. The former reservation boundaries are used for planning purposes by tribes and the Federal government. In the census, the entire area encompassing the former reservations was identified (excluding urbanized areas): individual former reservations were not identified separately. The parts inside urbanized areas were approximated in preparation for the 1980 Census. The historic areas of Oklahoma (excluding urbanized areas) were not identified in previous censuses.

IDENTIFIED AMERICAN INDIAN RESERVATIONS

American Indian reservations are areas with boundaries established by treaty, statute, and/or executive or court order. There are 278 American Indian reservations, and their boundaries were identified for the 1980 census by the Bureau of Indian Affairs (BIA) and State governments. The Federal and State reservations are located in 33 States and may cross State, country, minor civil division/census county division, and place boundaries. Three reservation areas are composed of lands that are jointly administered and or claimed by two reservations—San Felipe/Santa Ana Joint Area, New Mexico; San Felipe/Santo Domingo Joint Area, New Mexico; and other reservation lands in Montana. (U.S. Census, PC 80-2-ID, Appendix A)

If an Indian is defined as anyone who reports being such, in 1980 there were close to 1½ million. If an Indian is defined as living on a reservation and being enrolled in a tribe, there are only about 300,000. The legal definitions compromise and report about the average of these two numbers, around 800,000.

Take your choice.

CANADA

In 1981, there were reported to the census to be 293,000 status Indians, 75,000 nonstatus, and 98,000 Métis for a total of 466,000 (excluding the Inuits). These numbers result from self-identification (Catalogue 92-911, Table 1).

In 1980, the agency Indian and Inuit Affairs Program reported that there were 224,000 registered Indians who lived on reserves or Crown lands and 93,000 who lived elsewhere.

What is the "correct" number of Indians? 466,000 or 224,000 in 1981, or some number in between.

The 1986 sample census reported that there were 531,000 Indians and 129,000 Métis for a total of about 660,000.

Again, take your choice.

Vital Rates in
the Twentieth Century

NOTES ON THE SOURCES AND
INTERPRETATION OF BIRTHS AND DEATHS

Sources of Statistics

Birth and death rates are derived by combining information from two sources: (1) The births and deaths are recorded by local health departments. The recording of all information, including ethnicity or race, on the certificate is done by the attending physician or undertaker, or more likely a clerk. Each state or province in the past could determine what information to collect on the certificates; by the latter twentieth century the certificates are largely standardized nationwide, both in Canada and in the United States. (2) The denominator or number of people, including their race, is determined by the census counts. Because national censuses are conducted by central government agencies, the recording of ethnicity (for use in the denominator) is done by only one agency.

Different government agencies are responsible for the numerator and denominator, and therein lies the probability of trouble in assigning race or ethnicity to the vital event. A person may be classified as being of one ethnic group, American Indian, for example, in the numerator, and a different ethnicity in the denominator. How do we interpret the resulting rates?

Some Problems of Interpretation

Because we are interested in the Amerindians, let us note how their birth and death rates must be interpreted in light of the preceding procedural remarks as well as other, more general problems.

The Indians in the post-World War II years in many respects differ from those beloved by cultural anthropologists, popular writers, and moviemakers. Certainly they all differ in many respects from the Ancients. Hence, we ask: What is the meaning of changing birth and death rates?

It may be argued that meaningful interpretations over time can be made of the birth and death rates for a relatively homogeneous population. But even in these cases changes over time must be interpreted with caution. Is the New York City inhabitant or the Toronto citizen at the end of the twentieth century the same as the dwellers in these cities a century ago? For example, we know that in New York City two centuries ago, the people were largely of northwestern European origin. As the twenty-first century approaches, many of the people are of Latin American, Mediterranean, eastern European, African, and Asian origin. We know that the vital rates have changed over these two centuries. But have the original northwestern European people changed their behavior? Or have the vital rates changed because the people in 1990 are from cultures and lifestyles different from those of citizens of 1790? Or are both "causes" operative? No population, no matter how culturally homogeneous it may be at the beginning, remains consistently homogeneous and faithful to its origin.

The story about the changing vital rates of the Amerindians is much more complex than that for the Toronto or New York City people. We must explain, or any numbers presented may be misinterpreted.

The complexity in the Indian population, or any ethnic group, results from (a) intermarriage with members from different ethnic groups, a factor that may or may not be more important for the Indians than for others; and (b) the vagaries of the recording clerks.

Let us illustrate. Suppose that an Amerindian woman is married to a non-Indian and they have a child. Biologically that child is only half Indian. Should this birth be classified as "Indian"? As "half-an-Indian"? Or as non-Indian? In the United States and Canada the birth is classified as "Indian." The census cooperates by classifying all young children who are of mixed ancestry, that is, those who cannot themselves declare their race, as Indian. (If the non-Indian parent is of Asian or African origin, other classification rules may be invoked.) By changing the classification rules, a very different number of births and birthrates result. Classify the birth as of the non-Indian parent and immediately a large number of "Indian" births disappear. Classify the birth as "mixed," and we have a whole new population to analyze and interpret. What should we do? There is no satisfactory answer.

We illustrate. In the United States in the years 1974 to 1976, the average annual number of births in which both parents were reported as Indian was 12,380. The average number in which only one parent was so recorded was 15,510. In total there were 27,890 births (special tabulation from the Indian Health Service). Should we count the number of "Indian" births as *12,380* or *27,890?* Take your choice. There is no right or wrong answer.

Fewer than one-half of all "Indian" births in the 1970s were to parents both of whom reported themselves as Indian. By the 1980s (as we saw in Chapter 10), only about one-third of "Indian" births was to parents both of whom were classified as Indian. So how shall we interpret the changing Indian birthrate? More confusion and disputation.

Calculating Birth and Death Rates

Birthrates

The official birthrates presented in government reports generally are only the numbers of births per 1,000 population served by the agencies involved. Such data are insufficient for our purposes. We need estimates of TFR (or the gross reproduction rate) and the net production rate (or intrinsic rate of natural increase). To get these latter rates, we ought to have age-specific birthrates. They are unavailable for the entire twentieth century. So we proceeded as follows.

We used the age distributions of the Indian women as reported by the censuses over the last several decades and indirect standardization techniques (see Jaffe 1951). The estimated number of births was calculated from the reported number of children under 5 years of age as follows: one-fifth of those 0 to 4 years is the approximate number aged 2½; using life table values of survival from birth to age 2½, we inflate the estimated number of children aged 2½.

Censuses generally undercount young children, and we suppose that is the case with Indian children. But we have no way of determining the amount of undercounting, especially prior to World War II. Therefore, we simply tried to allow for this factor in the interpretation of the changes during the twentieth century. Suffice it to say that fertility has decreased considerably, especially since World War II.

The net reproduction rates are simply calculated from the estimated gross reproduction rates and the appropriate life tables, again with the help of indirect standardization.

Information about children ever born was obtained from census reports, and the sample 1980 census tape.

In some instances, when nonexistent historical information was needed, we estimated such in accordance with the procedures in Chapter 8, footnote 16.

Death Rates

The life tables posed no problems except for the beginning of the twentieth century. We used the tables prepared by government agencies. In the United States, the Indian Health Service provided the tables beginning with the earliest, that for 1939–41.

In Canada, life tables were prepared by Health and Welfare Canada based on the registered Indian population served by its Medical Services Branch. In some provinces, only the population living on reserves was included; in other provinces, registered Indians living off the reserves were included. Life tables were also prepared by Statistics Canada covering the total registered population living on and off the reserves. Considering all the technical details involved in collecting the death statistics, we conclude that there are no significant differences between these two sets of life tables.

For 1900 and 1910, we used life tables for blacks in the United States. Comparison of the Indian and black life expectancies in 1940 were remarkably close, as follows:

1940	At birth		Age 20		Source
	Male	Female	Male	Female	
Indians	51	52	44	44	IHS, unpublished
Blacks	52	56	40	42	Statistical Abstract, 1956, p. 65
Blacks					Glover 1921, pp. 76 ff.
1900–02	33	35	36	37	
1910	34	38	34	36	

Considering the poor quality and paucity of information for this early period, we feel that there is no significant difference between the two ethnic groups in the United States, in length of life. As for Canadian Indians, or Native People, demographically they are not very different from those south of the border. We have no way of knowing, or even guessing, how their life expectation might have compared with that of the U.S. Amerindians.

Hence, we used life expectancy for the blacks in 1910 as a proxy for that of the Indians, both in Canada and in the United States, for 1900 and 1910.

In closing, note that not all people who self-classify as Indians are included. The official life tables refer only to the registered (status) Indians in Canada and those U.S. Indians served by the IHS, insofar as we can ascertain. We think that those others who regard themselves as Indian or Native People and are omitted from the life tables that we used are reasonably similar to the general populations of the two countries; we were unable to locate any definitive information.

The 1980 Census Sample, United States

The information presented in Appendix Table 8.4 was obtained from the 1980 census sample file. The only change we made was to separate those who reported Indian as their race into two groups: (a) those who reported *only Indian ancestry* and (b) those who reported *non-Indian and Indian ancestry.* Thus, we duplicated the Canadian census that reported "single" and "multiple" ancestry.

Additional vital statistics follow:

1. Estimated Birthrates for Amerindians and All Women: United States, 1910 to 1970.
2. Children Ever Born per Woman Aged 35–44 for Amerindians and All Women: United States, 1960 to 1980.
3. Estimated Birthrates for Native People and All Women: Canada, 1931 to 1981.
4. Estimated Average Number of Children Ever Born to Married Indian Women Aged 35–44 by Several Characteristics: United States, 1980.
5. Estimated Years of Life Expectancy at Selected Ages: United States, 1910 to 1980.
6. Deaths per 1,000 Population for Status Indians: Canada, 1900 to 1979.
7. Estimated Years of Life Expectancy at Selected Ages: Canada, 1960–64 to 1982–85.

Appendix Table 8.1. Estimated Birthrates for Amerindians and All Women: United States, 1910 to 1980

| *Total fertility rate* | Amerindians | | | |
	Total	*Urban*	*Rural*	*Total U.S. population*
1910[a]	5.8	—	5.8	3.7
1920[a]	5.1	—	5.1	3.4
1930	4.7	3.0	5.0	2.6
1940	4.4	2.4	4.6	2.3
1950	4.6	3.3	4.9	3.0
1960	5.3	4.6	5.6	3.7
1970	3.3	2.8	3.9	2.6
1980	2.2	1.9	2.7	1.8
Net reproduction rate				
1910	1.6	—	1.6	1.4
1920	1.8	—	1.8	1.2
1930	1.8	1.1	1.9	1.0
1940	1.6	1.1	2.0	1.0
1950	1.8	1.4	2.1	1.1
1960	2.3	2.0	2.5	1.2
1970	1.4	1.2	1.7	1.1
1980	1.2	1.0	1.4	.95

[a]Almost all of the Indians were rural dwellers.

Appendix Table 8.2. Children Ever Born per Woman Aged 35 to 44 for Amerindians and All Women: United States, 1960 to 1980

	Indian	Total U.S. population
1960	4.2	2.5
1970	4.3	3.0
1980, total	3.5	2.6
Indian ancestry only	3.7	—
Indian and non-Indian ancestry	3.0	—

Appendix Table 8.3. Estimated Birthrates for Native People[a] and All Women: Canada, 1931 to 1981

Total fertility rate	Native People			Total Canada
	Total	Urban	Rural	
1931	5.1	b	5.1	3.2
1941	4.8	b	4.9	2.8
1951[c]	5.3	3.8	5.6	3.5
1961	5.3	3.1	5.8	3.9
1971	4.3	2.8	5.2	2.5
1981	2.8	2.2	3.3	1.8
Net reproduction rate				
1931	1.9	—	1.9	1.3
1941	1.7	—	1.8	1.2
1951	1.9	1.4	2.1	1.6
1961	1.7	1.0	1.9	1.8
1971	1.8	1.2	2.2	1.0
1981	1.4	1.1	1.7	0.8[d]

[a]Prior to 1981, it is not clear how the census classified the Métis, Inuits, and nonstatus Indians. In 1981, the status Indians constituted 60%, the nonstatus 15%, the Métis 20%, and the Inuit 5% of all Native People.
[b]Only about 5% were classified as urban.
[c]About 10% were urban in 1951, 20% in 1961, 40% in 1971, and 45% in 1981.
[d]Romaniuc, p. 14.

Appendix Table 8.4. Estimated Average Number of Children Ever Born to Married Indian Women Aged 35 to 44 by Several Characteristics: United States, 1980

	Historical Reservation Area		All other states	
Total	3.7		3.1	
Ancestry	*Indian only*	*Mixed*	*Indian only*	*Mixed*
	Urban			
Total	3.8	3.1	3.3	3.2
Years of schooling				
Under 12	4.6	3.9	4.0	3.8
12+	3.3	2.8	3.0	2.7
Under 12 years of schooling				
Husband				
Indian	4.8	NA	4.3	NA
Non-Indian	4.4	3.6	3.9	3.8
12+ years of schooling				
Husband				
Indian	3.8	NA	3.2	NA
Non-Indian	2.8	2.6	2.9	2.7
	Rural			
Total	4.3	3.3	3.9	3.1
Years of schooling				
Under 12	5.0	3.7	4.5	3.8
12+	3.4	3.0	3.3	2.7
Under 12 years of schooling				
Husband				
Indian	5.2	NA	4.7	NA
Non-Indian	4.0	NA	4.2	NA
12+ years of schooling				
Husband				
Indian	3.7	NA	3.4	NA
Non-Indian	2.9	3.1	3.1	2.7

Appendix Table 8.5. Estimated Years of Life Expectancy at Selected Ages: United States, 1910 to 1980[a]

	Amerindians					Total U.S.
	At birth	15	25	45	65	at birth
Men						
1900–02[a]	33	38	32	20	10	48[c]
1909–11[c]	34	37	30	19	10	50[c]
1939–41	51	48	41	26	14	62
1949–51	58	52	44	29	16	66
1959–61[b]	NA	NA	NA	NA	NA	67
1969–71	61	48	41	26	13	67
1979–81	67	54	46	29	15	70
Women						
1900–02	35	40	34	21	11	51
1909–11	38	39	33	20	11	54
1939–41	52	48	41	27	15	65
1949–51	62	55	47	32	18	71
1959–61[b]	NA	NA	NA	NA	NA	73
1969–71	71	59	50	34	19	75
1979–81	75	62	52	34	18	78

[a]The apparent inconsistencies in the Indian data from one decade to the next may result in part from changes in the states included in the compilation of Indian deaths. We have more confidence in the changes over the 80-year period than in decade to decade.
[b]For both sexes combined, life expectancy at birth was 62 years.
[c]Glover 1921.

Appendix Table 8.6. Deaths per 1,000 Population for Status Indians: Canada, 1900 to 1979[a]

1900–1904	31
1905–1909	31
1910–1914	30
1915–1919	30
1920–1924	30
1925–1929	29
1930–1934	29
1935–1939	27
1940–1944	25
1945–1949	21
1950–1954	17
1955–1959	14
1960–1964	10
1965–1969	9
1970–1974	8
1975–1979	7[b]

[a]Rates for the years 1900 to 1968 are from Latulippe-Sakamoto; 1969 to 1979 rates are from unpublished, photocopied tables from Indian and Northern Affairs.
[b]The rate for the total Canadian population in 1986 was 7 per 1,000, about the same as that of the status Indians.

Appendix Table 8.7. Estimated Years of Life Expectancy at Selected Ages: Canada, 1960–64 to 1980–85[a]

| | Status Indians | | | | | Total Canada |
	At birth	15	25	45	65	at birth
Men						
1960–65	60	52	44	28	14	68
1965–68	60	51	43	28	14	69
1976	60	50	42	27	15	70
1981	62	51	43	28	16	72
1982–85	64	52	45	29	15	72
Women						
1960–65	64	56	47	30	15	74
1965–68	66	55	46	30	16	75
1976	66	56	47	31	18	78
1981	69	57	48	31	11	79
1982–85	73	60	51	34	19	80

[a]The changes from one time to another are due to a variety of factors and do not necessarily indicate changes in mortality experience. As in the United States (Appendix Table 8.5), we have more confidence in the long-run changes from 1960 to 1985 than in the reported very short-run changes.

Appendix **9**

The Work Force and Occupational Classification

INTRODUCTION

For information covering the U.S. experiences through the first half of the twentieth century, see Jaffe and Stewart (1951). For information regarding the second half of this century, see, for example, the explanations in the decennial census volumes of the United States and Canada; the United Nations and the International Labour Organization have also published on this topic. The subject is vast.

Definitions

Work is the carrying on of activities needed to sustain life.
The *work force* is the total of all workers.
The *labor force* is another term for work force and involves very specific methods of collecting and processing the data.

Population versus Work Force

Originally

People lived under technologically underdeveloped conditions (in contrast to our advanced technology) and without a money economy. Hunters and gatherers and subsistence farmers fit this picture. Under these conditions, practically the entire band—every member of the band capable of contributing something, however little—worked. Firewood had to be collected, water carried, animal skins cleaned, and so forth. There was something for everyone to do. Consequently there was no distinction between the population and the work force; they were the same.

Twentieth Century

Time passes, millennium after millennium, and societies change drastically. Now there is considerable technological and scientific development, and people are paid money for their efforts. Now only part of the total population need work to obtain life's necessities for the entire population. Hence, that part of the total population that carries on activities for which they receive pay in money (perhaps excluding certain illegal activities) becomes the work force, or the labor force.

In the United States in 1988 there were close to 250 million people of all ages and shapes; only about half were in the labor force. In Canada we find much the same picture. A modern, technologically developed society does not need to have practically all its members in the work force.

Why we emphasize receipt of money as part of the description is explained in the following section.

Measuring the Work Force

In the United States, the idea of a measurable work force began to take shape in the early nineteenth century. Two factors combined to produce, eventually, statistics about the work force.

In the eighteenth century and earlier, there was almost no information about the economic conditions of the country. Indeed, there was no United States country until after the Revolution and the startup of the federal government following the revolution. With a central government instead of 13 independent-of-each-other colonies, there was a need to know what was happening on the economic side as well as the political side. How can the tax collector determine how much taxes can be collected and from where, until he/she has a statistical–economic map of the country?

But prior to the nineteenth century (or the very late eighteenth century), there was no mechanism by which the Feds could obtain that information. The Constitution came to the rescue of the statisticians. A decennial census of the population for purposes of Congressional representation was mandated. The first one was taken in 1790. No sooner was the 1790 census taken when it was recognized as the mechanism for collecting information regarding the economic and social conditions of the new nation. Thomas Jefferson, president of the American Philosophical Society, and Timothy Dwight, president of the Connecticut Academy of Arts and Sciences, submitted memorials to Congress in January

1800, suggesting and requesting that such information be collected in forth-coming censuses.

Jefferson's memorial was specific regarding the to-be-eventually work statistics.

> A curious and useful document of the distribution of society in these States, and of the conditions and vocations of our fellow-citizens [should be obtained via the census, showing] the number of free male inhabitants, of all ages, engaged in business . . . to wit: (1) Men of the learned professions, including clergymen, lawyers, physicians, those employed in the fine arts, teachers, and scribes in general. (2) Merchants and trades, including bankers, insurers, brokers, and dealers of every kind. (3) Marines. (4) Handicraftsmen. (5) Laborers in agriculture. (6) Laborers of other descriptions. (7) Domestic servants. (8) Paupers. (9) Persons of no particular calling. (Wright and Hunt 1900, pp. 18–20)

Now it is easy to obtain a count of the male work force. The census enumerator only need to ask every free male interviewed what his occupation is. Those who furnished an occupation were counted as being in the work force. Eventually women were also acknowledged to be workers. This is the origin of the *gainful worker* concept which was used from the census of 1820 through the census of 1930.

The Great Depression of the 1930s led to changes. Unemployment was very high, but no one knew just how high. The federal government, concerned about unemployment, needed to know how many unemployed there were in order to take some action, for example, the WPA (Works Projects Administration). But the gainful worker procedures produce no information about unemployment.

Such information is obtainable via the *labor force concept;* this was developed in the 1930s and first used in the 1940 census. Further, to make the information on the work force useful, however, data about employment and unemployment had to be available at least every month. Because a complete census could not be taken every month, a sample census, the CPS or Current Population Survey, was devised, initiated, and still continues.

As for the unemployed, the federal government was concerned only with those who had lost their jobs or who were new entrants into the work force but were unable to find employment for pay or profit. To help such people, unemployment insurance was introduced and various work programs undertaken. For all other teenage and older people, who were neither employed nor unemployed but who needed aid, various Social Security programs such as Old Age and Survivors Insurance were introduced.

Specific survey techniques had to be designed in order to implement this labor force program. Each respondent (over the specified minimum age) was asked whether he/she had worked for pay or profit during a specified week (1 week in each month). If not, did he/she look for work for pay or profit? Additional questions may be asked from time to time, or other changes made, in order to obtain more information about employment and unemployment.

Following these basic questions are additional enquiries regarding occupation, industry, and related items.

In summary: The labor force equals the *employed* plus the *unemployed,* both in the United States and Canada.

The Information about Occupations

Uses

Occupational information now serves as the first point in Jefferson's memorial, the "conditions . . . of our fellow citizens." By the latter part of the twentieth century, governments are collecting far more information about the state of the economy via other sources, and the work force statistics, especially employment, are not needed to the same extent as in the nineteenth century. The unemployment statistics, however, are thought to be needed, are in great demand, and are very often misused.

Some occupational data are used for such purposes as determining the ratio of medical doctors to population for public health purposes, of farmers to agricultural production, and other socioeconomic purposes. "We are short of engineers" or "we have too many engineers" are rallying cries for one pressure group or another.

Occupational Classification Systems

There are thousands of individual occupations, far too many for the average researcher to handle. Hence, the census groups them into more or less homogeneous categories. The conventional socioeconomic groups attempt to rank the occupations from "most" to "least" desirable. The top level generally receives the most income, requires the most schooling, and is held in higher esteem by the population; it is the most desirable. Each lower level or stratum is held in successively lower esteem.

All groupings of individual occupations are ad hoc compilations. Use an existing classification if it serves your purposes. If not, devise another classification system, if possible. The classification of military personnel, for example, from five-star general down to private, serves military purposes, but not necessarily civilian purposes. Compiling a tailormade classification, however, is very difficult, expensive, and time-consuming. For a private researcher, this is almost an impossible task.

The main problem with all occupational titles and classifications is that they are always changing. A few years ago there were no astronauts, but plenty of drivers of horse teams. Is one a replacement for the other? Is the word-processor operator comparable to the private secretary? What new occupations will appear next year? Next century?

Notwithstanding all of the statistical deficiencies in the census information about occupations, they can be useful if analyzed carefully. For example, do the ethnic groups protected under Equal Economic Opportunity legislation (EEO) have "better" or "poorer" jobs than do those workers not so covered? Do the Amerindians who live off reserves or reservations have "better" or "poorer" jobs than do the reserve dwellers? In Chapter 12, we compared the socioeconomic position of the Amerindians with that of the general U.S. population. Do the children of immigrants have "better" jobs than their immigrant parents? How do the people living in the largest cities compare with those living in the smaller cities? And so on.

Appendix *10*

Some Additional Statistics

> DISCIPLES: Master, of what use are statistics? Most people are not statisticians and are afraid of the word.
>
> MASTER: All people use numbers whether or not you call them statistics. Every time you play the lottery you use numbers. Statistics are simply numbers so organized as to tell a tale. A sheet of paper with numbers on it may not appeal to some people, but without these numbers sensible conclusions cannot be drawn.
>
> *Analects of Peng Shun Lu,* No. 73

Following are several tables (10.1–10.5) of data that are not easily obtainable elsewhere. The chapter to which each table is most pertinent is given.

For the large majority of statistics about Indians, see especially the explanations and tables in the censuses of Canada and the United States.

THE LIST

1. Estimated Percentage of Live Births Who Became Orphaned, by Age of Mother and Father: Pre-European Period (Chapter 5).
2. Average Number of Children Ever Born to Married Indian Women Aged 35 to 44 by Characteristics of Women: United States, 1980 (Chapter 9).
3. Percentage of Indian Women Married to Non-Indian Men, by Characteristics of Women: United States, 1980 (Chapter 10).
4. Ethnic Group of Husband by Ethnic Group of Wife for Native/Nonnative Persons: Canada, 1981 (Chapter 10).
5. Indian Gainful Workers 10 Years Old and Over, by Sex and Socioeconomic Groups: United States, 1930 and 1910 (Chapter 12).

Appendix Table 10.1. Estimated Percentage of Live Births Who Became Orphaned, by Age of Mother and Father: Pre-European Period[a]

	Age of parents											
	Nonagriculture						Agriculture					
	15	20	25	30	35	40	15	20	25	30	35	40
Infant survives 5 years												
Not orphan	80	68	58	55	51	44	80	71	65	61	58	51
Orphan, total	20	32	42	45	49	56	20	29	35	39	42	49
Both parents die	1	3	5	7	8	11	1	3	4	5	6	8
Mother only dies	11	21	23	23	24	27	10	15	18	18	18	20
Father only dies	8	8	13	16	18	18	9	11	14	16	18	21
Total	100	100	100	100	100	100	100	100	100	100	100	100
Infant survives 10 years												
Not orphan	49	34	30	26	19	12	57	46	40	35	29	21
Orphan, total	51	66	70	74	81	88	43	54	60	65	71	79
Both parents die	9	17	20	24	32	43	6	10	13	16	21	29
Mother only dies	24	29	29	28	26	23	21	25	26	25	24	24
Father only dies	18	20	21	22	23	22	16	19	21	23	25	26
Total	100	100	100	100	100	100	100	100	100	100	100	100
Infant survives 15 years												
Not orphan	27	18	14	10	6	3	37	28	23	18	12	7
Orphan, total	73	82	86	90	94	97	63	72	77	82	88	93
Both parents die	23	32	39	46	58	69	15	22	27	33	42	54
Mother only dies	29	29	27	24	19	14	27	29	27	25	22	19
Father only dies	21	20	20	20	17	14	21	21	23	24	23	20
Total	100	100	100	100	100	100	100	100	100	100	100	100

Note: Due to rounding, columns may not add to 100%. The line "Not orphan" indicates the probability of a parent couple remaining intact. For example, if both parents were age 15, after 5 years 80% of the couples would remain intact.
[a]At time of child's birth, both parents were the same age.

Appendix Table 10.2. Average Number of Children Ever Born to Married Indian Women Aged 35 to 44 by Characteristics of Women: United States, 1980

	Urban	Rural
All women	3.4	4.0
Historical Reservation Area	3.7	4.2
Ancestry Indian only	3.8	4.3
Schooling less than 12 years	4.6	5.0
Husband Indian	4.8	5.2
Husband non-Indian	4.4	4.0
Schooling 12 or more years	3.3	3.4
Husband Indian	3.8	3.7
Husband non-Indian	2.8	2.9
Ancestry mixed	3.1	3.3
Schooling less than 12 years	3.9	3.7
Husband Indian	*	*
Husband non-Indian	3.6	*
Schooling 12 or more years	2.8	3.0
Husband Indian	*	*
Husband non-Indian	2.6	3.1
All other states	3.3	3.7
Ancestry Indian only	3.3	3.9
Schooling less than 12 years	4.0	4.5
Husband Indian	4.3	4.7
Husband non-Indian	3.9	4.2
Schooling 12 or more years	3.0	3.3
Husband Indian	3.2	3.4
Husband non-Indian	2.9	3.1
Ancestry mixed	3.2	3.1
Schooling less than 12 years	3.8	3.8
Husband Indian	*	*
Husband non-Indian	3.8	*
Schooling 12 or more years	2.7	2.7
Husband Indian	*	*
Husband non-Indian	2.7	2.7

*Too few cases in sample to show separately.

Appendix Table 10.3. Percentage of Indian Women Married to Non-Indian Men by Characteristics of Women: United States, 1980

All women	Urban	Rural
Historical Reservation Area		
Ancestry Indian only	48	22
Schooling less than 12 years	45	17
Schooling 12 or more years	49	29
Ancestry mixed	73	76
Schooling less than 12 years	66	68
Schooling 12 or more years	76	81
All other states		
Ancestry Indian only	69	39
Schooling less than 12 years	65	31
Schooling 12 or more years	72	47
Ancestry mixed	75	71
Schooling less than 12 years	69	60
Schooling 12 or more years	78	79

Appendix Table 10.4. Ethnic Group of Husband by Ethnic Group of Wife for Native/ Nonnative Persons: Canada, 1981[a]

	Ethnicity of wife						
	Single response: Native Person				Multiple response: Native and nonnative	Nonnative	Total
Ethnicity of husband	Inuit	Métis	Nonstatus Indian	Status Indian			
Single response:							
Native Person							
Inuit	2,775	5	10	40	30	310	3,170
Métis	30	4,855	345	1,125	190	4,740	11,285
Nonstatus Indian	15	210	2,360	940	110	3,895	7,530
Status Indian	35	715	780	29,430	480	5,885	37,325
Multiple response:							
Native and nonnative	60	215	110	540	1,500	8,075	10,500
Nonnative	585	5,745	5,180	9,380	9,475	5,511,330	5,541,695
Total	3,500	11,745	8,785	41,455	11,785	5,534,235	5,611,505

[a]Derived from Question 26, Census of Population 1981. See Norris 1989.

Appendix Table 10.5. Indian Gainful Workers 10 Years Old and Over by Sex and Socioeconomic Groups: United States, 1930 and 1910

Gainful workers	1930		1910	
	Number	Percentage	Number	Percentage
Total	98,148	100.0	73,916	100.0
Professional persons	2,355	2.4	1,284	1.7
Proprietors, managers, and officials	29,280	29.8	23,013	31.1
Farmers (owners and tenants)	28,038	28.6	21,997	29.8
Wholesale and retail dealers	625	0.6	520	0.7
Other proprietors, managers, and officials	517	0.6	496	0.7
Clerks and kindred workers	2,494	2.5	1,027	1.4
Skilled workers and foremen	4,228	4.3	2,056	2.8
Semiskilled workers	11,755	12.0	8,052	10.9
Semiskilled workers in manufacturing	8,016	8..2	6,728	9.1
Other semiskilled workers	3,739	3.8	1,324	1.8
Unskilled workers	48,036	48.9	38,484	52.1
Agricultural laborers	28,245	28.8	26,490	35.8
Factory and building construction laborers	7,084	7.2	3,656	4.9
Other laborers	8,323	8.5	4,873	6.6
Servant classes	4,384	4.5	3,465	4.7
Males	80,306	100.0	59,206	100.0
Professional persons	1,531	1.9	927	1.6
Proprietors, managers, and officials	27,615	34.4	21,765	36.8
Farmers (owners and tenants)	26,521	33.0	20,841	35.2
Wholesale and retail dealers	569	0.7	462	0.8
Other proprietors, managers, and officials	525	0.7	442	0.7
Clerks and kindred workers	1,630	2.0	859	1.5
Skilled workers and foremen	4,204	5.2	2,021	3.4
Semiskilled workers	4,278	5.3	1,511	2.6
Semiskilled workers in manufacturing	1,632	2.0	673	1.1
Other semiskilled workers	2,646	3.3	838	1.4
Unskilled workers	41,048	51.1	32,123	54.3
Agricultural laborers	25,124	31.3	23,293	39.3
Factory and building construction laborers	6,973	8.7	3,571	6.0
Other laborers	8,277	10.3	4,772	8.1
Servant classes	674	0.8	487	0.8

(continued on page 300)

Appendix Table 10.5. Indian Gainful Workers 10 Years Old and Over by Sex and Socioeconomic Groups: United States, 1930 and 1910 (*continued*)

Gainful workers	1930		1910	
	Number	Percentage	Number	Percentage
Females	17,842	100.0	14,710	100.0
Professional persons	824	4.6	357	2.4
Proprietors, managers, and officials	1,665	9.3	1,248	8.5
Farmers (owners and tenants)	1,517	8.5	1,156	7.9
Wholesale and retail dealers	56	0.3	38	0.3
Other proprietors, managers, and officials	92	0.5	54	0.4
Clerks and kindred workers	864	4.8	168	1.1
Skilled workers and foremen	24	0.1	35	0.2
Semiskilled workers	7,477	41.9	6,541	44.5
Semiskilled workers in manufacturing	6,384	35.8	6,055	41.2
Other semiskilled workers	1,093	6.1	486	3.3
Unskilled workers	6,988	39.2	6,361	43.2
Agricultural laborers	3,121	17.5	3,197	21.7
Factory and building construction laborers	111	0.6	85	0.6
Other laborers	46	0.3	101	0.7
Servant classes	3,710	20.8	2,978	20.2

Summary

	Men				Women			
	1930		1910		1930		1910	
	Number	Percentage	Number	Percentage	Number	Percentage	Number	Percentage
Agriculture	51,645	64	44,134	74	4,638	26	4,353	30
Nonagriculture	28,661	36	15,072	26	13,204	74	10,357	70
Total	80,306	100	59,206	100	17,842	100	14,710	100

Appendix **11**

Population of Canada
by Provinces, 1701 to 1981

For the analysis in Chapter 7, we needed population counts or estimates of all the provinces (see Appendix Table 11.1) from the beginning of the eighteenth century to almost the end of the twentieth. With Chapter 7, Figure 7.8, and the population as shown in Appendix Table 11.1, we can trace the impingement of the expanding white population upon the Indians and Indian territory. We were unable to find such information. The census reports include all provinces only since 1951; this was the first time that Newfoundland, including Labrador, was included. Information is available for all provinces except Newfoundland back to 1871. Earlier there is but a scattering of numbers collected by others than Statistics Canada.

Another source is the "Historical Compendium for the Royal Commission on the Economic Union and Development Prospects for Canada," prepared by Statistics Canada (June 1984, photocopy). This document contains scattered provincial data back to 1665–66 when Lower Canada (Quebec) was credited with having 3,215 of European origin.

Numbers for Newfoundland prior to 1951 were found in *The Book of Newfoundland,* edited by J. R. Smallwood in 1937. Considerable information was found in Robert Montgomery Martin's *History of the Colonies of the British Empire* (1843). On the basis of the "Historical Compendium . . . " and Martin, we reconstructed, or estimated, the numbers prior to 1871.

Note that the population history of the Canadian provinces is rather complicated:

1. From the beginning of the sixteenth century, unknown numbers of European traders, explorers, fishermen, soldiers, and other government

Appendix Table 11.1. Census Counts and Estimated Numbers by Province: Canada, 1701 to 1981 (Numbers in Thousands)

Province	1981	1971	1961	1951	1941	1931	1921	1911	1901	1891	1881	1871	1861	1851	1841	1831	1821	1801	1751	1701
Total Canada	24,084	21,569	18,239	14,009	11,828	10,659	9,051	7,450	5,592	5,035	4,511	3,850	3,378	2,552	1,655	1,140	798	360	100(?)	25(?)
Maritime	2,214	2,058	1,898	1,618	1,451	1,291	1,264	1,181	1,115	1,082	1,057	920	804	644	505	350	240	75	40	10(?)
Newfoundland (including Labrador)	564	522	458	361	321	282	263	243	221	202	186	153	140	110	85	60	50	25	20	
Prince Edward Island	121	112	105	98	95	88	89	94	103	109	109	94	81	63	50	25				
Nova Scotia	840	789	737	643	578	513	524	492	460	450	441	388	331	277	220	160	190	50	20	
New Brunswick	689	635	598	516	457	408	388	352	331	321	321	285	252	194	150	105				
Quebec (Lower Canada)	6,369	6,028	5,259	4,055	3,332	2,875	2,360	2,006	1,649	1,489	1,359	1,192	1,112	890	690	553	435	215	60	15(?)
Ontario (Upper Canada)	8,534	7,703	6,236	4,597	3,788	3,432	2,934	2,527	2,183	2,114	1,927	1,621	1,396	952	455	235	123	70	5(?)	1(?)
Prairie	4,184	3,542	3,179	2,549	2,422	2,354	1,956	1,327	419	153	62	25	7	5	5	2				
Manitoba	1,014	988	922	777	730	700	610	461	255	153	62	25	7	5	5	2				
Saskatchewan	956	926	925	832	896	922	758	492	91	NA	NA	NA	NA	NA	NA	NA				
Alberta	2,214	1,628	1,332	940	796	732	588	374	73	NA	NA	NA	NA	NA	NA	NA				
Yukon	23	18	15	9	5	4	4	9	27	99	56	56	7	6	NA	NA	Unknown			
Northwest Territory	46	35	23	16	12	9	8	7	20											
British Columbia	2,714	2,185	1,629	1,165	818	694	525	393	179	98	50	36	52	55	NA	NA				

personnel wandered all over Canada and most probably were rarely if ever counted.

2. Boundary lines demarcating provinces were shifted about from time to time. Originally the French settled in what are now the Maritime Provinces and along the Lower St. Lawrence River Valley. Along the St. Lawrence was much good farmland, and the area became known as Lower Canada, or New France; much of it became the present province of Quebec.

3. The English also began as fishermen on the Atlantic coast and in the Maritime Provinces and then worked their way westward along the St. Lawrence Valley past the French areas, and following the good farmland. This area was called Upper Canada and finally became the province of Ontario.

4. Except for British Columbia, there was little elsewhere to attract settlers. Only fur traders, Amerindians, and Inuits were interested in these other areas. The Hudson Bay Company, which began in the fur business, was given most of this land and named it Rupert's Land. The fur business was a good business. Rupert's Land was the drainage basin of Hudson Bay and comprised most of the land of the provinces of Quebec and Ontario north of about Quebec City and west of Labrador, all of the provinces of Manitoba and Saskatchewan and the southern half of Alberta, and the southeastern corner of what is now the Northwest Territory. If anyone kept count of the number of European-origin people in Rupert's Land, such a count did not follow present-day province lines.

5. British Columbia had its own set of problems. The English, Spanish, Americans (people from the United States), and Russians all claimed jurisdiction during the eighteenth century, and all sent out expeditions to explore, survey, and look for fur business. By the end of the century, Spain had abandoned the Northwest Coast. In 1846, the boundary between Canada and the United States was agreed upon at the forty-ninth parallel, and British Columbia now had a southern boundary. The Russians who had first exploited the Alaskan fur trade gradually worked their way south along the coast; they may be responsible for the Alaskan panhandle along what would have been the northern coast of British Columbia if the Russians had not preceded the British. In 1867, the Russians sold Alaska to the United States.

Very few European-origin people had settled in British Columbia. As late as 1871 there were only about 36,000 nonnatives in the province, according to that census. The large increases in population, except for the Native People, occurred in the twentieth century as the frostbitten eastern Canadians found their Miami in southern British Columbia near the Pacific Ocean.

We can continue to illustrate some of the practical problems involved in reconstructing province numbers back to the beginning of the eighteenth century, but enough is enough.

How accurate may our estimates be as shown in Appendix Table 11.1? Sufficiently accurate for our purpose of trying to demonstrate the encroachment of the nonnative people upon the Canadian Amerindians during the eighteenth and nineteenth centuries. We make no claim that these numbers will serve all purposes but maybe almost all.

Population Growth and Scientific and Technological Innovations: An Aspect of Social Change

How does a small band of people, using the most primitive stone tools, eventually become a modern, technologically developing, state-of-the-art society?

We offer the following model to describe this process. Further, we believe that there is sufficient archaeological and historical material to permit testing it. This process is but one part of a more complicated model; however, our present study is not the place to attempt a fully developed model.

We make two assumptions: (1) The proportion of the total population of a band or nation, which is capable of inventions and innovations, is and was constant at least since the emergence of *Homo sapiens s.* (2) Scientific and technological innovations, including social inventions, are produced by combining previously known scientific principles or technologies.

From these assumptions we deduce: (a) as population increases, there are more people capable of innovating, and (b) as the number of innovations increases, more innovations can be produced.

Let us begin with a situation in which the people live in small, isolated bands, as the original first Asian immigrants may have lived, and as may have been found in many parts of the world as recently as the nineteenth century. These bands averaged 100 people, let us assume—500 if you wish. Most importantly there is but minimum contact and exchange of ideas among the bands. Someone may have innovated in one band but is unable to exchange such knowledge and experiences with other innovators in other bands if further innovations are to be forthcoming.

Innovators who lived on communication routes were in a better position to exchange knowledge with outsiders; actual population size of the band or tribe may have been of less importance to them except in warfare. Perhaps this accounts for part of the success of the eastern Mediterranean and southwestern Asia people in building their civilizations.

Over the millennia, population increases; some bands expand by absorbing others, and some may have favorable environments that facilitate population growth. Remember that we are thinking in terms of tens and tens of millennia; *Homo sapiens s.* may have been in existence for over 100,000 years. So innovations as well as populations increase but slowly.

In the meantime, some of these innovations lead to improved means of communication, thereby increasing the rate of growth of innovations. Other innovations contribute to an increased food supply, improved spear or arrowheads for hunting game, as well as agriculture. An increased food supply permits further population increase over the many millennia. And more people implies more potential innovators.

We have a slowly accelerating curve over the many millennia.

Obviously, this process of population and innovation growth, aided and abetted by means of communication, also can create negative effects. Technologically modern warfare may return the world's people to living in small, isolated bands. Who knows? The modern airplane can transmit diseases very rapidly around the globe; admittedly, the seventeenth-century Europeans, without the aid of the airplane, managed to spread European diseases rather rapidly in the Western Hemisphere.

The process that we have just described illustrates the process itself. Models and some research on the growth of innovations—they used to be called "inventions"—and of population growth have long been in existence. We only tried to put them together.

May we hypothesize that our model may help to explain some of the differences between the Indians north and south of the Rio Grande in pre-European times? We think that enough archaeological material is available to permit some testing.

Appendix *13*

Dogs, Directives, and Circulars:
How Bureaucrats Think

Indian and Northern Affairs
Ottawa, Ont. K1A 0M4

July 30, 1975

To All Regional Directors

Circular W-17

It has been brought to our attention that the number of dogs on Indian Reserves has been increasing at a rate far beyond the capacity of this Department or the Indians to administer them.

The Indian Reserve Dog Regulations are optional in nature, and though the last revision of these was on June 10, 1954, few reserves have put them into effect. It has therefore been found desirable, in concurrence with our general review of the Department's policies through the publication of program and policy guide-lines, to establish a definitive statement of our position on this question.

In view of the apparent attachment of many Indians to their dogs, it can be expected that this Circular will meet with some opposition on the local level, but with proper moves on the Department's part to forestall any fears the Indians may have, there should be no real problems in the implementation of this policy. It should be noted that this Circular is of a preliminary nature. Proposals for change should be directed to J. Wright, Director of Program Development, Local Government Program. It can be explained to the Bands in your districts that the Department's intention is not to do away with dogs altogether, but merely to ensure that they are properly administered, and that any improvement in dog administration will be to the advantage of all concerned in the long run. No program can function efficiently without some rules for its planning and its day-to-day operations, and surely this axiom applies to the Indian dog situation as well.

Indian Band Dog Guidelines

Policy Circular W-17

1.1. These guidelines govern all dogs on Indian reserves, whether they be male or female, old or young, and owned by residents of the reserve or by others, except that dogs owned or kept by employees of the Department of Indian and Northern Affairs shall be exempted from the provisions of paragraphs 3 and 7 of these guidelines.

1.2. All dogs on Indian reserves shall be registered and placed on the Band Dog List for that Band. A copy of the Band Dog List shall be kept at the Regional Office and amendments, additions or deletions to the list shall be communicated to the Regional Office within one week after they are made at the Band Level.

1.3. Where the sire of a litter of pups can be ascertained, the pups shall be entered under his Band Dog List number until such time as they receive names or reach the age of three months, whichever comes last.

1.4. Where the sire of the litter cannot be ascertained, the pups shall be listed under the Band Dog List number of the mother, except that where it is known that the sire is not a Dog resident on the reserve or belonging to a member of the Band, then the pups shall not be included in the Band Dog List.

1.5. Pups born to a Reserve Dog mother and a Non-Reserve dog sire shall be considered enfranchised and shall not be subject to the provisions of those guidelines.

2.1. Where a Reserve Dog that is registered on the Band Dog List has not, after three months have elapsed from its date of birth, been given a name, that Dog shall be known by the Band Dog List Number assigned to it. This provision does not apply to Dogs that are enfranchised or die within that three-month period.

2.2. Reserve Dogs shall not chase automobiles or other vehicles registered in the name of Her Majesty in right of Canada or to the Department of Indian and Northern Affairs.

2.3. Failure to comply with the provisions of 2.2 may result in action taken by the Regional Director to:

(a) remove the Dog's name from the Band Dog list.

(b) require that the dog be subject to co-management by the Department and the Indian or Indians the Band Dog List describes as its Owners.

(c) outright denial (as a last resort) of Core Funding to the Reserve with respect to all dogs.

3.1. It shall be the responsibility of the Chief and Council of the Band to ensure that all Dogs on the Reserve shall be of Good behaviour and shall not be vicious or engage in the excessive consumption of alcoholic beverages, drugs, or other intoxicants.

Ottawa, July 23, 1975

Circular W-7

Sir;

It is observed with alarm that the holding of dances by the Indians on their reserves is on the increase, and that these practices tend to disorganize the efforts the Department is putting forth to make them self-supporting.

I have, therefore, to direct you to use your utmost endeavours to dissuade the Indians from excessive indulgence in the practice of dancing. You should suppress any dancing which causes waste of time, interferes with the occupations of the Indians, unsettles them for serious work, injures their health or encourages them in sloth and idleness. You should also dissuade, and, if possible, prevent them from leaving their reserves for the purpose of attending fairs, exhibitions, etc. when their absence would result in their own farming and other interests being neglected. It is realized that reasonable recreation and amusement should be enjoyed by the Indians, but they should not be allowed to dissipate their energies and abandon themselves to demoralizing amusements. By the use of tact and firmness you can obtain control and keep it, and this obstacle to continued progress will then disappear.

The rooms, halls or other places in which Indians congregate should be under constant inspection. They should be scrubbed, fumigated, cleaned or disinfected to prevent the dissemination of disease. The Indians should be instructed in regard to the matter of proper ventilation and the avoidance of over-crowding rooms where public assemblies are being held and proper arrangement should be made for the shelter of their horses and ponies. The Agent will avail himself of the services of the medical attendant of his agency in this connection. Except where further information is desired, there will be no necessity to acknowledge receipt of this circular.

Yours very truly,

J. McGilp

References

Ackerman, E. C., Reid, J. G. G., Roe, M. E., & Campbell, C. R. (1984). *The prehistoric occupation of Heceta Island, Southeastern Alaska.* Washington State University (photocopy received from author).

Acsadi, G., & Nemeskeri, J. (1970). *History of human life span and mortality.* Budapest: Publishing House of the Hungarian Academy of Sciences.

Adler, H. J., & Brusegard, D. A., (Eds.). (1980). *Perspective Canada III.* Ministry of Supply and Services, Canada. Ottawa, Catalogue Number 11-511E, p. 173.

Adovasio, J. M., Donahue, J., Cushman, K., Carlisle, R. C., Stuckenrath, R., Gunn, J. D., & Johnson, W. C. (1983). Evidence from Meadowcroft Rockshelter. In R. Shutler, Jr. (Ed.), *Early man in the New World* (Chapter 13). Beverly Hills: Sage Publications.

Allison, M. J. (Guest Ed.) (1976). *Medical College of Virginia Quarterly, 12*:2.

Angel, J. L. (1971a). *The people of Lerna.* Washington, DC: The Smithsonian Press.

Angel, J. L. (1971b). Early Neolithic skeletons from Catal Huyuk: Demography and pathology. *Anatolian Studies, 21.*

Armelagos, G. J., & Medina, C. M. (1977). The demography of prehistoric populations. *Eugenics Society Bulletin, 9*, 8–14.

Atlas of Canada. (1981). Published by Readers Digest Association (Canada), Ltd. in conjunction with the Canadian Automobile Association.

Austerlitz, R. (1980). Language–family density in North America and Eurasia. In *Ural-Altic Yearbook.* Bloomington, Indiana: Wiesbaden.

Bamforth, D. B. (1988). *Ecology and human organization on the Great Plains.* New York: Plenum Press.

Bard, E., Hamelin, B., Fairbanks, R. G., & Zindler, A. Calibration of the ^{14}C timescale over the past 30,000 years using mass spectrometric U-Th ages from Barbados Corals. *Nature, 345*, 31 May 1990, pp. 405 ff.

Benedict, J. B. (June 1989). Age of punctate pottery from the Caribou Lake site: Comparison of three physical dating methods. *Southwestern Lore, 55*:2.

Berger, R. (1983). New dating techniques. In R. Shutler, Jr. (Ed.), *Early man in the New World.* Beverly Hills: Sage Publications.

Betancourt, J. L., & Van Devender, T. R. (1981). Holocene vegetation in Chaco Canyon, New Mexico. *Science, 214*, 656–658.

Birdsell, J. S. (1968). Some predictions for the Pleistocene based on equilibrium systems among recent hunters-gatherers. In R. B. Lee & I. Devore (Eds.), *Man the hunter.* Chicago: Aldine.

Bongaarts (9 May 1980). Does malnutrition affect fecundity? A summary of evidence. *Science, 208,* 564–569.

Borden, C. E. (9 March 1979). Peopling and early cultures of the Pacific Northwest. *Science, 203.*

Bordes, F. (1978). Preface. In A. L. Bryan (Ed.), *Early man in America.* Alberta: University of Alberta, Archaeological Research International.

Boserup, E. (1965). *The conditions of agricultural growth.* Chicago: Aldine.

Bourgeois-Pichat, J. See *United Nations* (1973), p. 75.

Boyer, E. L. (1989). *Tribal colleges: Shaping the future of Native America.* Princeton: The Carnegie Foundation for the Advancement of Teaching.

Brothwell, D., & Brothwell, P. (1969). *Food in antiquity.* London: Thames and Hudson.

Brothwell, D., Brothwell, P., & Sandison, A. T. (1967). *Disease in antiquity.* Springfield, IL: Charles C Thomas.

Bryan, A. L. (1978a). The contribution of J. M. Cruxent to the study of the Paleo-Indian problem in the New World. In *Unidad y variedadas: Ensanyos en homenaje a Jose M. Cruxent.* Caracas, Venezuela: Centro de Estudio Avanzados.

Bryan, A. L. (Ed.). (1978b). *Early man in America.* Alberta: University of Alberta, Archaeological Research International.

Bryan, A. L. (1983). South America. In R. Shutler, Jr. (Ed.), *Early man in the New World.* Beverly Hills: Sage Publications.

Buikstra, J. E. (1981). Mortuary practices, paleodemography, paleopathology. In R. Chapman, I. Kinnes, & K. Randsborg (Eds.), *Archaeology of death.* New York: Cambridge University Press.

Canada, Census. (1981a). Statistics Canada. Total population showing urban–rural distribution by sex and age and by ethnic origin (photocopied).

Canada, Census. (1981b). Census families showing ethnic origin of husband by ethnic origin of wife (Native Persons) for Canada and the provinces (photocopied).

Canada, Census. (1981c). Catalogue Number 92-911. Population, ethnic origin.

Canada's Native People. (1984). Statistics Canada Catalogue Number 99-937. Introduction. (Prepared by M. S. Devereaux.)

Canadian Indian, The. (1986). Ottawa: Indian and Northern Affairs, pp. 54–61.

Cardinal, H. (1977). *The rebirth of Canada's Indians.* Alberta: Hurtig Publishers.

Cassidy, C. M. See Greene & Johnston.

Catlin, G. (1844). *Letters and notes . . . of North American Indians.* Dover Publications. (Unabridged republication of 1844 edition published in London.)

Chang, K.-C. (1977). *The archaeology of ancient China.* New Haven: Yale University Press.

Chavez, F. A. (1973). *Origins of New Mexico families.* Albuquerque: University of Albuquerque in collaboration with Calvin Horn Publishers.

Chen, T. (1946). *Population in modern China.* Chicago: University of Chicago Press.

Childers, W. M., & Marshall, H. L. (April 1980). Evidence of early man exposed at Yuka Ointo Wash. *American Antiquity, 45:*2.

Clabeaux, M. S. (April 1977). Investigator sex and bias in skeletal sexing. Paper read at the American Association of Physical Anthropologists Annual Meeting.

Clark, S. N. (1877). Are the Indians dying out? Washington, DC: Office of Indian Affairs, Department of the Interior.

Clem, R. (1992). The frontier and colonialism in Russia and Soviet Central Asia. In Lewis (Ed.), *Perspectives in Soviet Central Asia.* New York and London: Rutledge.

Clissold, S. (1962). *The seven cities of Cibola.* New York: Clarkson N. Potter.

Cockburn, T. A. (1971). Infectious diseases in ancient populations. *Current Anthropology, 12:*1.

Cohen, M. N. (1978). *Population pressure and the origins of agriculture.* New Haven: Yale University Press.

Columbia encyclopedia (1950, second edition).

Cowgill, G. L. (1975). On causes and consequences of ancient and modern population changes. *American Anthropologist, 77,* 505.

Culliton, B. J. (19 January 1990). *Science, 247,* 279–280.

Cybulski, J. S. (1981). Homo Erectus: A synopsis. In *Homo Erectus—Papers in honor of Davidson Black.* Toronto, University of Toronto Press.

Cybulski, J. S. (personal communication). Physical anthropology and paleopathology.

Dahlberg, F. (Ed.). (1981). *Woman the gatherer.* New Haven: Yale University Press.

Day, A. G. (1964). *Coronado's guest.* Berkeley and Los Angeles: University of California Press.

Deloria, V., Jr., & Lytle, C. M. (1983). *American Indians, American justice.* Austin: University of Texas Press.

Derevianko, A. P. (1978). On the migrations of ancient man from Asia to America in the Pleistocene era. In A. L. Bryan (Ed.), *Early man in America* (p. 70). Alberta: University of Alberta, Archaeological Research International.

Devereaux, M. S. See *Canada's Native People.*

Dobyns, H. F. (1976). *Native American historical demography.* Bloomington and London: Indiana University Press.

Driver, H. E. (1961). *Indians of North America.* Chicago: University of Chicago Press.

Driver, H. E., & Massey, W. C. (1957). Comparative studies of North American Indians. *Transactions of the American Philosophical Society, 47*:2, pp. 260 ff.

Dublin, L. I., & Lotka, A. J. (1936). *Length of life,* p. 43. New York: Ronald Press.

Eckholm, G. F. (1964). Transpacific contacts. In J. D. Jennings & E. Norbeck (Eds.), *Prehistoric man in the New World.* Chicago: University of Chicago Press.

Embrie, J., & Embrie, K. (1979). *Ice ages: Solving the mystery.* Hillside, NJ: Enslow Publishers.

Encyclopedia Canadiana. (1976). Grolier of Canada.

Ericson, J. E., Sullivan, C. H., & Boaz, N. T. (1981). Diets of Pleistocene mammals from Omo, Ethiopia, deduced from isotopic ratios in tooth apatite. *Palaeogeography, Palaeoclimatology, Palaeoecology, 36,* 69–73.

Erlandson, J. M. (1988). The role of shellfish in prehistoric economies: A protein perspective. *American Antiquity, 53*:1.

Fagan, B. M. (1987). *The great journey.* London: Thames and Hudson.

Fairholt, F. W. (1876). *Tobacco: Its history and associations.* London.

Fladmark, K. R. (1983). Times and places . . . . In R. Shutler, Jr. (Ed.), *Early man in the New World.* Beverly Hills: Sage Publications.

Fladmark, K. R. (November 1986). Getting one's bearings. *Natural History,* pp. 8 ff.

Folsom, F., & Folsom, M. E. (1983). *America's ancient treasures.* Albuquerque: University of New Mexico Press.

Foreman, G. (1982). *Indian removal.* Norman: University of Oklahoma Press.

Fowler, C. S. (1986). Subsistence. In *Handbook of the North American Indians, 11,* (pp. 64–97). Washington, DC: Smithsonian Institution.

Frazier, K. (1986). *People of Chaco.* New York: W. W. Norton & Co.

Funk, R. E. (1978). Post-Pleistocene adaptation. In *Handbook of the North American Indians, 15,* (pp. 16–27). Washington, DC: Smithsonian Institution.

Ganteaume, C. R. (December 1986). Native peoples of the Southeast. *Museum of the American Indian Newsletter, XI*:3.

Gibson, A. M. (1980). *The American Indian: Prehistory to the present.* Norman: University of Oklahoma Press.

Gidley, M. (1979). *With one sky above us.* Seattle: University of Washington Press.

Gilbert, A. S., & Singer, B. H. (June 1982). Reassessing zooarchaeological quantification. *World Archaeology, 14*:1, 23–24.

Glover, J. W. *United States life tables.* U.S. Bureau of the Census, 1921.

Gould, R. A. (1980). *Living archaeology.* New York: Cambridge University Press.

Greenberg, J. See Lewin 1988.

Greenberg, M., Popper, F., & Carey, G. (5 December 1985). *New England Journal of Medicine,* 482–483.

Greenberg, M., Popper, F., & Carey, G. (Spring 1987). *The public interest,* pp. 38 ff.

Greene, E. B., & Harrington, V. D. (1932). *American population before the federal census of 1790.* New York: Columbia University Press.

Greene, L. S., & Johnston, F. E. (Eds.). (1980). *Social and biological predictors of nutritional status, physical growth, and neurological development.* New York: Academic Press.

Guthrie, R. D., & Guthrie, M. L. (July 1980). On mammoth's dusty trail. *Natural History.* (Also in D. M. Hopkins (Ed.). (1982). *Mammals of the mammoth steppe as paleoenvironmental indicators* (Chapter 19). New York: Academic Press.)

Hambright, T. Z. (1960). Comparability of marital status, race, nativity, and country of origin on the death certificates and matching census record: U.S. May–August 1960. *U.S. Public Health Service, National Center for Health Statistics,* 2:34.

Handbook of the North American Indians (various volumes and editors, 1970–1990). Washington, DC: Smithsonian Institution.

Harison, J. D. (1985). *Métis.* Vancouver/Toronto: The Glenbow–Alberta Institute in association with Douglas & McIntyre.

Hassan, F. A. (1981). *Demographic archaeology.* New York: Academic Press.

Hart, G. D. (Ed.). (1983). *Disease in ancient man.* Toronto: Clarke Irwin.

Heizer, R. F., & Napton, L. W. (8 August 1969). Biological and cultural evidence from prehistoric human caprolites. *Science, 165,* 563–568.

Helm, J., Rogers, E. S., & Smith, J. G. E. Intercultural relations and cultural changes in the shield and MacKenzie borderlands. In *Handbook of North American Indians, 15* (pp. 146 ff.). Washington, DC: Smithsonian Institution.

Hishinuma, S. (1977). Historical review on the longevity of human beings. *Institute of Actuaries in Japan* (photocopy).

Hogg, A. G. (1982). *Application of radiocarbon dating techniques.* Hamilton, New Zealand: Radiocarbon Laboratory, University of Waikato (photocopy).

Hopkins, D. M. (1967). The Cenozoic history of Beringia—A synthesis. In D. M. Hopkins (Ed.)., *The Bering land bridge.* Stanford: Stanford University Press.

Hopkins, D. M., Mathews, J. V., Jr., Schweger, C. E. & Young, S. B. (Eds.). (1982). *Paleoecology of Beringia.* New York: Academic Press.

Huddleston, L. E. (1967). *Origins of the American Indians: European concepts 1492 to 1729.* Austin: University of Texas Press.

Hunt, W. C. (1915). *Indian population in the United States and Alaska.* U.S. Census Bureau.

Ikawa-Smith, F. (1978). Lithic assemblages from the early and middle upper Pleistocene formations in Japan. In A. L. Bryan (Ed.), *Early man in America* (pp. 42–53). Alberta: University of Alberta, Archaeological Research International.

Imbrie, J., & Imbrie, K. (1979). *Ice ages: Solving the mystery.* Hillside, NJ: Enslow Publishers.

Indian health care. (1986). U.S. Congress, Office of Technology Assessment. Washington, DC: GPO.

Indian health service. Washington, DC.

Indian land tenure, economic status, and population trends. (1935). Part X of the Supplementary Report of the Land Planning Committee to the National Resources Board. Washington, DC: GPO.

Indian population in the United States and Alaska, 1910. (1915). Prepared under the supervision of W. C. Hunt. Washington, DC: GPO.

Innes, H. A. (1956). *The fur trade in Canada.* Toronto: University of Toronto Press.

International encyclopedia of the social sciences. (1968). D. L. Sills (Ed.). The Macmillan Company and The Free Press.

Jaffe, A. J. (1951). *Handbook of statistical methods for demographers.* U.S. Census Bureau. Washington, DC: GPO.

Jaffe, A. J. (April 1962). Notes on the population theory of Eugene Michael Kulischer. *Milbank Memorial Fund Quarterly,* XL:2.

Jaffe, A. J. (1969). *Handbook of statistical procedures for long-range projections of public school enrollment.* U.S. Census Bureau. GPO. Appendix B.

Jaffe, A. J., & Spirer, H. F. (1987). *Missed statistics—Straight talk for twisted numbers.* New York: Marcel Dekker.

Jaffe, A. J., & Stewart, C. D. (1951). *Manpower resources and utilization.* New York: John Wiley & Sons.

Jaffe, A. J., Cullen, R. M., & Boswell, T. D. (1980). *The changing demography of Spanish Americans.* New York: Academic Press.

Jia, L. (1980). *Early men in China.* Beijing: Foreign Language Press.

Johanson, D., & Maitland, E. (1981). *Lucy: The beginnings of humankind.* New York: Simon and Schuster.

Johnson, E. (17 January 1969). Archaeological evidence of utilization of wild rice. *Science, 163,* 276–277.

Josephy, A. M., Jr. (1982). *Now that the buffalo's gone.* New York: Alfred A. Knopf.

Kalbach, W. E., & McVey, W. W. (1971). *The demographic bases of Canadian society.* Toronto: McGraw-Hill Ryerson.

Katz, S. H., Hediger, M. L. & Valleroy, L. A. (17 May 1974). Traditional maize processing techniques in the New World. *Science, 184.*

Keeper, J. Problems of Indians and Métis in rural areas. In D. R. Sealey & V. J. Kirkness (Eds.), *Indians without tipis* (Chapter 7). Manitoba: William Clare Publisher.

Kelly, L. C. (1983). *The assault on assimilation: John Collier and the origins of Indian policy reform, part II.* Albuquerque: University of New Mexico Press.

Kendrick, F. (1986). *People of Chaco.* New York: W. W. Norton & Co.

Kerr, D. D. (1975). *Historical atlas of Canada, third revised edition.* Ontario: Thomas Nelson & Sons.

Kessel, J. L. (1979). *Kiva, cross, and crown.* U.S. National Park Service.

Kulischer, E. M. See Jaffe (1962).

Lallo, J., Armelagos, G. J., & Rose, J. C. (1978). Paleoepidemiology of infectious disease in the Dickson Mounds population. *MCV Quarterly, 14:1,* 17–23.

Larsen, C. S. (1981). Skeletal and dental adaptations to the shift to agriculture. *Current Anthropology, 22:4.*

Latulippe-Sakamoto, C. *Estimation de la mortalite des Indies du Canada–1900 to 1968.* Doctoral dissertation number MCF 45495. Ottawa: National Library of Canada.

Leakey, R. E., & Lewin, R. (1978). *People of the lake.* New York: Anchor Press.

Lewis R. A., Roland, R., & Clem, R. (1976). *Nationality and population change in Russia and the USSR.* New York: Praeger Publishers. (See especially Chapter 4.)

Lewin, R. (24 June 1983). Isotopes give clues to past diets. *Science, 220,* 1369.

Lewin, R. (26 October 1984). Reading old bones. *Science, 226.*

Lewin, R. (25 November 1988). Linguists search for the mother tongue. *Science, 242,* 1128–1129.

Lewis, T. M. N., & Kneberg, M. (1958). *Tribes that slumber.* Knoxville: University of Tennessee Press.

Lower, J. A. *Canada on the Pacific Rim.* Toronto: McGraw-Hill Ryerson.

Loy, T. H. (17 June 1983). Prehistoric blood residue's detection on tool surfaces and identification of species of origin. *Science, 220,* 1269–1271.

Madigan, L. (1956). *The American Indian relocation program.* Association of American Indian Affairs. *Mammoth trumpet.* Orono: Center for the Study of Early Man, University of Maine.

Mangelsdorf, P. C., MacNeish, R. S., and Galinat, W. C. (1964). Domestication of corn. *Science, 143,* 538–545.

Marquis of Lansdowne. (Ed.). (1928). *The Petty–Southwell correspondence, 1676–1687.* London: Constable & Co.

Marshall, E. (16 February 1990). Paleoanthropology gets physical. *Science, 247.*

Martin, P. S. (October 1987). Clovisia the beautiful. *Natural History,* 10–13.

Martin, R. M. (1843). *History of the colonies of the British Empire.*

Mason, R. J. (1981). *Great Lakes archaeology.* New York: Academic Press.

McKinley, K. B. (1971). Survivorship in gracile and robust Australopithecines: A demographic comparison and a proposed birth model. *American Journal of Physical Anthropology, 34,* 417–426.

McNeill, W. H. (1976). *Plagues and peoples.* New York: Anchor Books.

Mehringer, P. J., Jr. (1986). Prehistoric environments. *Handbook of North American Indians, 11.* Washington, DC: Smithsonian Institution.

Meyer, M. L., & Thornton, R. (1988). Indians and the numbers game: Quantitive methods in American native history. In C. G. Calloway (Ed.), *New direction in American Indian history* (Chapter 1). Norman: University of Oklahoma Press.

Milisauskas, S. (1978). *European prehistory.* New York: Academic Press.

Mochanov, I. A. (1978). The Paleolithic of northeast Asia and the problem of the first peopling of America. In A. L. Bryan (Ed.), *Early man in America,* (p. 67). Alberta: University of Alberta, Archaeological Research International.

Mooney, J. (1928). The aboriginal population of America north of Mexico. *Smithsonian Miscellaneous Collections, 8:7.*

Moore, A. M. T. (n.d.). The excavation of Tell Abu Hureyra in Syria: A preliminary report (with contributions by G. C. Hillman & A. J. Legge). *The Prehistoric Society.*

Moore, A. M. T. (August 1979). A Pre-Neolithic farmers' village on the Euphrates. *Scientific American, 241:2,* 62–70.

Moore, J. H., & Campbell, G. R. (1989). An ethnographical perspective on Cheyenne demography. *Journal of Family History, 14:1,* 17–42.

Morison, S. E. (1971). *The European discovery of America: The Northern voyages.* New York: Oxford University Press.

Murphy, J. L. (5 March 1971). Maize from an Adena mound in Athens County, Ohio. *Science, 171.*

Nelson, D. E., Morlan, R. E., Vogel, J. S., Southon, J. R., & Harington, C. R. (9 May 1986). New dates on northern Yukon artifacts. *Science, 232.*

Nicholas, G. P. (Ed.). (1988). *Holocene human ecology in northeastern North America.* New York: Plenum Press.

Niethammer (1978). *American Indian food and lore.* New York: Collier Publishers.

Ninth census of the United States, 1870. Population and social statistics.

Norris, M. J. (1989). Demography of aboriginal people in Canada. Ottawa: Statistics Canada (photocopied).

Ogburn, W. F. (1922). *Social change.* New York: Viking Press.

Ogburn, W. F. (1933). *Recent social trends in the U.S.* New York: McGraw-Hill.

Ogburn, W. F. (1937). Change, social. In *Encyclopedia of the social sciences.*

Olson, E. A. (1963). *The problem of sample contamination in radiocarbon dating* (doctoral dissertation). Columbia University, Faculty of Pure Science.

Otlet, R. L. (1976). An assessment of laboratory errors in liquid scintillation methods of ^{14}C dating. *Proceedings of the Ninth International Conference on Radiocarbon Dating.* Los Angeles and San Diego.

Patterson, E. P., II. *The Canadian Indian: A history since 1500.* Collier–Macmillan Canada.

Pelletier, A. J. (prior to 1931). Canadian census of the seventeenth century. Proceedings of the Canadian Political Science Association. *Perspective Canada III.* (1980). H. J. Adler and D. A. Brusegard (Eds.). Minister of Supply and Services, Canada, Catalogue Number 11-511E.

Pfeiffer, S. (1977). *The skeletal biology of Archaic populations of the Great Lakes region.* National Museum of Canada, Archaeological Survey of Canada, Paper Number 64, pp. 153 ff.

Prehistoric Denmark. (1970). Copenhagen: Danish National Museum.

Price, J. A. (1979). *Indians of Canada.* Scarborough, Ontario: Prentice-Hall of Canada.

Qoyawayma, P. (1964). *No turning back.* Albuquerque: University of New Mexico Press.

Reed, C. A. (Ed.). (1978). *Origins of agriculture.* The Hague: Mouton Publishers.

Reynolds, T. E. G. (1986). Toward peopling the New World. *American Antiquity, 51:2.*

Richman, I. B. (1965). *California under Spain and Mexico, 1535–1847.* New York: Cooper Square Publishers.

Rick, J. W. (1980). *Prehistoric hunters of the High Andes.* New York: Academic Press.

Roberts, L. (10 February 1989). *Science, 243,* pp.–235 ff.

Robicsak, F. (1978). *The smoking gods: Tobacco in Maya art, history, and religion.* Norman: University of Oklahoma Press.

Romaniuc, A. (n.d.) Transition from traditional high to modern low fertility: Canadian aboriginals. Ottawa: Statistics Canada. (Photocopy of paper prepared after 1981 census data become available.)

Roosevelt, A. C. (1980). *Parmana.* New York: Academic Press.

Rosenwaike, I. (1972). *Population history of New York City.* Syracuse: Syracuse University Press.

Rouse, I. The Arawak: Handbook of South American Indians, Vol. 4 (pp. 507 ff.). Washington, DC: Smithsonian Institution (Cooper Square Publishers, 1963 reprint).

Ruhlen M. (March 1987). Voices from the past. *Natural History,* 6–10.

Sauer, C. O. (1968). *Northern mists.* Berkeley and Los Angeles: University of California Press.

Scalinger's chronology. See Marquis of Lansdowne.

Schlaifer, R. (1961). *Introduction to statistics for business decisions.* New York: McGraw-Hill.

Schoeninger, M. J., Deniro, M. J., & Tauber, H. (24 June 1983). Stable nitrogene isotope ratios of bone collagen reflect marine and terrestrial components of prehistoric human diet. *Science, 220,* 1381–1383.

Schwartz, D. W. (1983). In *Handbook of the North American Indians, 10* (Havasupai), pp. 13–24. Washington, DC: Smithsonian Institution.

Shapiro, H. L. (1981). Davidson Black: An appreciation. In B. A. Sigmon & J. S. Cybulski (Eds.), *Homo Erectus—Papers in honor of Davidson Black.* Toronto: University of Toronto Press.

Sharp, A. (1964). *Ancient voyagers in Polynesia.* Berkeley and Los Angeles: University of California Press.

Shumway, G., Hubbs, C. L., & Moriarty, J. R. (4 December 1961). Scripps Estates Site, San Diego, California: A La Jolla site dated 5460 to 7370 years before the present. *Annals of the New York Academy of Sciences, 93:3.*

Shutler, R., Jr. (Ed.). (1983). *Early man in the New World.* Beverly Hills: Sage Publications.

Shryock, H., & Siegel, J. (1971). *The methods and materials of demography, 2.* U.S. Bureau of the Census, pp. 687 ff.

Siggner, A. J. (1979). *An Overview of demographic, social, and economic conditions among Canada's registered Indian population.* Indian and Northern Affairs, Canada.

Simmons, A. H., Köhler-Rollefson, I., Rollefson, G. O., Mandel, R., & Kafafi, Z. (1 April 1988). 'Ain Ghazal: A major Neolithic settlement in Central Jordan. *Science, 40.*

Slobodin, R. D. (1981). Subarctic Métis. In *Handbook of the North American Indians*, 6 (pp. 361–371). Washington, DC: Smithsonian Institution.

Smith, B. D. (22 December 1989). Origins of agriculture in eastern North America. *Science, 246*, 1566–1571.

Smith, J. G. E. (1981). Western Woods Cree. In *Handbook of the North American Indians*, 6 (pp. 257–270). Washington, DC: Smithsonian Institution.

Spencer, P.S. *et al.* (31 July 1987). Guam amyotrophic lateral sclerosis-Parkinsonism—Dementia linked to a plant excitant neurotoxin. *Science, 237*, pp. 517 ff.

Spinden, H. J. (1950). *Tobacco in America.* New York Public Library, pp. 14 ff.

Spooner, B. (1972). *Population growth: Anthropological implications.* Cambridge: MIT Press.

Statistical abstract of the United States. (1989). Washington, DC: GPO.

Statistics Canada. (1984). In *Canada's Native People* (Introduction).

Sterud, E. L. (1978). Prehistoric populations of the Dinaric Alps: An investigation of interregional interaction. In C. L. Redman, M. J. Berman, E. V. Curtain, W. T. Langhorne, Jr., N. M. Versaggi, & J. C. Wanser (Eds.), *Social archaeology* (Chapter 17). New York: Academic Press.

Stewart, T. D. (1973). *The people of America.* New York: Charles Scribners & Sons.

Stringer, C. (18 February 1988). The dates of Eden. *Nature, 331.*

Stuiver, M., & Polach, H. A. (1977). Reporting of ^{14}C data. *Radiocarbon, 19*:3.

Such, P. (1978). *Vanished peoples: The archaic Dorset and the Beothuk people.* Toronto: NC Press.

Sutherland, S. H. (1936). *Population distribution in colonial America.* New York: Columbia University Press.

Tannahill, R. (1973). *Food in history.* New York: Stein and Day.

Taylor, C. E. (1979). *The Métis and nonstatus Indian population: Numbers and characteristics.* Canada: Department of the Secretary of State (photocopied).

Taylor, R. E., Payen, L. A., Gerow, B., Donahue, D. J., Zabel, T. H., Jull, A. J. T., & Damon, P. E. (17 June 1983). Middle Holocene age of the Sunnyvale human skeleton. *Science, 220*, 171–173.

Trovato, F. (1987). A macrosociological analysis of native Indian fertility in Canada: 1961, 1971, 1981. *Social Forces, 66*:2.

Tuck, J. A. (1981). Northern Iroquoian prehistory. In *Handbook of the North American Indians*, 15 (p. 325). Washington, DC: Smithsonian Institution.

Turner, C. G., II. (1983). Dental evidence for the peopling of the Americas. In R. Shutler, Jr. (Ed.), *Early man in the New World* (Chapter 13). Beverly Hills: Sage Publications.

Turner, C. G., II. (January 1987). Telltale teeth. *Natural History*, 6–10.

Ubelaker, D. H. (1974). Reconstruction of demographic profiles from ossuary skeleton samples. *Smithsonian Contribution to Anthropology, 18.*

Ubelaker, D. H. (1978). *Human skeletal remains.* Washington, DC: Taraxacum.

Ubelaker, D. H. (1980). *Human bones and archaeology.* U.S. Department of Interior.

Ubelaker, D. H. (1988). American Indian population size, A.D. 1500 to 1985. *American Journal of Physical Anthropology, 77*, 289–294.

United Nations demographic yearbook (annual).

United Nations. (1973). *Determinants and consequences of population trends.* New York.

U.S. Bureau of the Census, Washington, DC. *Historical statistics of the United States: Colonial times to 1957.*

United States Census (1870). *Population and social statistics*, p. xvii.

United States Census (1910). *Indian population in the U.S. and Alaska.*

United States Census (1930). *The Indian population of the United States and Alaska, 1930.*

United States Census (1940). *Comparative occupation statistics, 1870 to 1940.*

United States Census (1970). *American Indians*, PC(2)IF.

Urquhart, M. C., & Buckley, K. A. H. (1965). *Historical statistics of Canada.* The Macmillan Company of Canada.

Valladas, H., Reyss, J. L., Joron, J. L., Valladas, G., Bar-Yossef, O., & Vandermeersch, B. (18 February 1988). Thermoluminescence dating of Mousterian 'Proto-Cro-Magnon' remains from Israel and the origin of modern man. *Nature, 331.*

Vallois, H. J. (1961). Vital statistics in prehistoric population as determined from archaeological data. *Viking Fund Publications in Anthropology, 28.*

Vazsonyi, A., & Spirer, H. F. (1984). *Quantitative analysis for business.* Englewood Cliffs, NJ: Prentice-Hall.

Viola, H. J. (1974). *Thomas L. McKenney, architect of America's early Indian policy, 1816–1830.* Chicago: Sage Books, The Swallow Press.

Waldman, C. (1985). *Atlas of the North American Indians.* New York: Facts on File Publications.

Waldram, J. B. (1986). The other side . . . In F. L. Barron and J. B. Waldram (Eds.), *1885 and after: Native society in transition.* Regina, Saskatchewan: Canadian Plains Research Center, University of Regina.

Wassen, S. H. (1965). The use of some specific kinds of South American Indian snuff and related paraphernalia. *Etnologiska studier* (Chapter VII): Goteborg, Sweden: Etnografiska Museet.

Weaver, M. P. (1972). *The Aztecs, Maya, and their predecessors.* New York: Seminar Press.

Weiss, K. M. (April 1963). Demographic models for anthropology. *Memoirs of the Society for American Anthropology, 38:2,* part 2.

Whitehead, D. R. (12 November 1965). Prehistoric maize in southwestern Virginia. *Science, 150.*

Willey, P., & Mann, B. (1986). The skeleton of an elderly woman. *Plains Archaeologist, 141–152.*

Wills, W. H. (1988). Early agriculture and sedentism in the American Southwest: Evidence and interpretations. *Journal of World Prehistory, 2:4,* pp. 445 ff.

Wing, E. S., & Brown, A. B. (1979). *Paleonutrition.* New York: Academic Press.

Woodbury, R. B., & Zubrow, E. B. W. (1979). Agricultural beginnings, 2000 B.C.–A.D. 500. In *Handbook of North American Indians, 9,* (pp. 43–60). Washington, DC: Smithsonian Institution.

Wormington, H. M. (1983). Early man in the New World: 1970–1980. In R. Shutler, Jr. (Ed.), *Early man in the New World.* Beverly Hills: Sage Publications.

Wright, C. D., & Hunt, W. C. (1900). *History and growth of the U.S. census.* Washington, DC: GPO.

Wright, J. L., Jr. (1981). *The only land they knew.* New York: The Free Press.

Yesner, D. R. (1980). Nutrition and cultural evolution. In N. W. Jerome, R. E. Kandel, & G. H. Pelto (Eds.), *Nutional anthropology.* Pleasantville, NY: Redgrave Publishing Co.

Zegura, S. L. (July 1987). Blood test. *Natural History.*

Zimmerman, M. R. (1980). *Foundations of medical anthropology.* Philadelphia: W. B. Saunders Co.

Zivanovic, S. (1982). *Ancient diseases.* New York: Pica Press.

Index